Kodiak

Alaska's Emerald Isle

Carol M. Sturgulewski

Kodiak, Alaska's Emerald Isle

Text by Carol M. Sturgulewski
Contribution to the Kodiak's Seafaring Legacy section
    courtesy of the Kodiak Maritime Museum
Design by Edward Bovy and Alissa Crandall
Cartography by Jim Green

Cover photos: City of Kodiak, Marion Owen
    Boats in St. Herman Harbor, Marion Owen
    Kodiak brown bear, Steve Gilroy
    Karluk church, Marion Owen
Page 4 photo: Wildflowers, Vance Gese
Page 5 photo: Fireweed, Alissa Crandall
Back cover photo: Rain forest, Vance Gese

ISBN 0-936425-82-2 softcover
ISBN 0-936425-83-0 hardcover

Published by:
Greatland Graphics
(www.alaskacalendars.com)
Printed in China

Produced and distributed for the
Kodiak Chamber of Commerce
P.O. Box 1485
Kodiak, Alaska 99615
www.kodiak.org

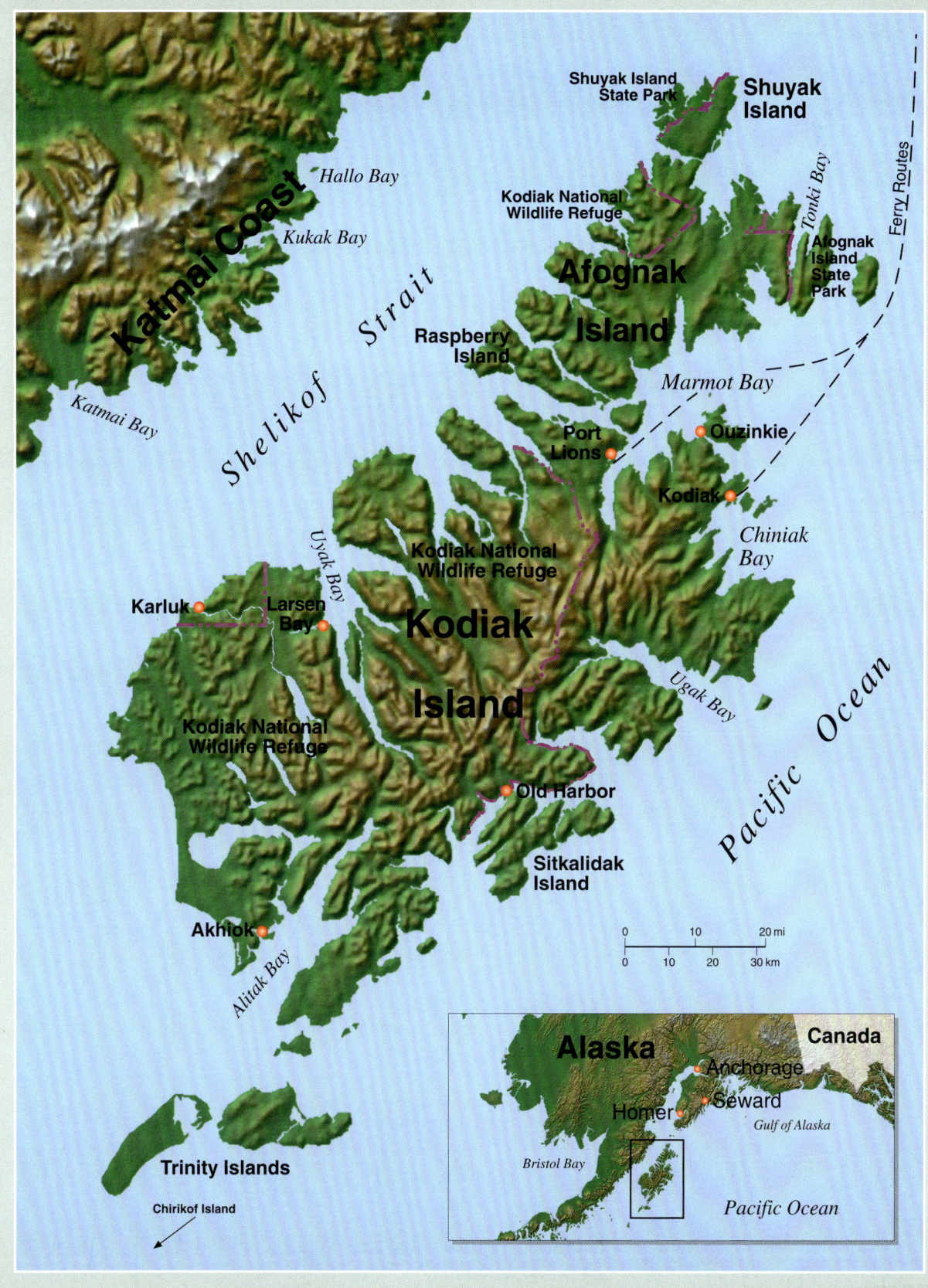

Shuyak Island
State Park

Shuyak Island

Hallo Bay

Katmai Coast

Kukak Bay

Kodiak National
Wildlife Refuge

Tonki Bay

Afognak
Island
State
Park

Afognak Island

Ferry Routes

Shelikof Strait

Katmai Bay

Raspberry Island

Marmot Bay

○ **Ouzinkie**

Port
Lions ○

Kodiak ○

Chiniak Bay

Uyak Bay

Kodiak National
Wildlife Refuge

Karluk ○

Larsen Bay ○

Kodiak Island

Ugak Bay

Pacific Ocean

Kodiak National
Wildlife Refuge

○ **Old Harbor**

Sitkalidak Island

Akhiok ○

Alitak Bay

0	10	20 mi
0	10	20	30 km

Trinity Islands

← Chirikof Island

Alaska

Canada

Anchorage ○

Homer ○

Seward ○

Gulf of Alaska

Bristol Bay

Pacific Ocean

Contents

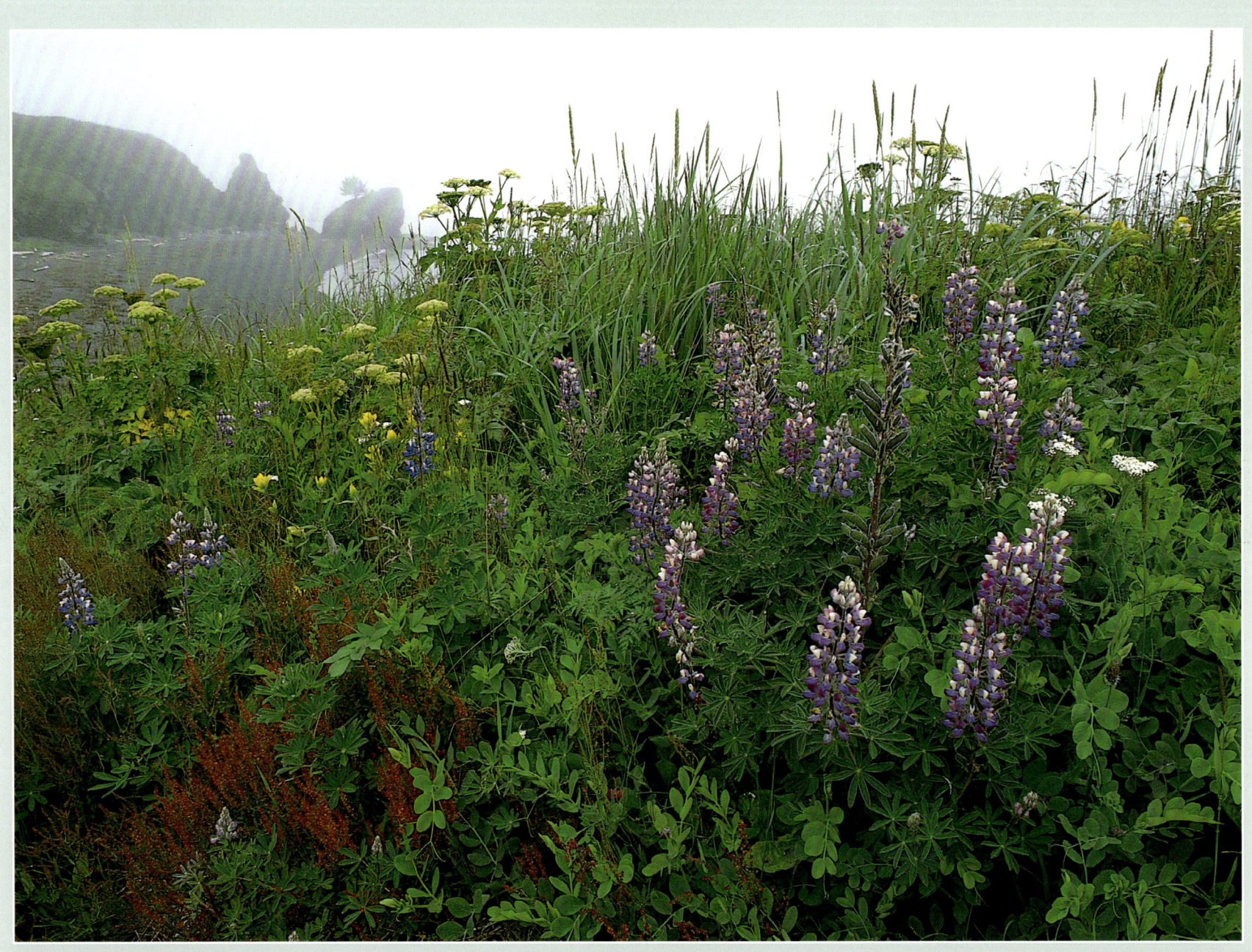

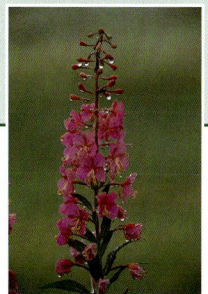

Kodiak I think won a place in the hearts of all of us.

Our spirits probably touched the highest point here. If we had other days that were epic, these days were lyric. To me they were certainly more exquisite and thrilling than any before or after.

I feel as if I wanted to go back, to Kodiak, almost as if I could return there to live. So secluded, so remote, so peaceful; such a mingling of the domestic, the pastoral, the sylvan, with the wild and the rugged; such emerald heights, such flowery vales, such blue arms and recesses of the sea, and such a vast green solitude stretching away to the west, and to the north and to the south. Bewitching Kodiak!

The spell of thy summer freshness and placidity is still upon me.

John Burroughs, Alaska: The Harriman Expedition, 1899

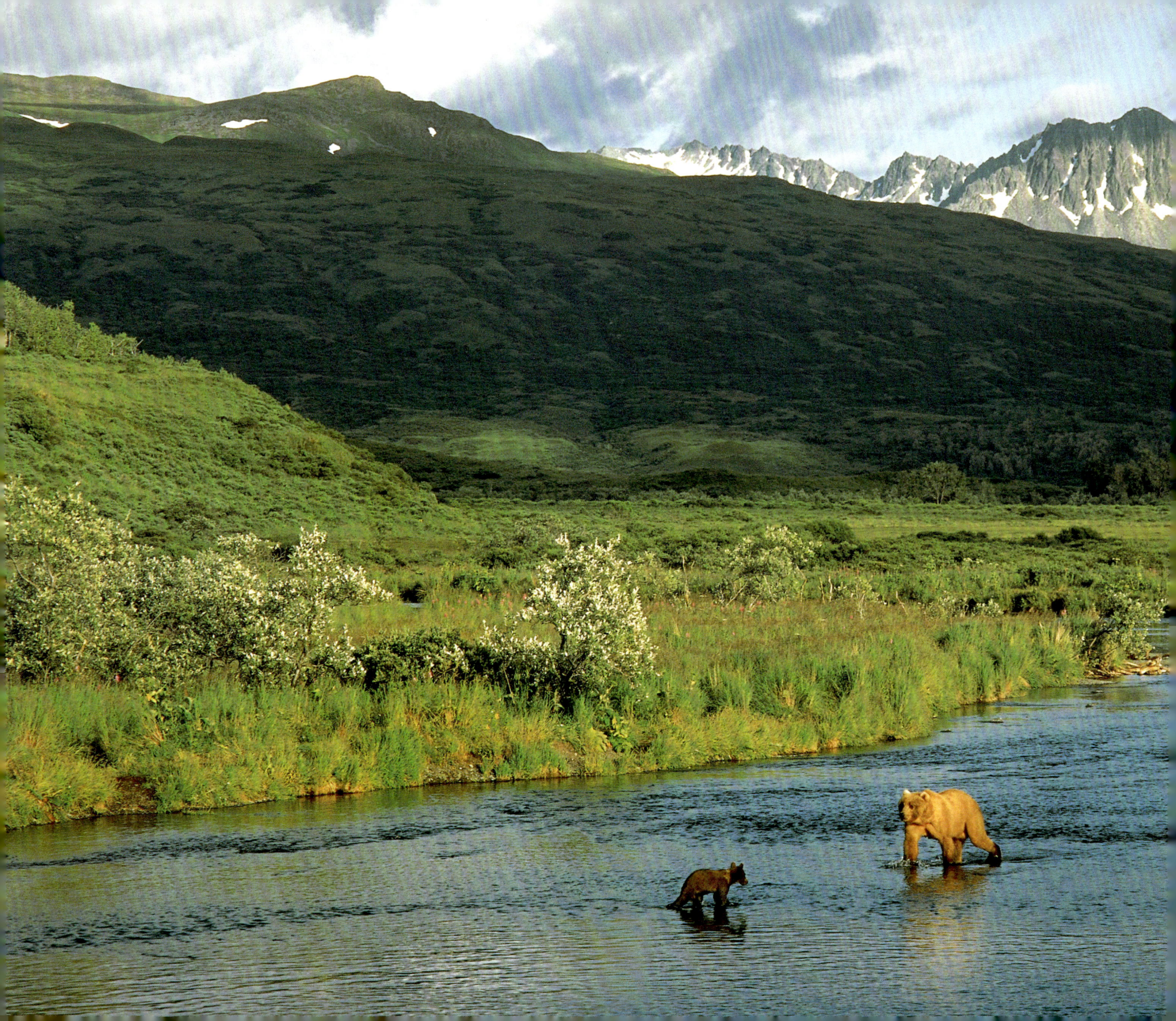

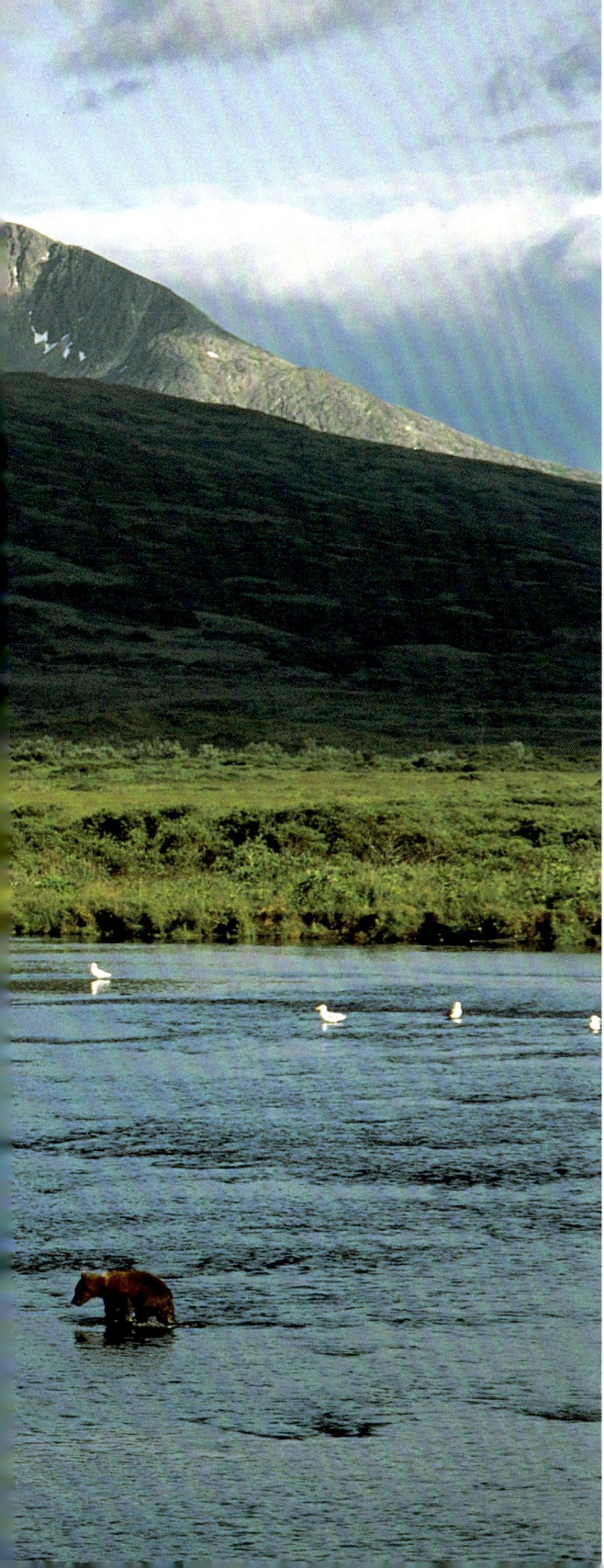

The *L*and

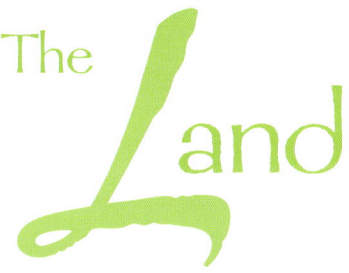

IT'S CALLED "THE EMERALD ISLE."

The name evokes the glory of vibrant, green, velvet hills that wrap this gem in spring and summer. But there is also the crystalline beauty of a wintry waterfall, the pearly fog of autumn rain. Kodiak is a jewel in any season.

It rests amid the billowing blue folds of the sea, ringed with polished ebony cliffs and capped with diamond-sparked snows. Although it seems a speck of land in the mass of the great Pacific, Kodiak is one of the largest islands in the United States, second only to Hawaii's Big Island. And this is an island of extremes: glaciers and sand dunes, bare tundra and mossy forest, low-lying bogs and 4,000-foot peaks. To the south, broad, gentle valleys drain into smooth stretches of sand and marsh. North, across the treacherous Shelikof Strait, lies the craggy, moon-scaped Valley of Ten Thousand Smokes, amid one of the world's most active volcanic centers.

Extremes of nature sculpted the Kodiak archipelago. Steaming volcanoes erupted from undersea turmoil, creating the tips of these islands. Eons later, blue glaciers did their part to birth mountains and valleys, with icy fingers clutching and kneading the rock. Earthquakes shifted and split the land. Storm-tossed waves carved away cliffs, exposing fossils of creatures placed there 10 million years ago.

left Brown bears in river.
(Don Pitcher/Alaska Stock)

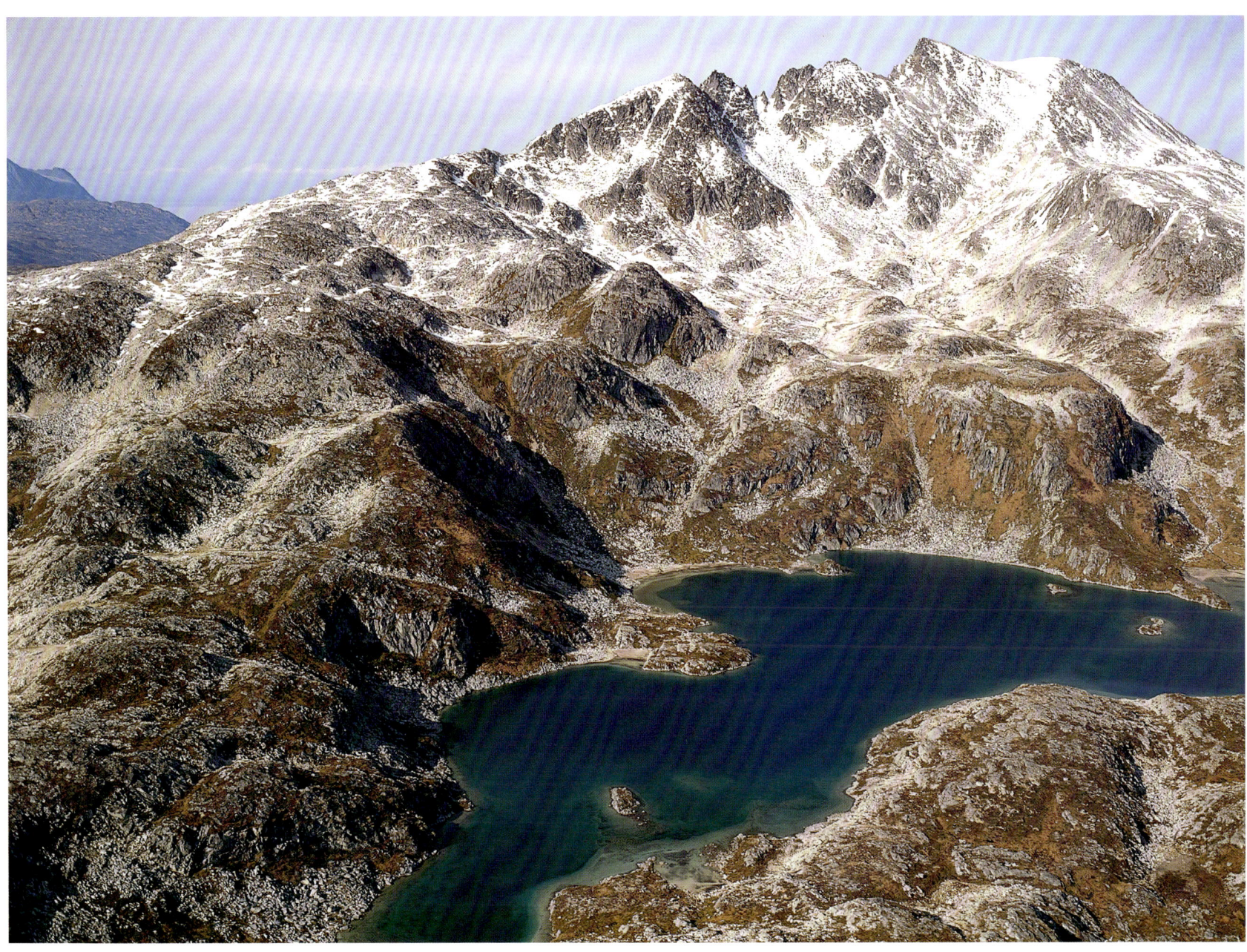

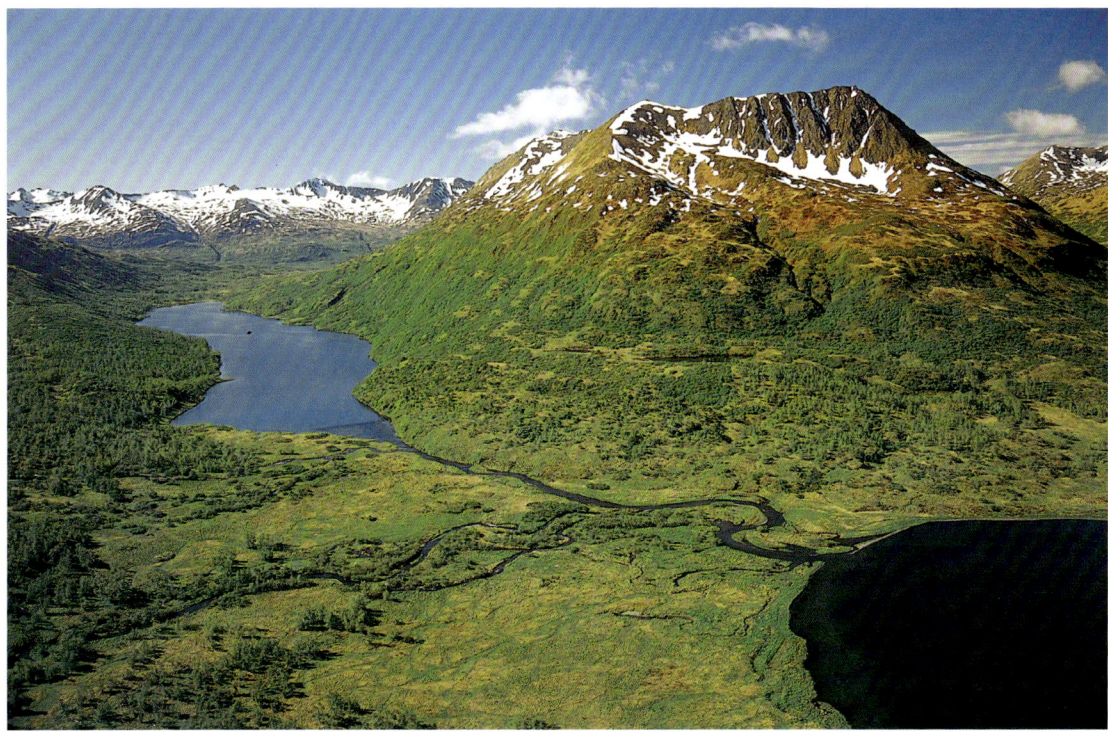

The wind brought gifts—seeds of grasses, plants and trees from the mainland. The great coniferous forest that stretches across the entire North American continent abruptly reveals its borders here. The northeastern part of the archipelago is forested with towering Sitka spruce, the only unmixed stand in the world. But on the northern end of Kodiak Island, the treeline suddenly gives way to steep, grassy hills. The forest slowly stalks to the south, invading about a mile of tundra every hundred years.

From the air, most of the island appears a hiker's paradise, rock bones draped in close-cropped velveteen grass. On the ground, reality: smooth passage is interrupted by dense alder thickets where brown bears rest. Steep, rocky mountains drop into ravines choked with fern and devil's club in summer and with ice in winter. Thick carpets of grass can grow taller than a person in a short summer's growth. But the hard going is worth the work.

When snow is on the mountains, skiers and snowboarders struggle to the top, celebrating the season in dizzying

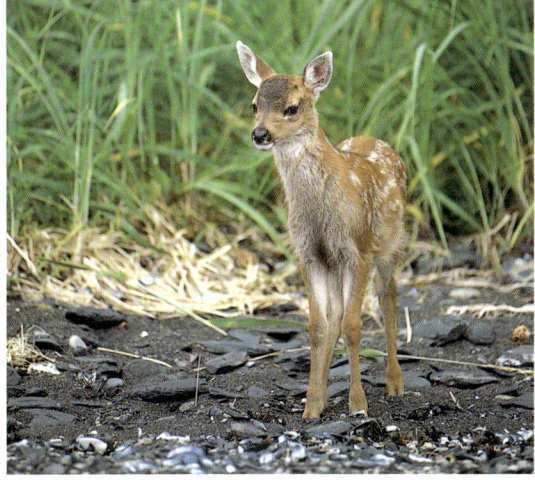

far left Aerial view of Lake Leanne with a dusting of snow in the surrounding mountains. (Fred Hirschmann)

above Lush vegetation gives Alaska's Emerald Isle its name. (Calvin Hall)

left Sitka black-tailed deer fawn. The deer are an introduced species. (Tom Walker)

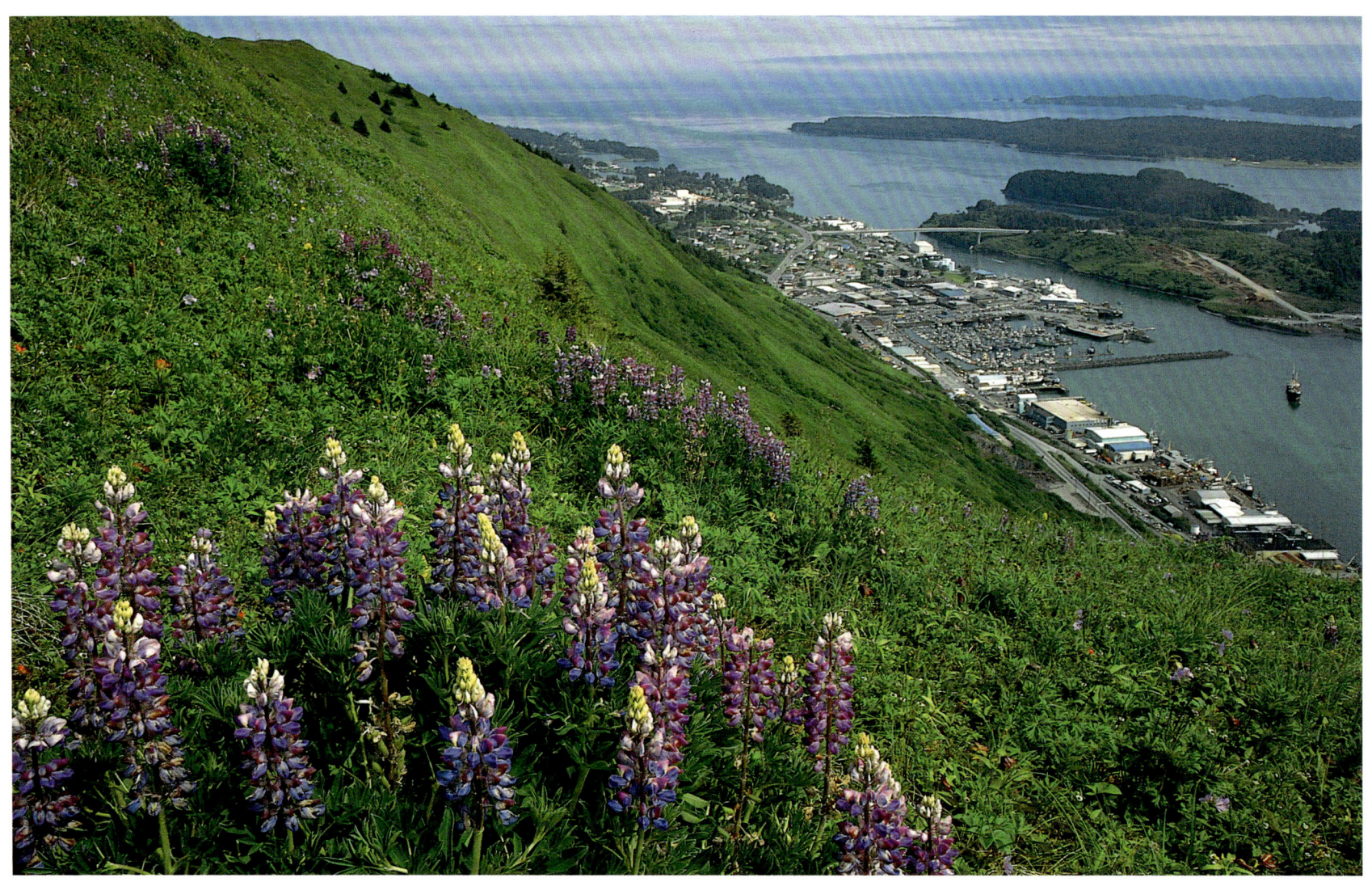

above City of Kodiak
from Pillar Mountain with
summer lupine.
(Marion Owen)

right Savannah sparrow.
More than 200 species of
birds have been identified
in the Kodiak archipelago.
(Ron Niebrugge)

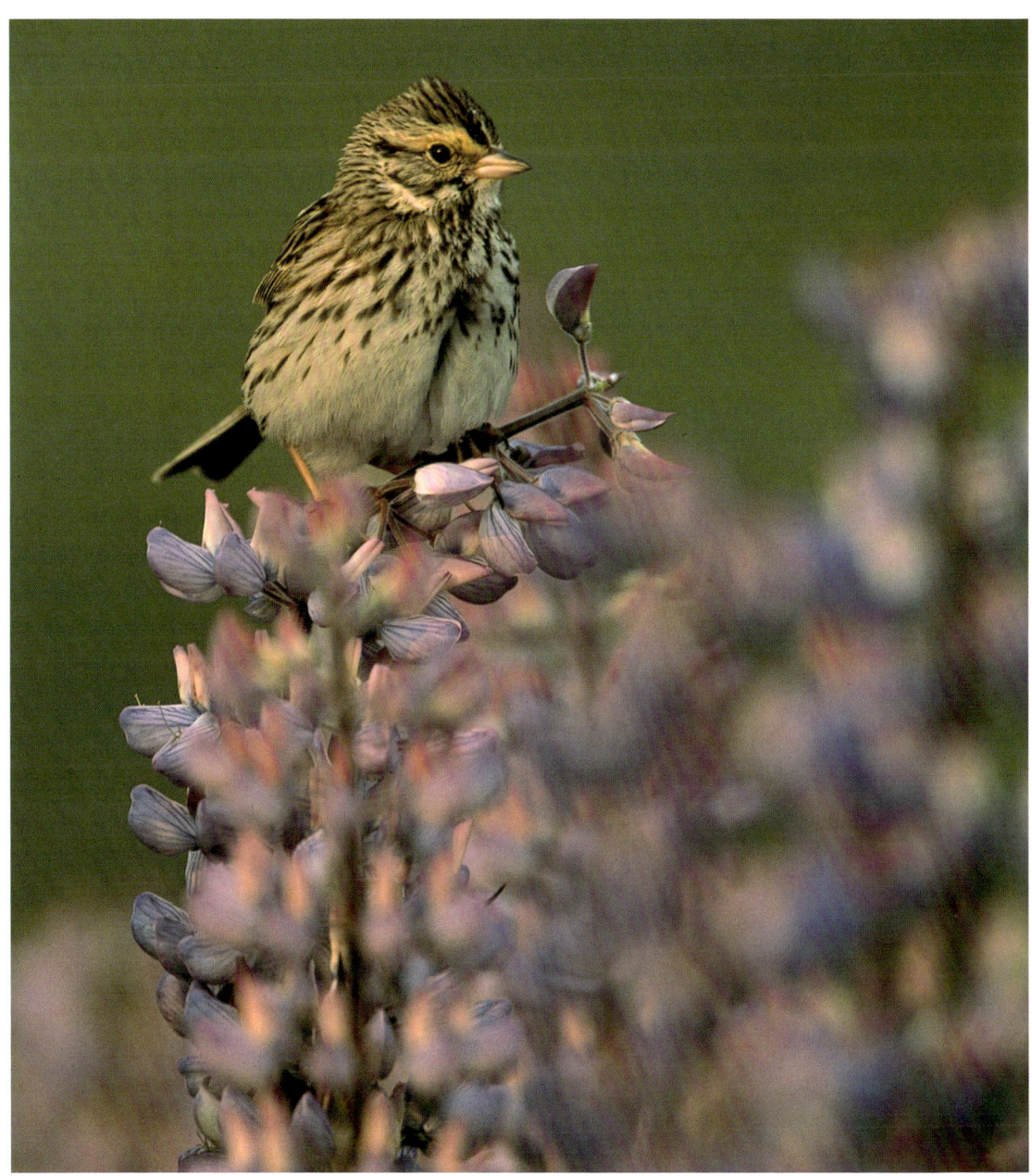

runs downhill. In spring and summer those alpine hills are dappled with delicate wildflowers. The sky's rainbow is reflected in the meadow's colors: deep purple iris, lavender wild geranium, sunny yellow paintbrush, sky-blue lupine. Oversized bumblebees, heavy enough to anchor themselves in a stiff island breeze, wander amid the heady scents of white bog orchid and pink wild rose, dodging the pungent chocolate lily. There are healing plants here–spiky green plantain, feathery white yarrow– and the deadly poison of the blue monkshood once used on Alutiiq hunting spears. There is food in abundance, for the people and animals who know how to find it: lamb's quarters and wild chives, beach pea and goosetongue. Crowberry and cranberry, salmonberry and blueberry have fed life on Kodiak for uncounted years.

The bears are happy here, feasting on berries and in salmon-rich streams. They reign over the islands and the neighboring Katmai coast with an assurance that matches their massive size. Humans keep a respectful distance, clanging bells and singing loudly in the

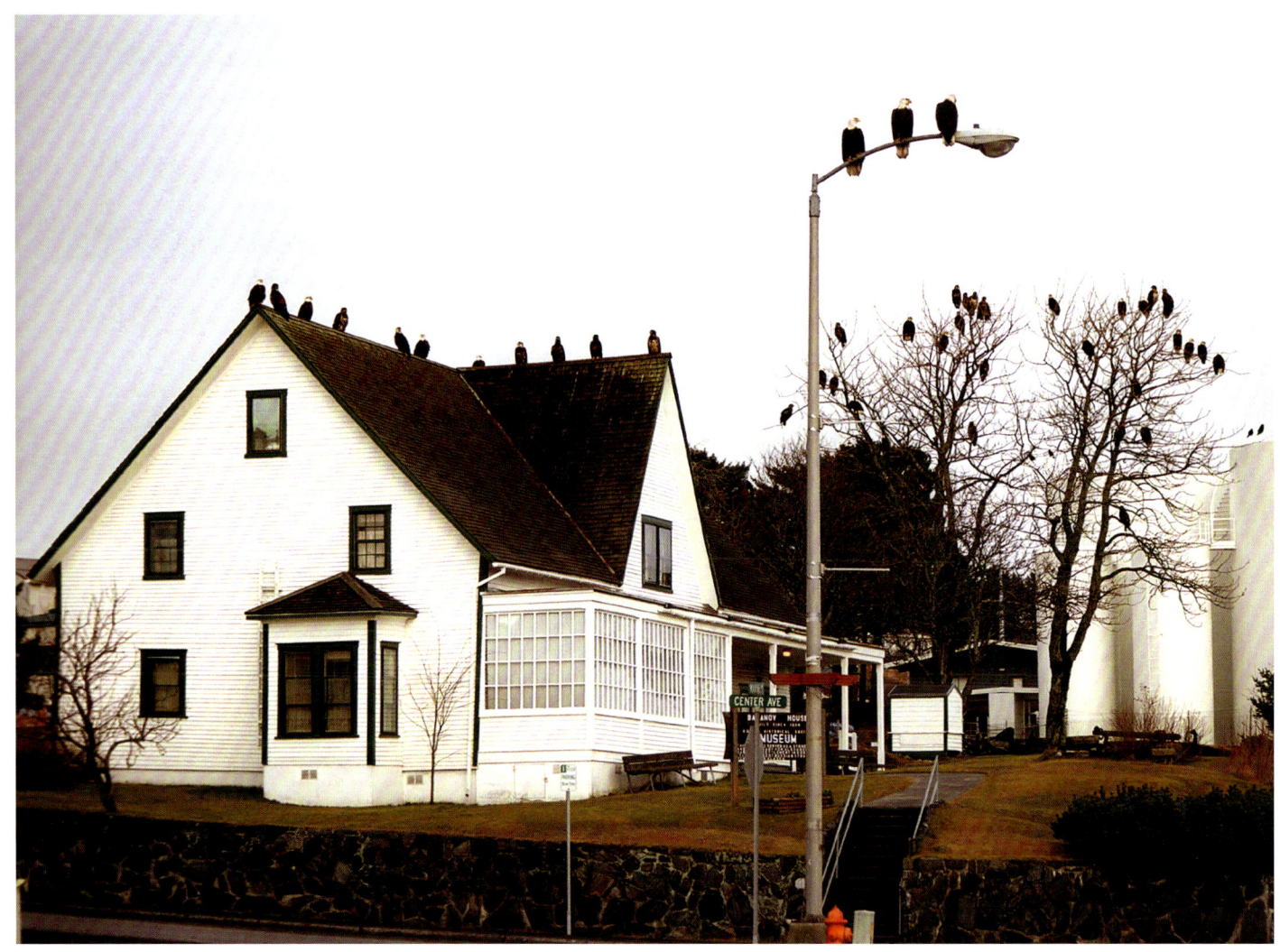

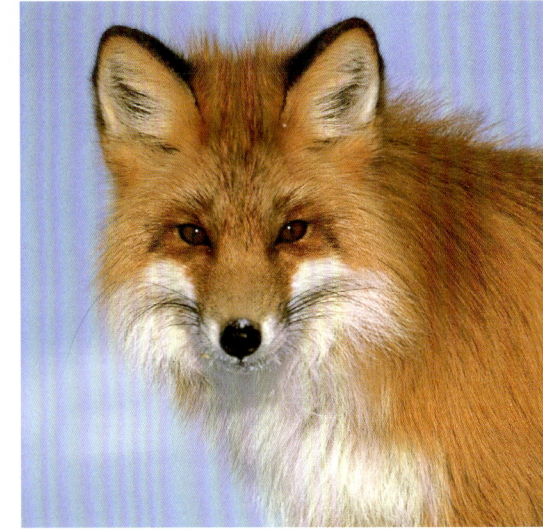

right Red fox are native to the Kodiak archipelago. (Patrick Endres)

below A rare sighting of Kodiak brown bears on the road. Bears usually prefer the more remote parts of the island. (Elysia Leake)

left Eagles frequent the Baranov Museum at the Kodiak waterfront in the fall and winter to scavenge food from off-loading fishing boats. (Elysia Leake)

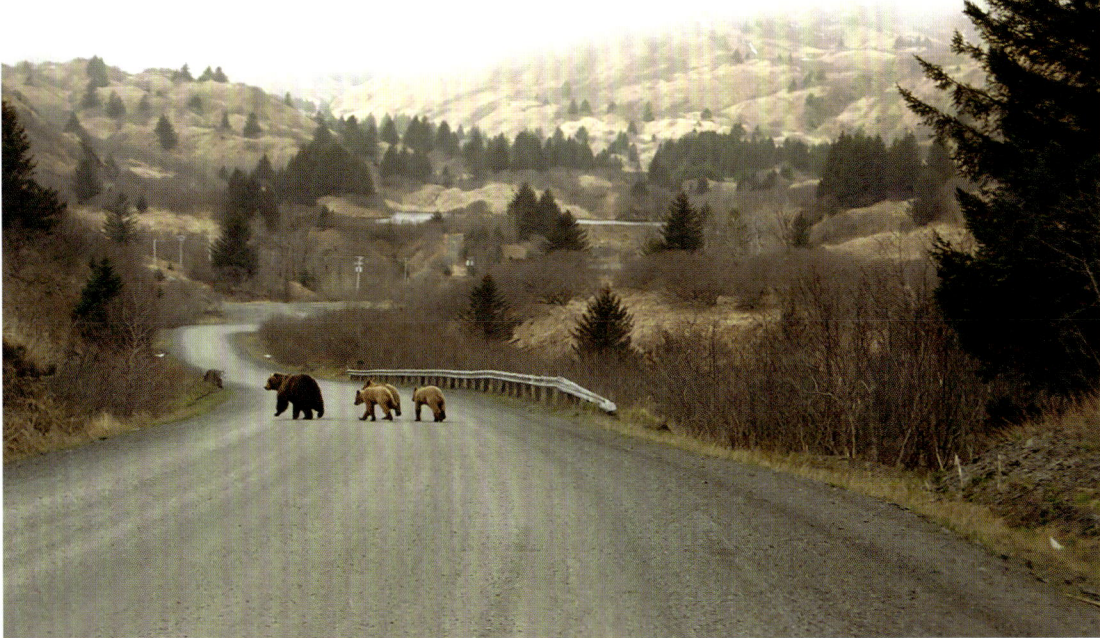

wild, fretting over bear-proof garbage containers in town.

The bears and their brethren usually prefer the solitude of the more remote parts of the island, but there are always surprises: a Sitka black-tailed deer browsing outside the hospital doors, or a red fox taking a shortcut down a village street. The eagle, still rare in so many parts of our country, is a common sight here. More than 500 have been counted within driving distance of Kodiak city on some annual Audubon Christmas bird counts. Look amid the cottonwood trees clustering above Kodiak's waterfront and there they are, supervising harbor traffic with a critical eye. They reign over more than 200 bird species in the archipelago, from the tiny, sweet-voiced golden-crowned sparrow, to the elegant and elusive trumpeter swan.

The native mammals are few: river otter, red fox, short-tail weasel, little brown bat, tundra vole and brown bear. Man introduced the first horses and cattle in Alaska here, along with ground squirrels, deer, mountain goat, Roosevelt elk, snowshoe hare, beaver, muskrat and red squirrel. And there's no surprise like

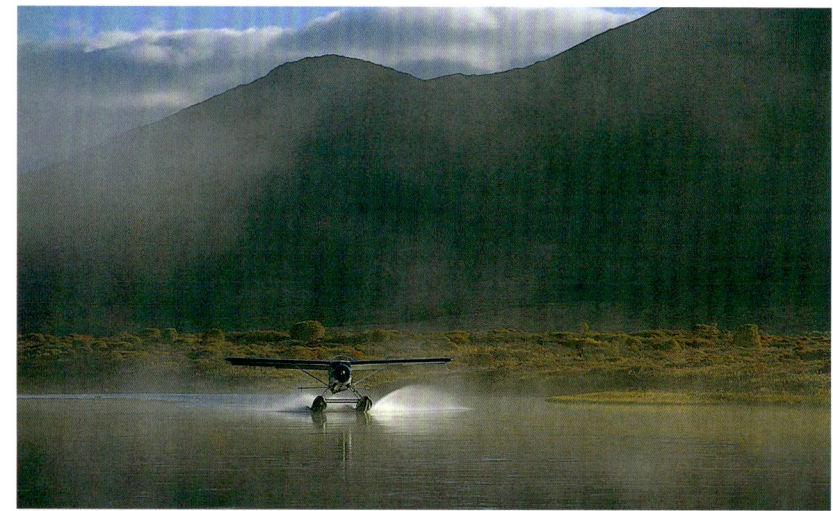

right A floatplane lands on the Karluk River, known for salmon fishing and bear viewing. Floatplanes and charter boats can take you to great fishing on remote rivers and lakes. (Tom Evans)

left Domestic herds of bison roam the Narrow Cape area. (Hank Pennington)

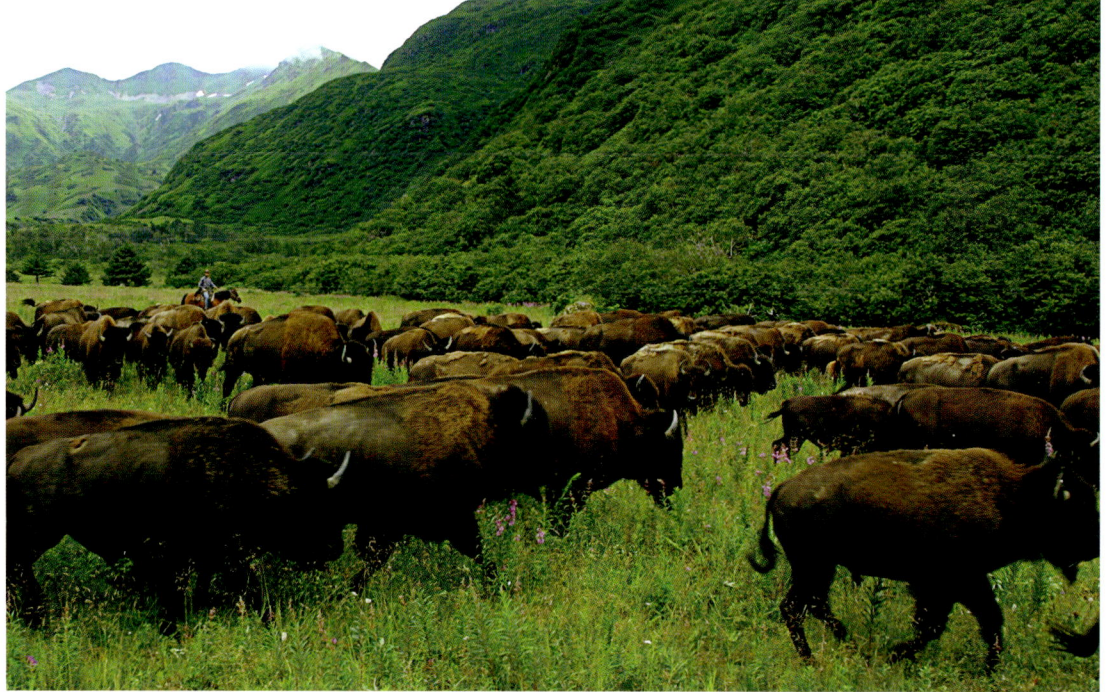

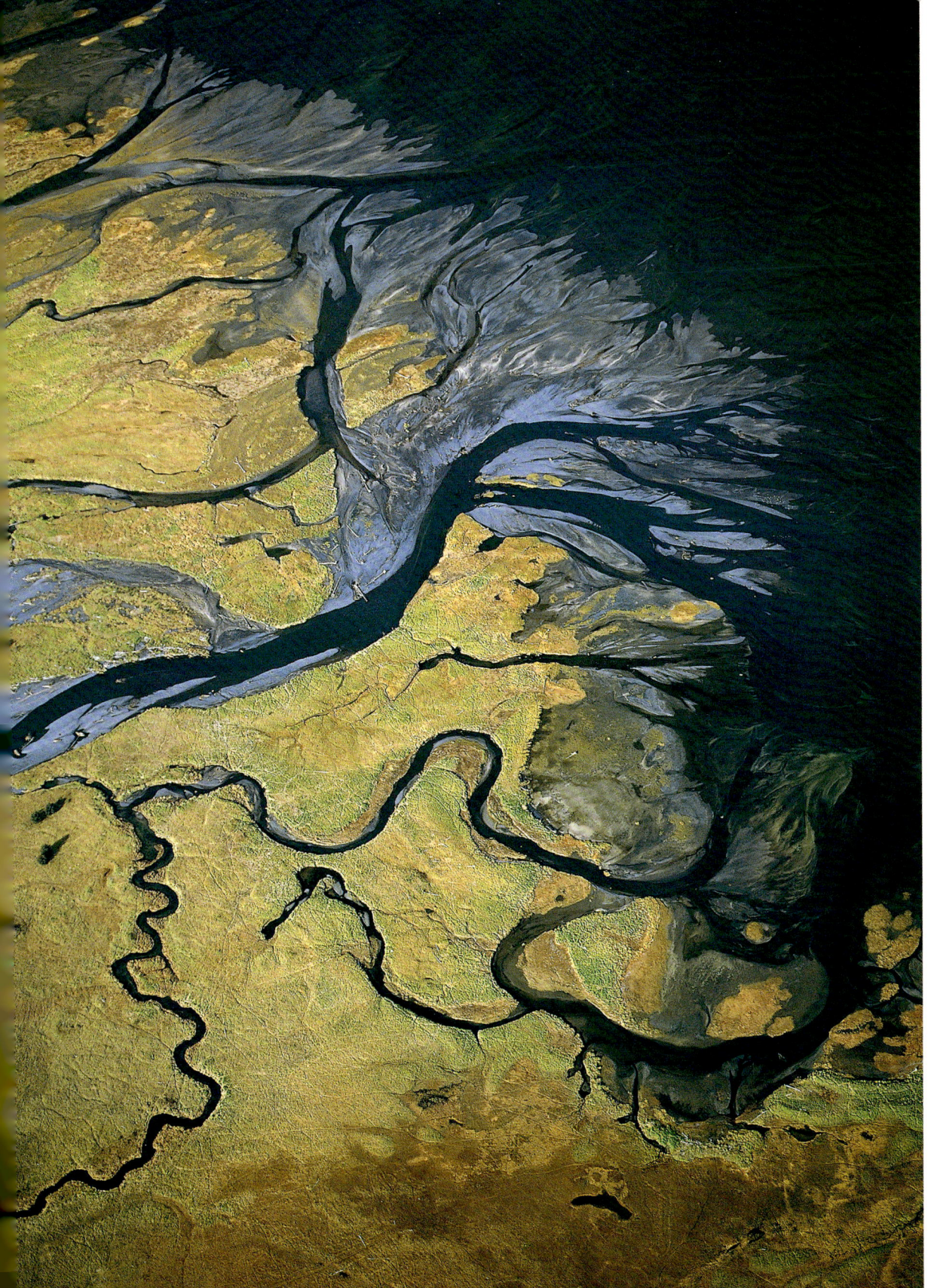

looking up from the peaceful Pasagshak River to find a herd of bison, complete with cowboys, thundering along the sandy beach.

Despite the changes man has brought, the land is so massive that it dwarfs any human or animal presence. On Kodiak Island alone, the coastline meanders for more than 1,270 miles. Rarely is nature's design interrupted. Just six villages and one city are scattered along the water's edge, every one with its toes in the sea. Thin lines of road trace ancient coastal pathways; soft outlines of Alutiiq sod houses and ruined World War II Quonset huts remind us of older times.

Even after nearly 8,000 years of the human touch, our imprint on this mighty land is faint.

left Aerial pattern of drainages on the tidal flats at the head of Kizhuyak Bay on the northern end of Kodiak Island. (Fred Hirschmann)

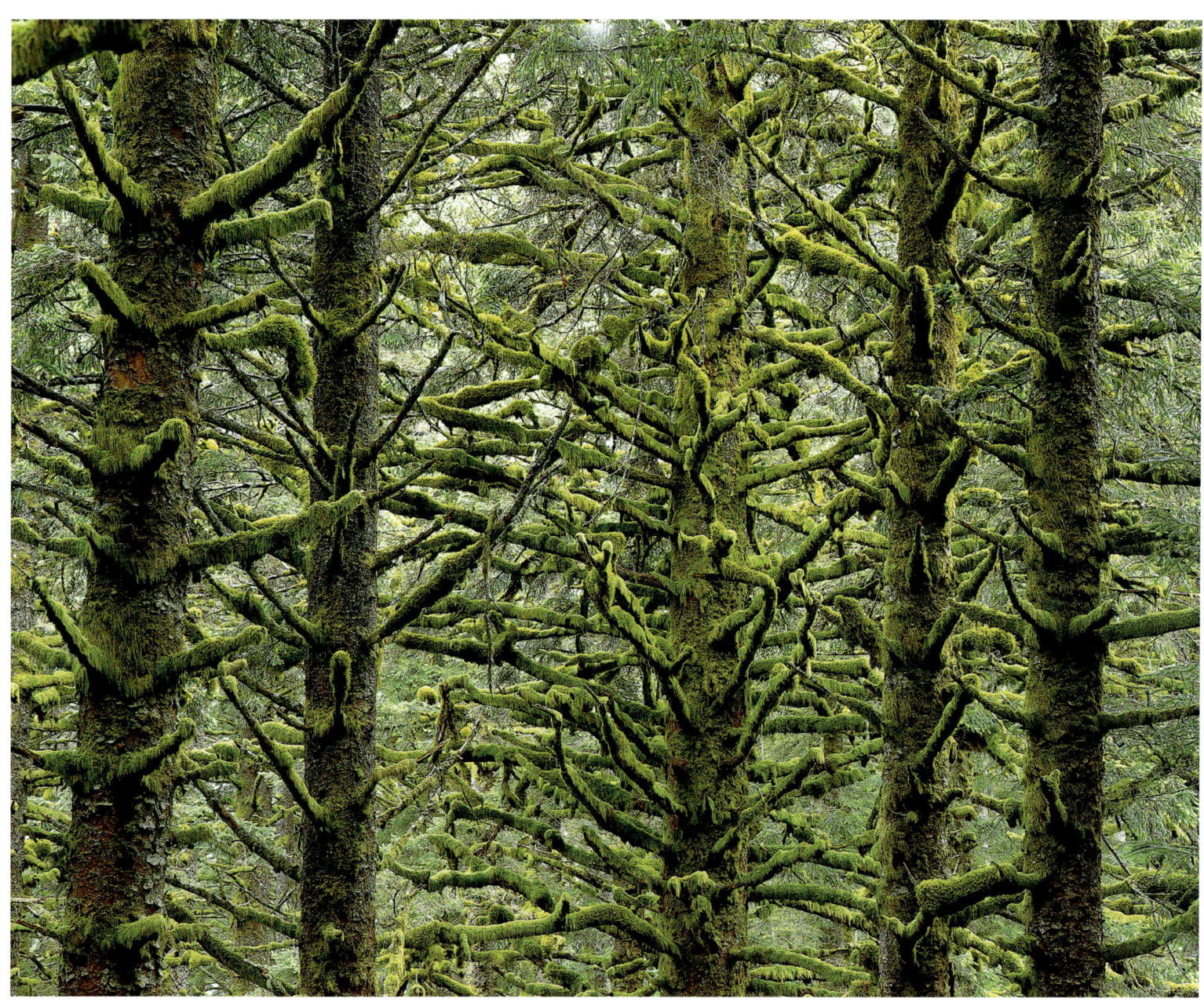

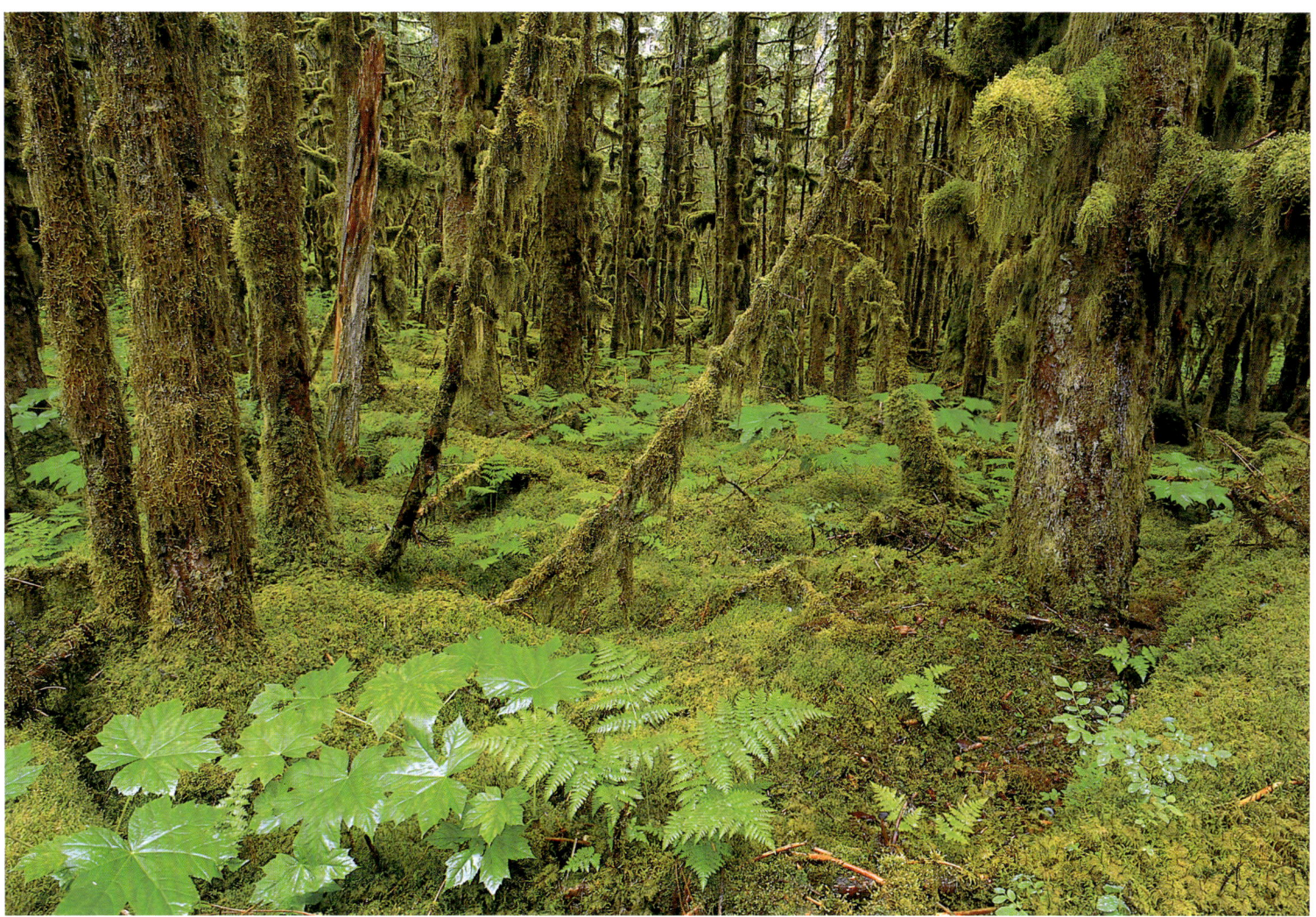

left The northeast part of the archipelago is covered with thick Sitka spruce forests—the only unmixed stand in the world. (Vance Gese)

above Heavily laden with moss, massive Sitka spruce shelter a variety of shade-tolerant plants in the rain forest. (Vance Gese)

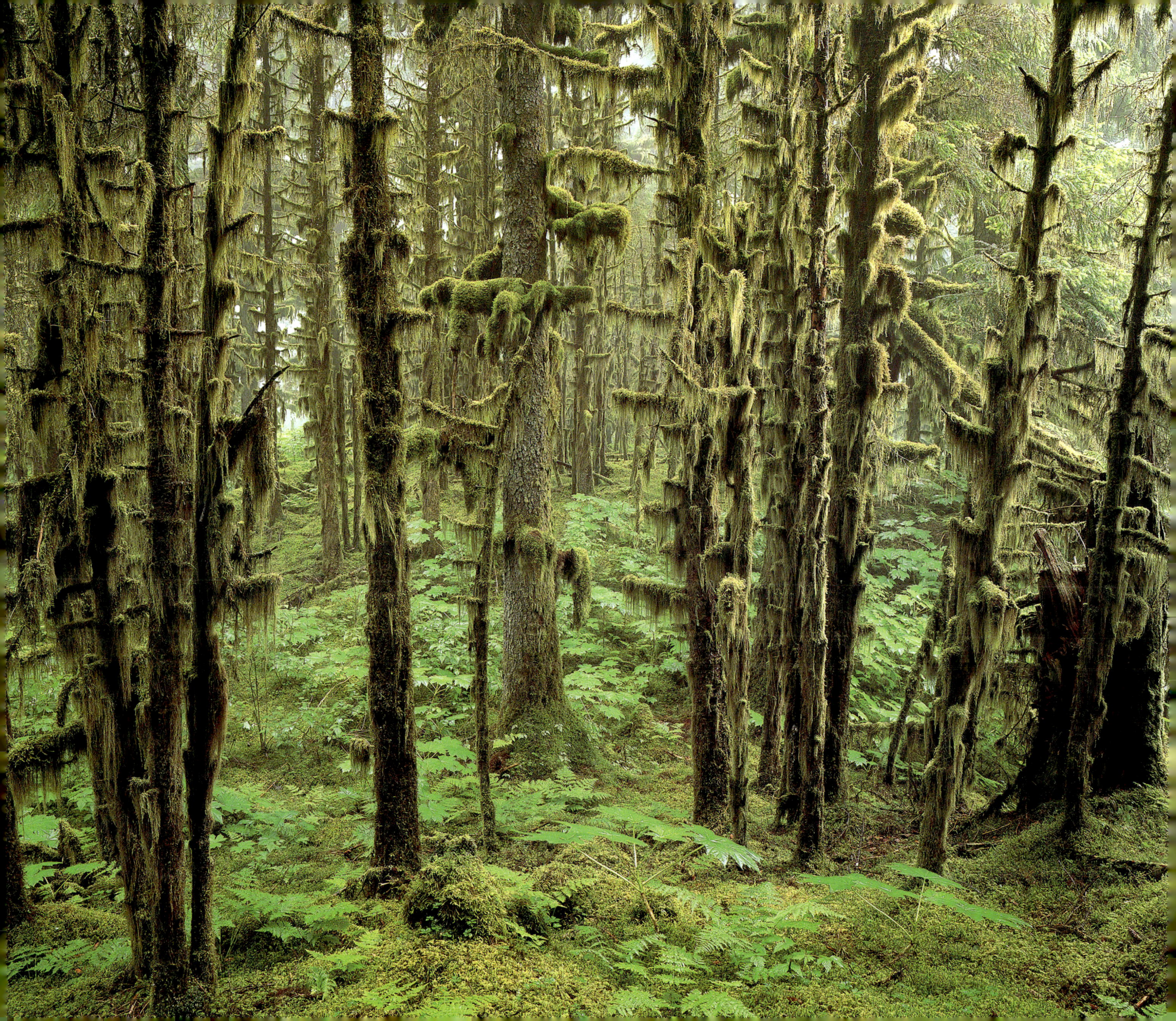

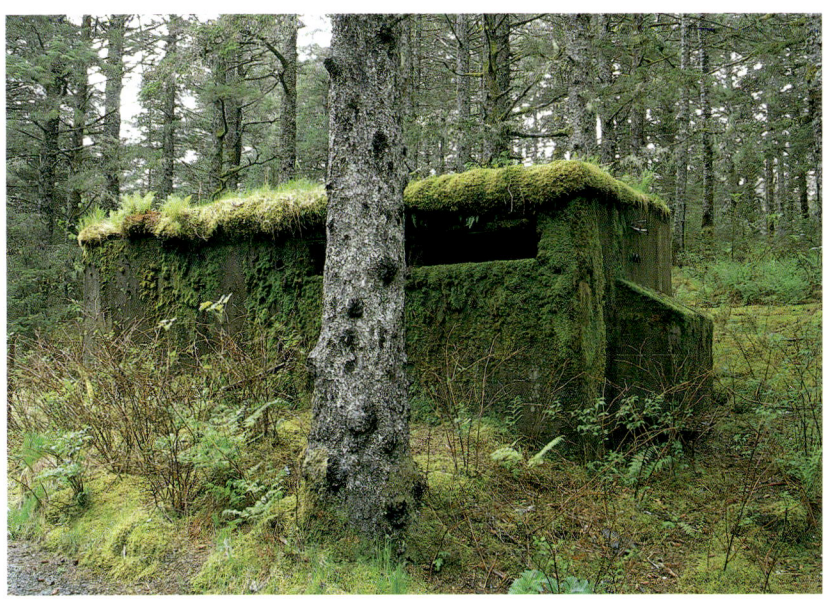

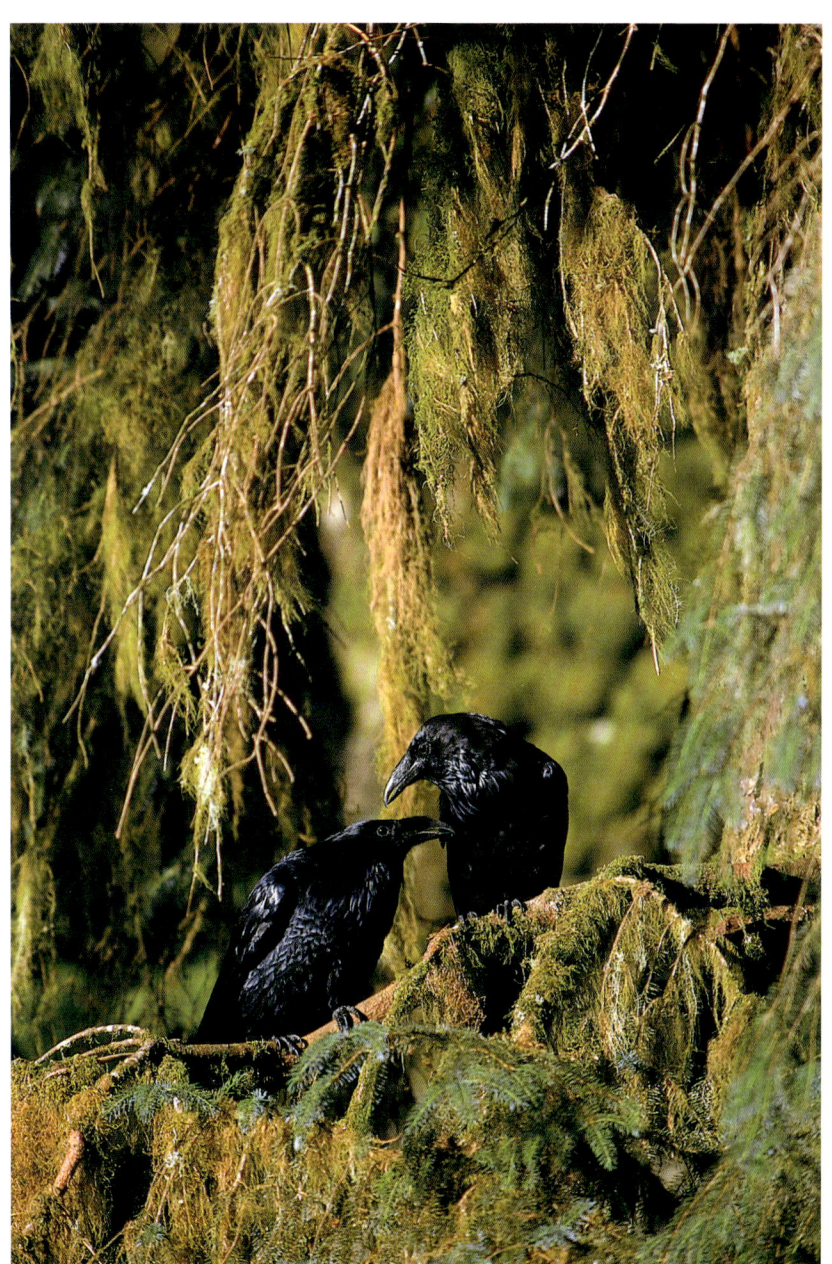

left Summer fog creeps in behind a spruce forest. (Vance Gese)

above A WWII bunker is tucked in the rain forest at Ft. Abercrombie State Historical Park. The 183-acre park holds many reminders of its past as a military outpost. (Calvin Hall)

right A pair of common ravens preen in a Sitka spruce tree. (Gary Schultz.)

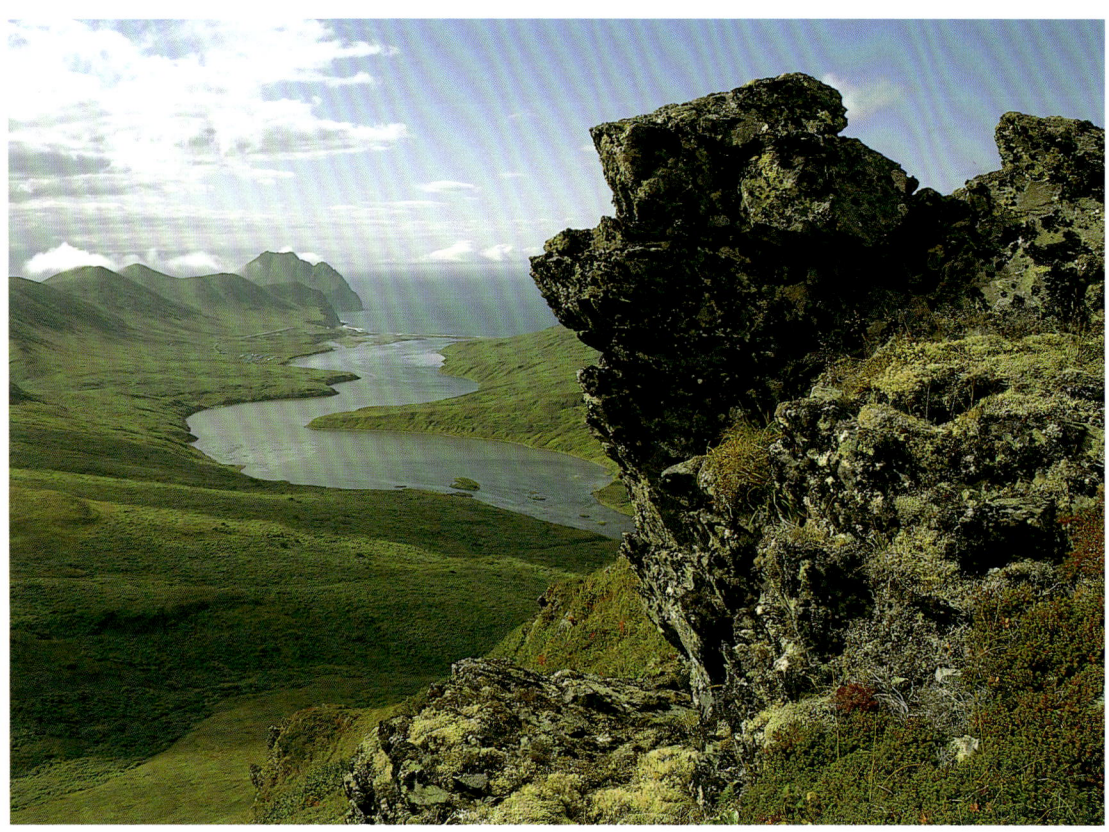

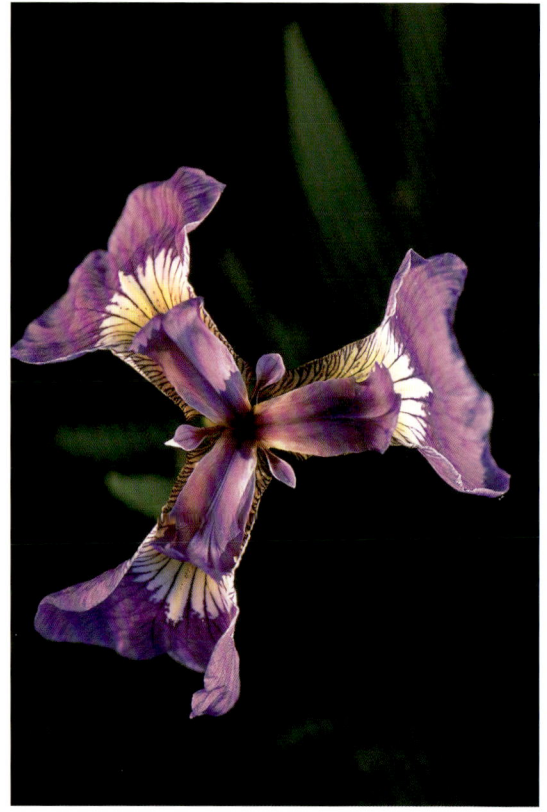

above The Karluk River and Cape Karluk. (Don Pitcher/Alaska Stock)

right Deep purple iris thrive in bogs found throughout the island group. (Ron Niebrugge)

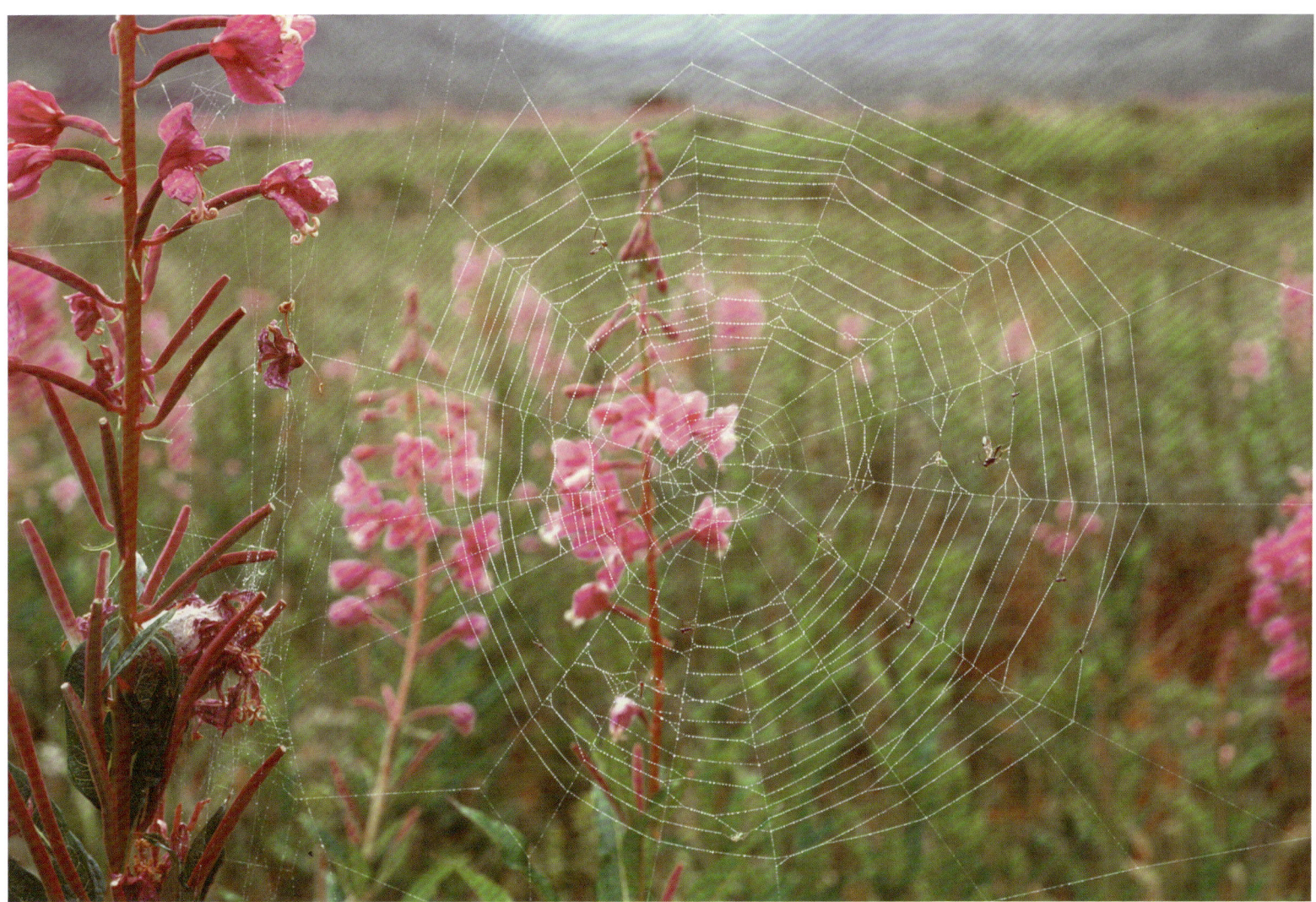

above Dewy spiderweb
on fireweed in the Kodiak
National Wildlife Refuge.
(Steve Kaufman)

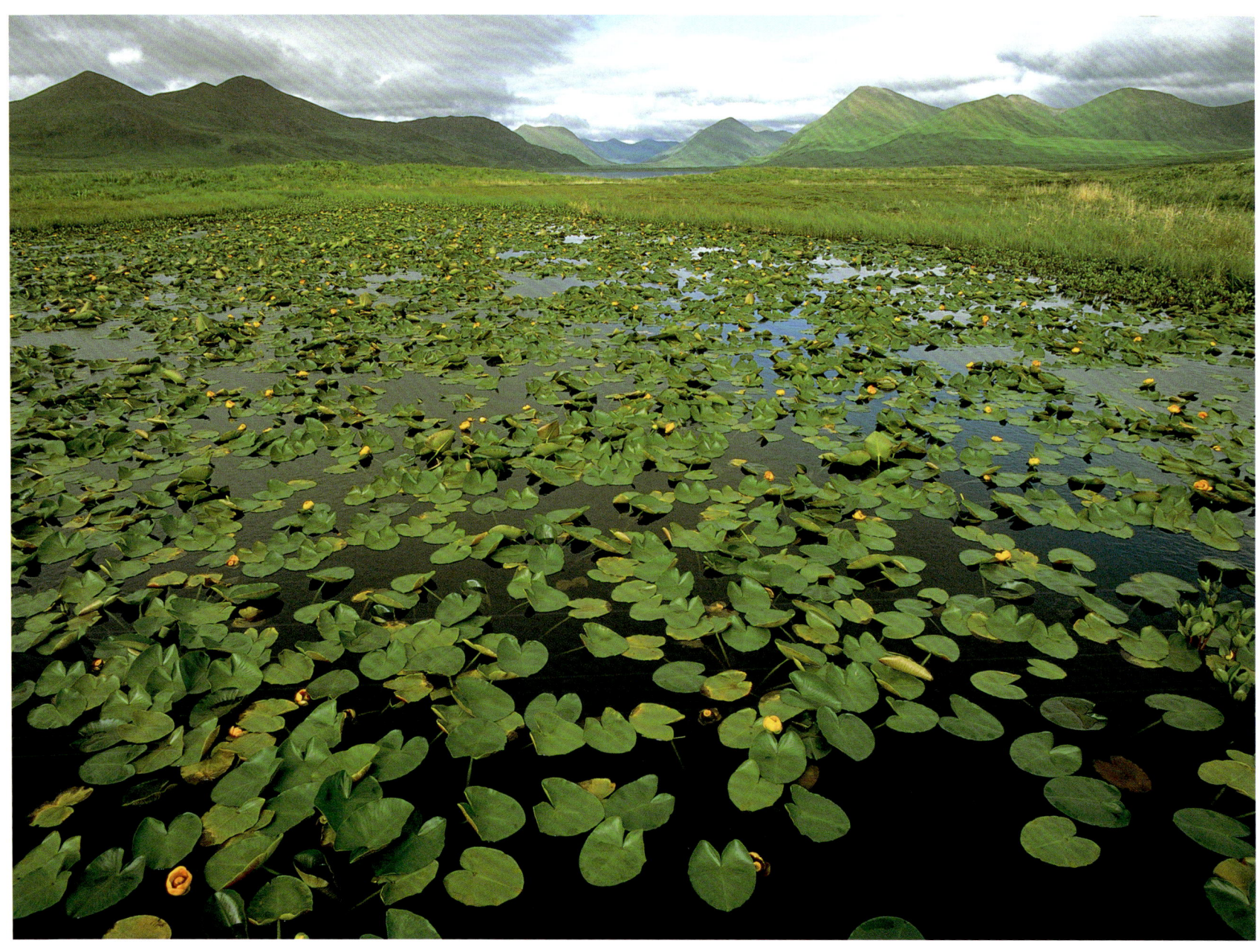

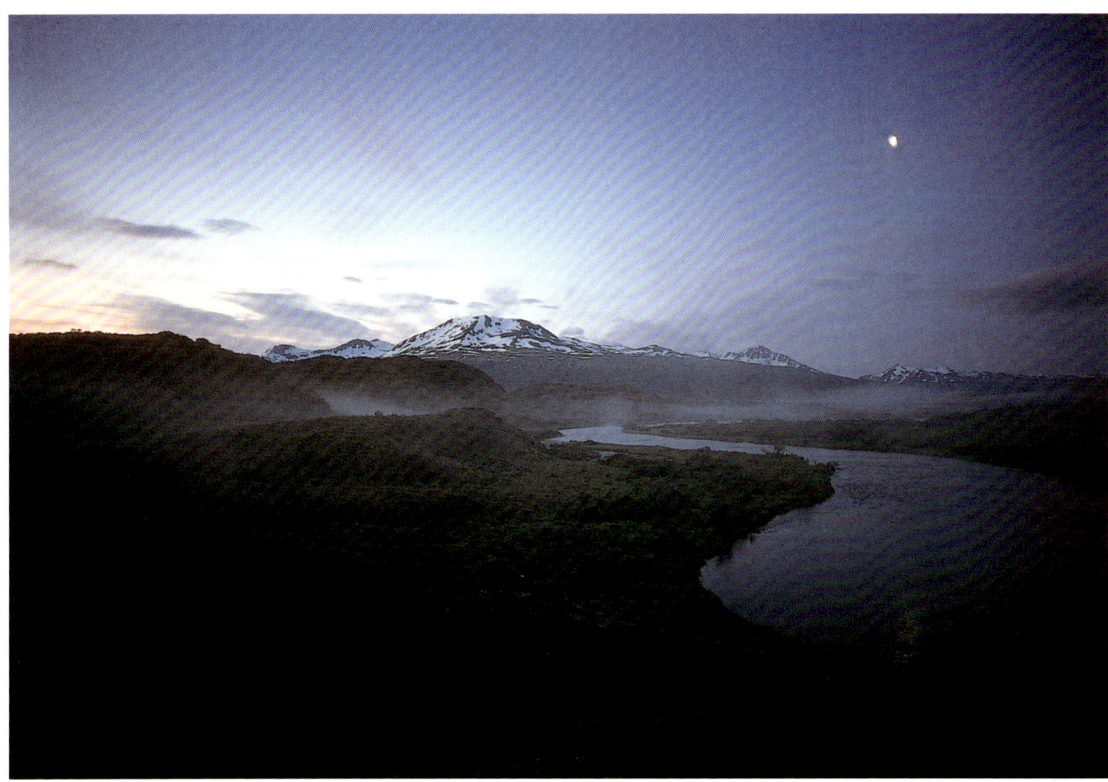

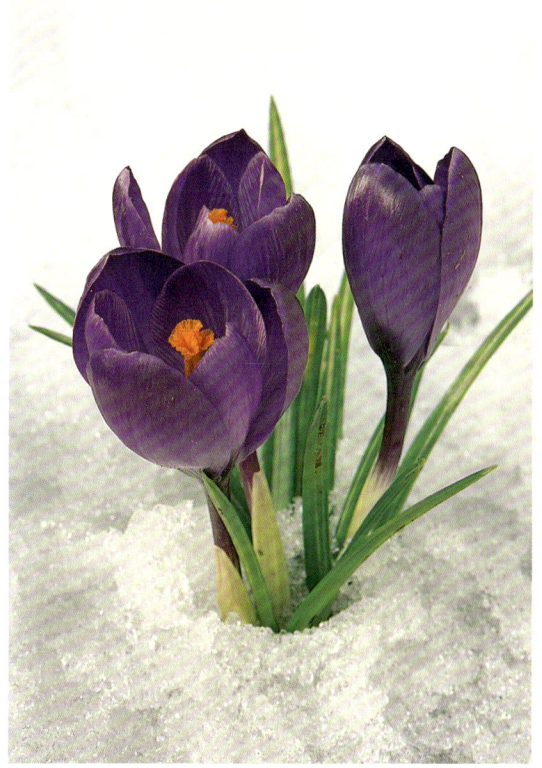

below Purple crocus bloom through a spring snow. (Marion Owen/ Alaska Stock)

left Tundra pond and lily pads at Olga Bay. (Don Pitcher/Alaska Stock)

above Dog Salmon River and Grayback Mountain with a summer moon. (Don Pitcher/Alaska Stock)

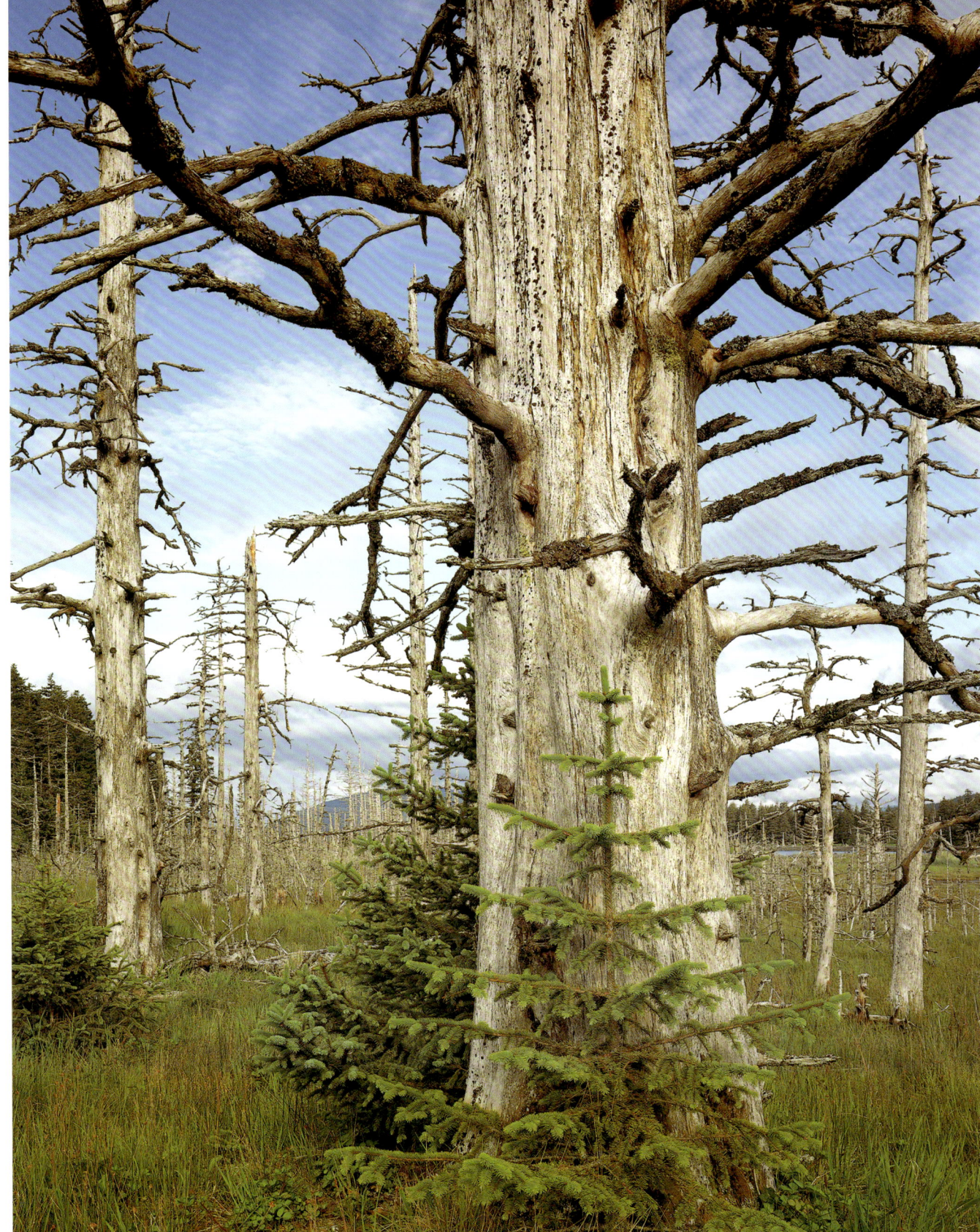

right On Afognak Island, new forest life grows among the relics left behind by the 1964 earthquake. (Jeff Gnass)

far right Russet cottongrass and headlands on Shuyak Island overlook Shelikof Strait, Shuyak Island State Park. (Jeff Gnass)

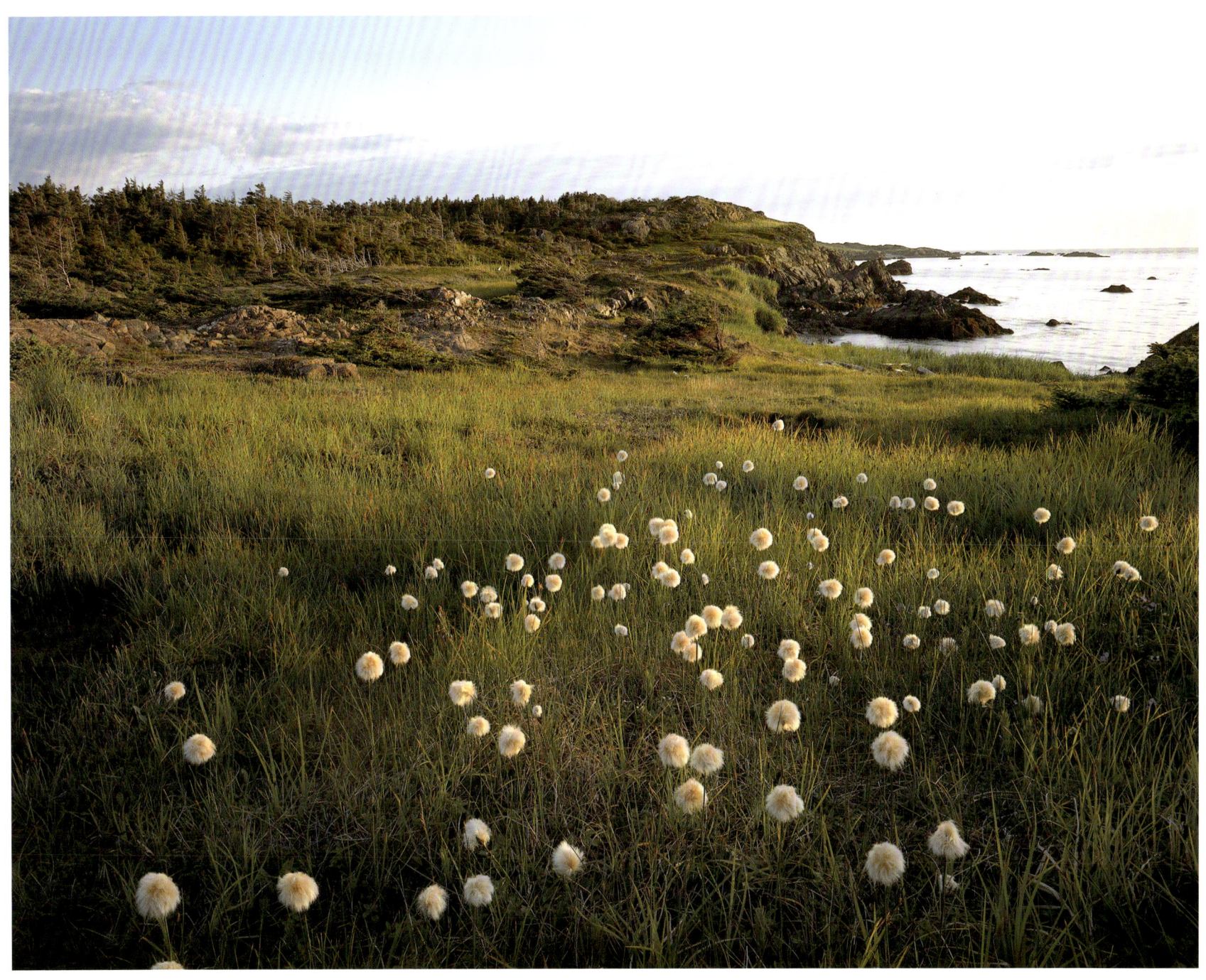

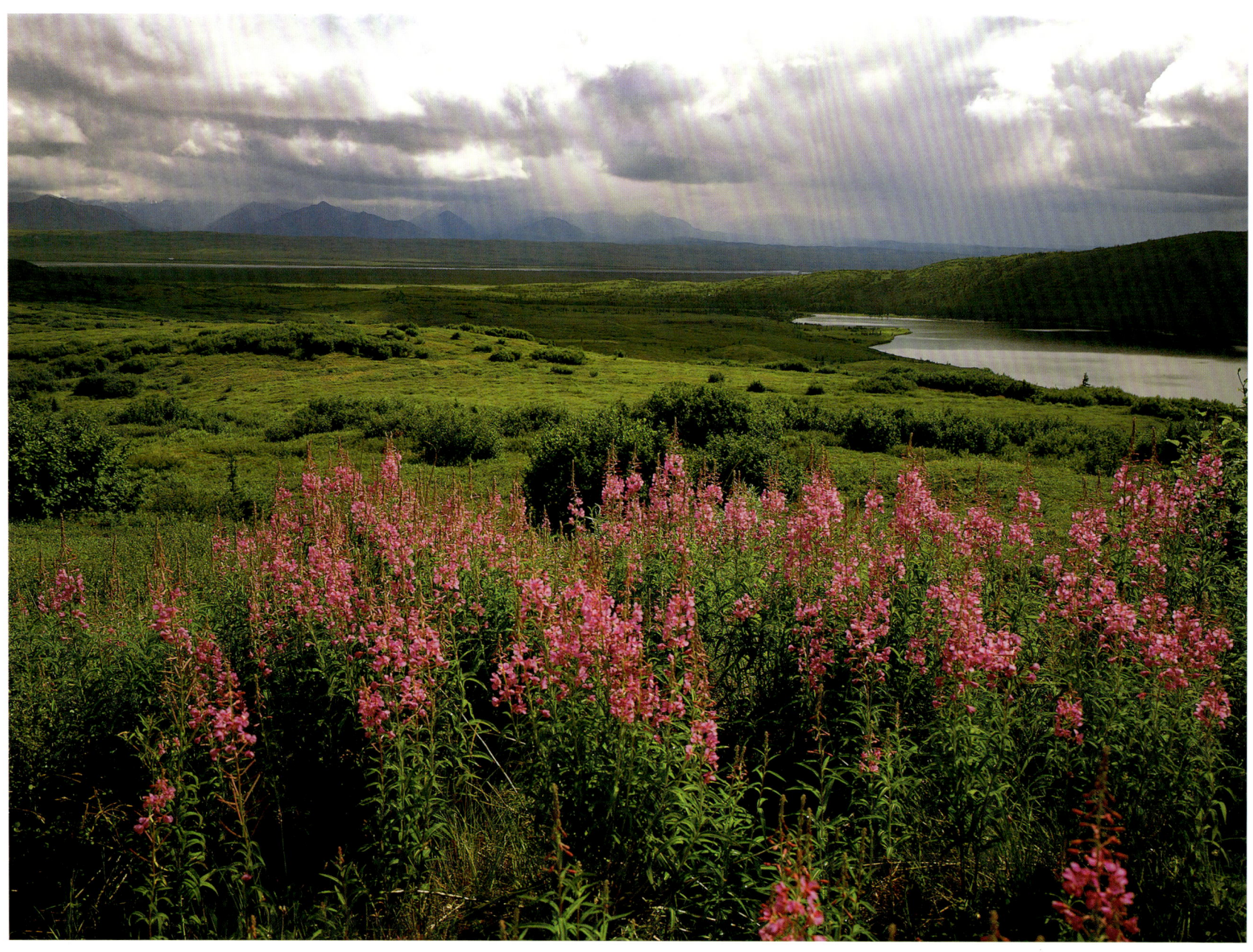

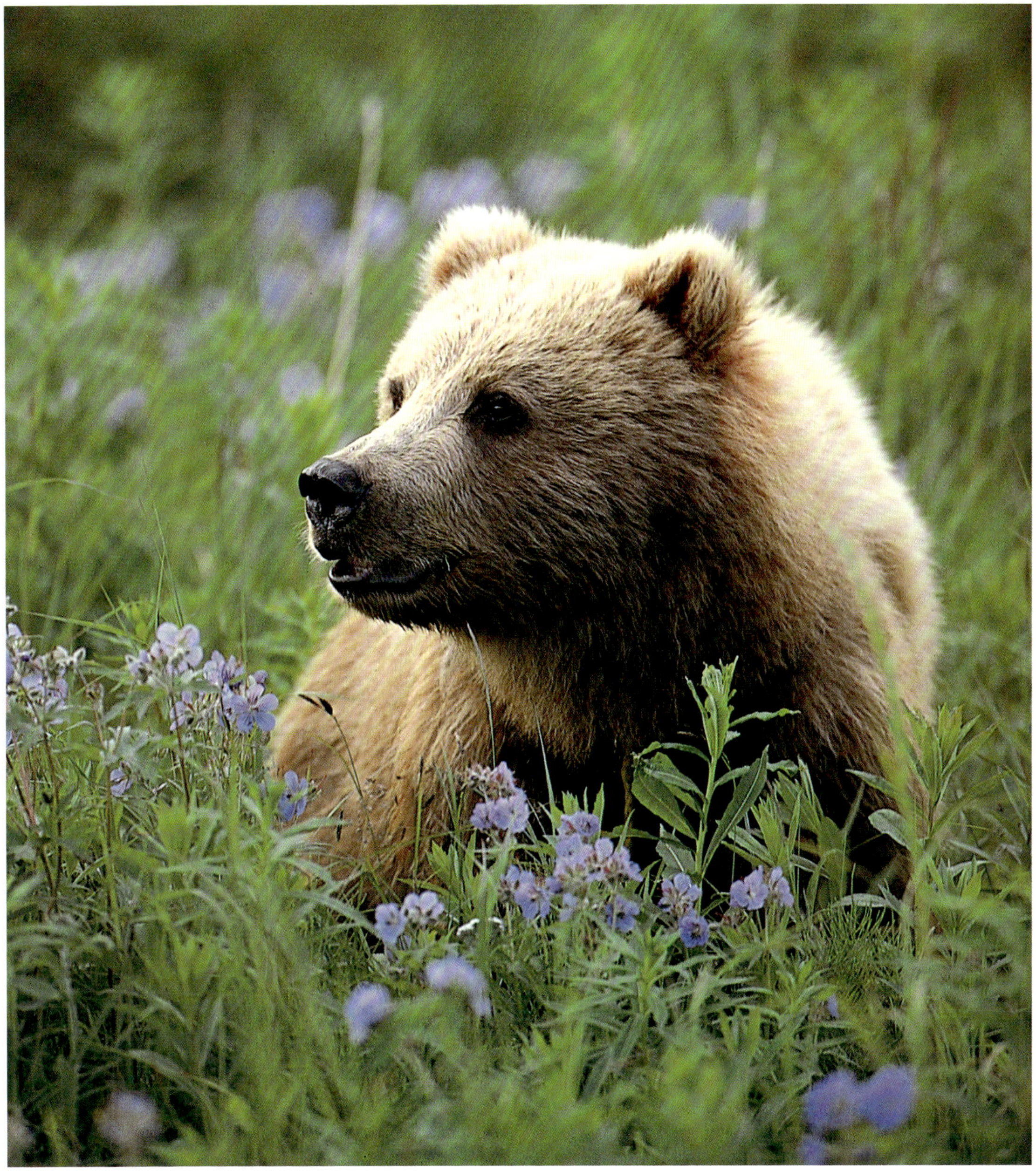

far left Bold fireweed brightens a midsummer afternoon. (Steve Gilroy)

left Kodiak brown bear in wild geranium. About 3,000 bears live on the islands with many more inhabiting the Katmai coast. (Tom Walker)

below The forget-me-not is the Alaska state flower. (Cathy Hart)

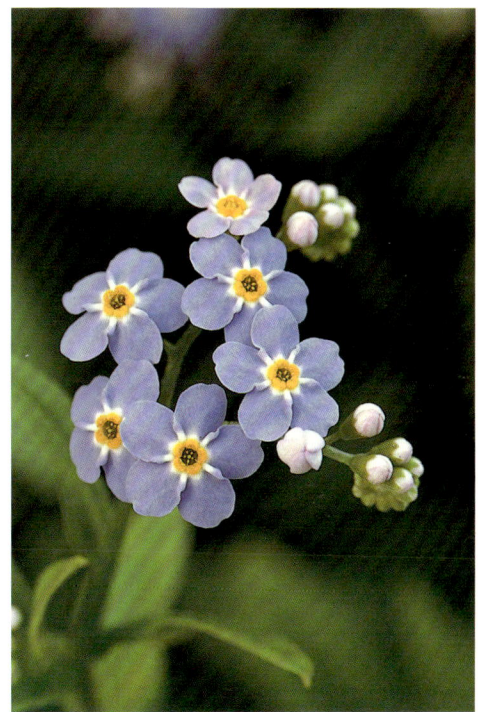

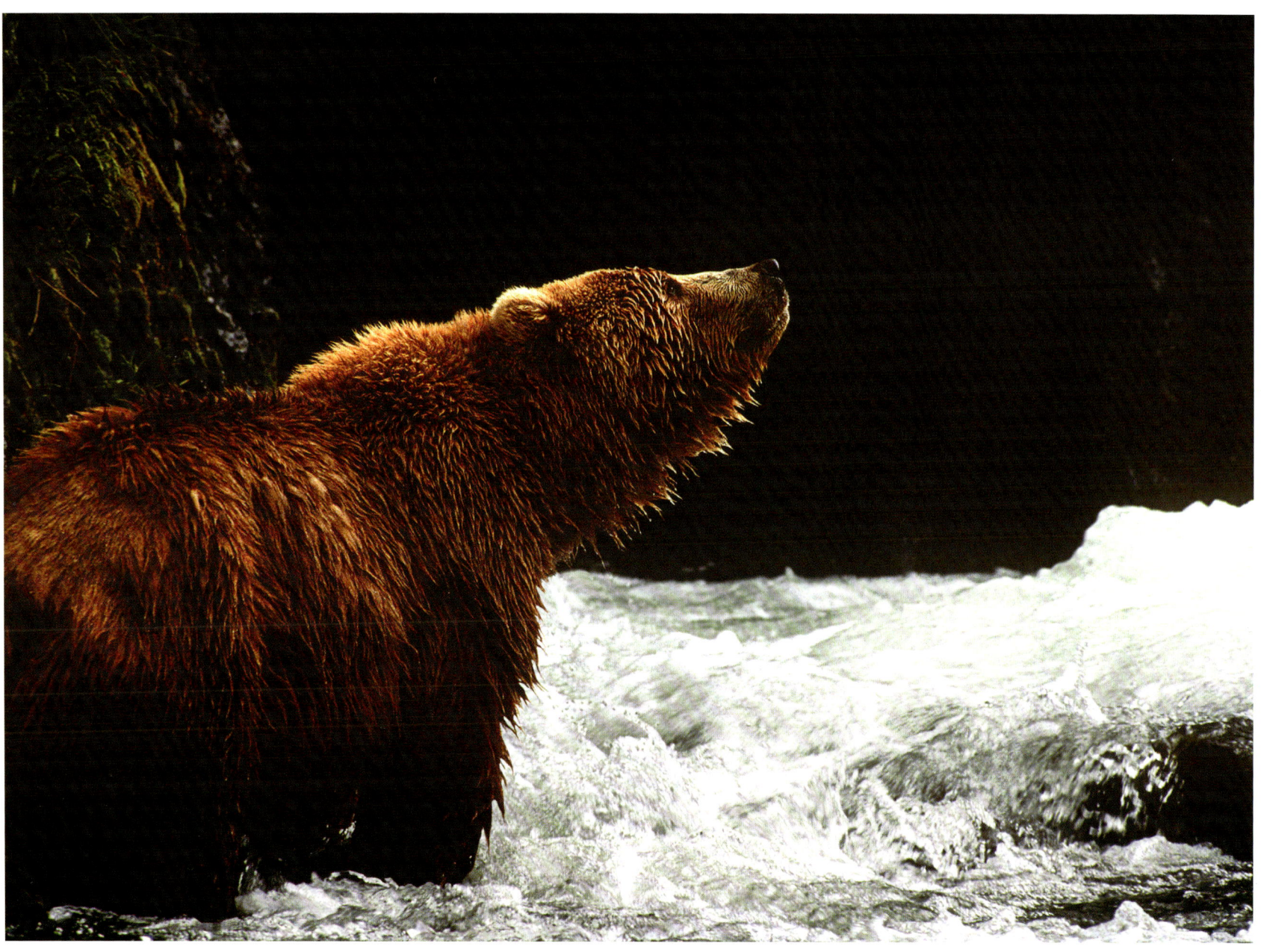

Kodiak's Bears

Say "Kodiak" and the world says "bear."

The great bruins are synonymous with the great island that shares their name. A Kodiak brown bear is a bear of superior strength and majesty, a bear found nowhere else in the world.

Kodiak's bears are a distinct subspecies of the grizzly bears found in other parts of North America. Separated from the mainland by the Gulf of Alaska and the Shelikof Strait, they are isolated physically and genetically, and have differently-shaped skulls. The mild winters, lush vegetation and rich salmon runs of the archipelago and Katmai coast allow them to grow larger than their inland cousins. The biggest males can be as heavy as 1,500 pounds and stand nearly 10 feet tall. With their long claws, small eyes and ears, and shaggy coats ranging from dark brown to blond, they are the classic portrait of Bear.

There are nearly 3,000 brown bears in the Kodiak archipelago, with more on the neighboring Katmai coast on the Alaska Peninsula across the Shelikof Strait. Over-hunting led to the creation of the Kodiak National Wildlife Refuge in 1941 to protect bears and other wildlife. The refuge covers about two-thirds of Kodiak Island as well as several smaller islands, encompassing and preserving prime bear habitat. Katmai National Park and Preserve, across the Shelikof Strait, multiplies the opportunities for bear viewing.

The bears usually emerge from their dens in April. They head for the snowline, searching for roots, buds, new grass, and unwary ground squirrels. When salmon return to fresh water for spawning, the bears line up along stream banks and lakes for their midsummer feast. Berries arrive on the menu in late summer and by late November, the bruins are asleep again.

Every summer, *Ursus arctos middendorffi* makes a gift to the island's economy. When the bears follow the salmon, people follow the bears, hoping to catch a rare glimpse of the lords of the islands. Flight services offer day trips to the far corners of the archipelago for bear viewing or fly visitors to Kodiak and Katmai lodges for longer visits. Remote camps and cabins house hunters, photographers and researchers. The economic ripples spread to charter boats, restaurants, hotels, sporting good stores and souvenir shops. From the stuffed high school mascot to the real bruin fishing outside the lodge window, Kodiak bears are a constant yet elusive presence.

While they usually shy away from humans, there's nothing like a fragrant garbage dump or an unattended campsite to attract a curious, hungry bear. Their attacks are few but are always serious and sometimes deadly. The rules of bear safety are taught early and repeated often in this part of the world. Berry-pickers are careful to leave something for the bears and hikers always make enough noise to let Mama Bear know that visitors are in her woods.

After all, the bears were here first. They are part of the island. Sometimes, they might *be* the island. On clear autumn days when Kodiak's smooth, cinnamon-brown hills resemble tawny fur and rippling muscles, the great bear and the great island seem as one.

left Kodiak brown bear at Frazer Lake falls. (Hank Pennington)

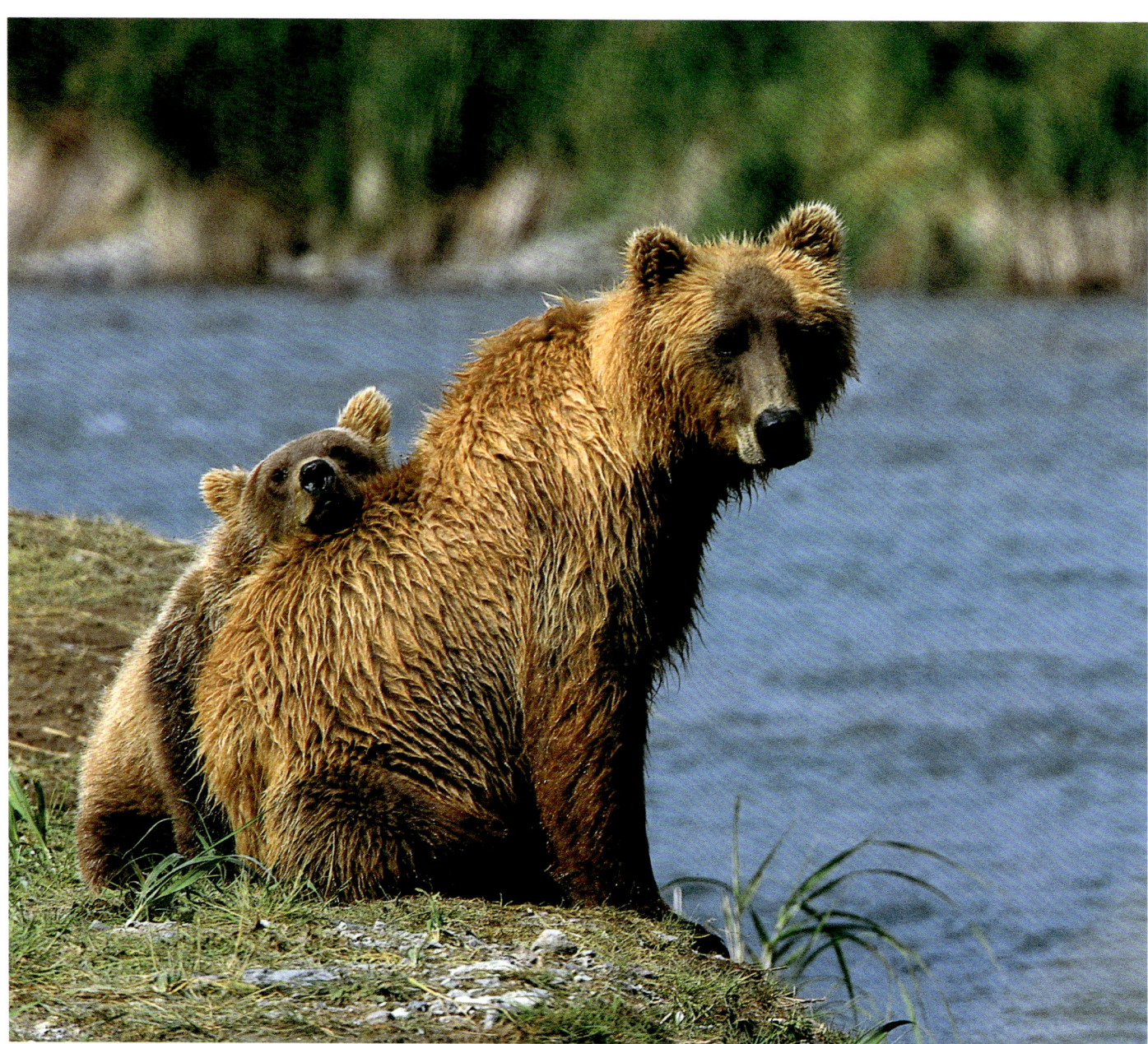

right Alaska brown bear sow with yearling cub on the Katmai coast. (Steve Gilroy)

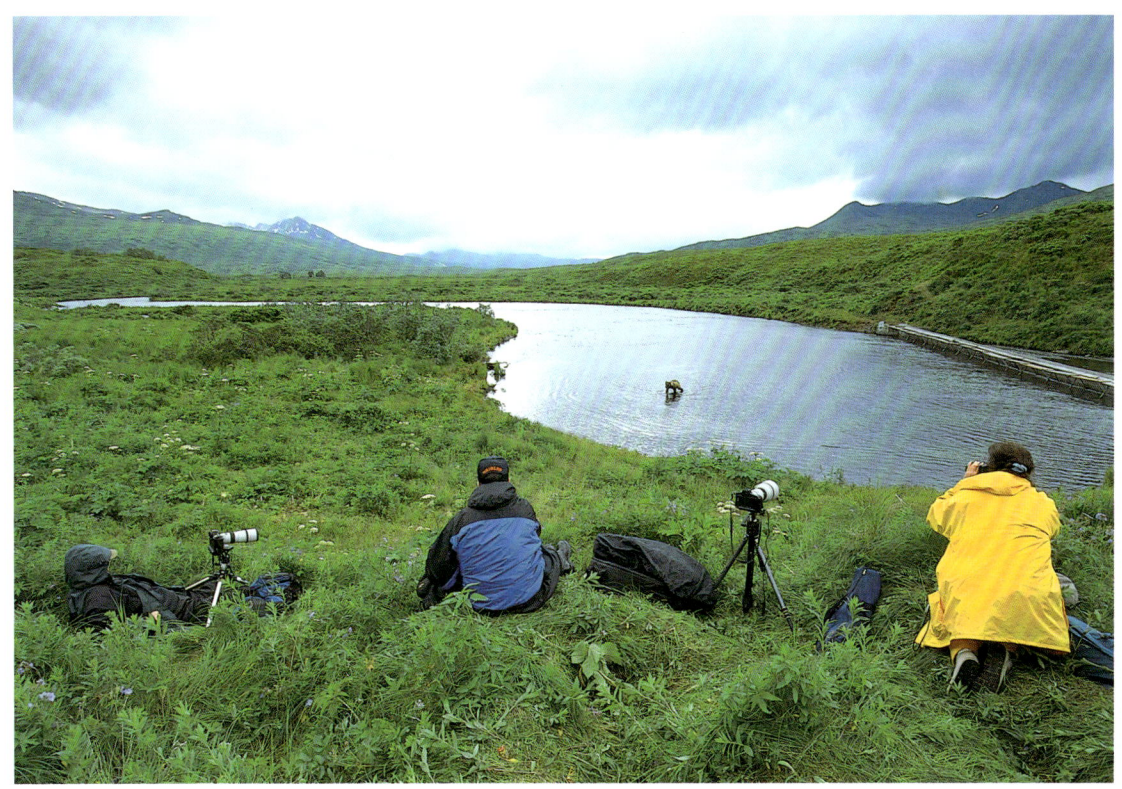

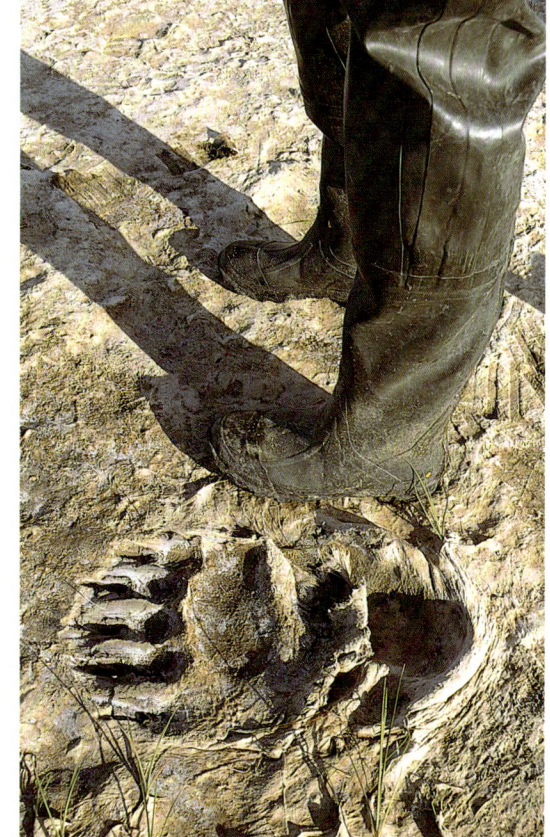

above Bear viewing above the fish weir at Dog Salmon Creek, Kodiak National Wildlife Refuge. (Steve Gilroy)

right Alaska brown bear footprint, on the Katmai coast. (Steve Gilroy)

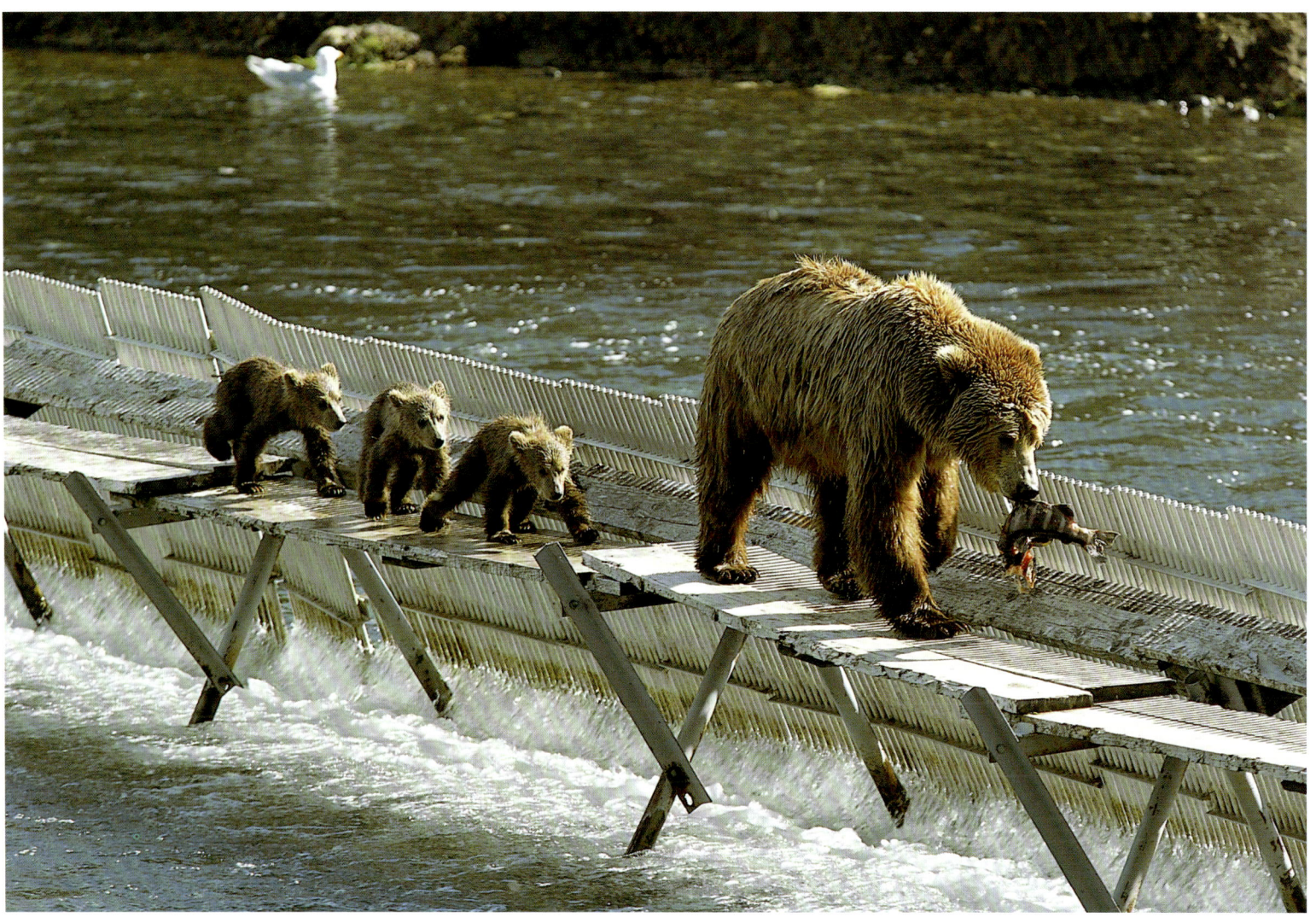

above Kodiak brown
bear family on fish weir.
(Heather L. Johnson)

33

below Red fox with sockeye salmon on the Thumb River, Kodiak National Wildlife Refuge. (Steve Gilroy)

right Kodiak brown bear yearling cub, Kodiak National Wildlife Refuge. The refuge encompasses more than two-thirds of Kodiak Island. It was established in 1941 to protect bear and other wildlife habitat. (Steve Gilroy)

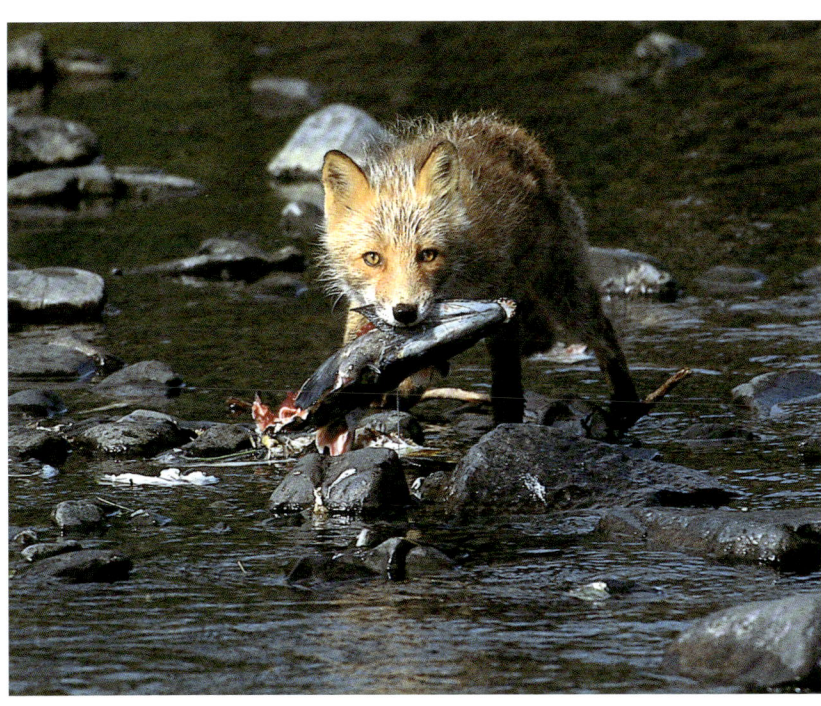

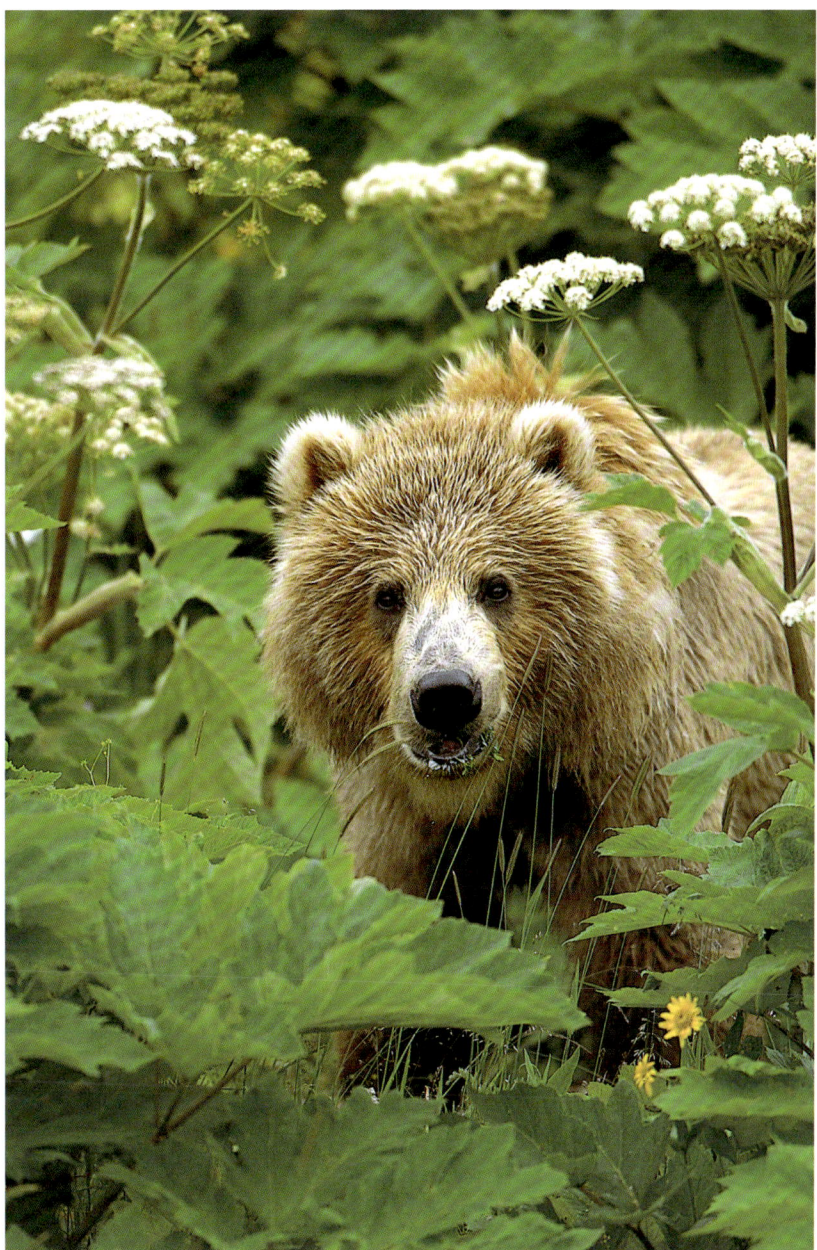

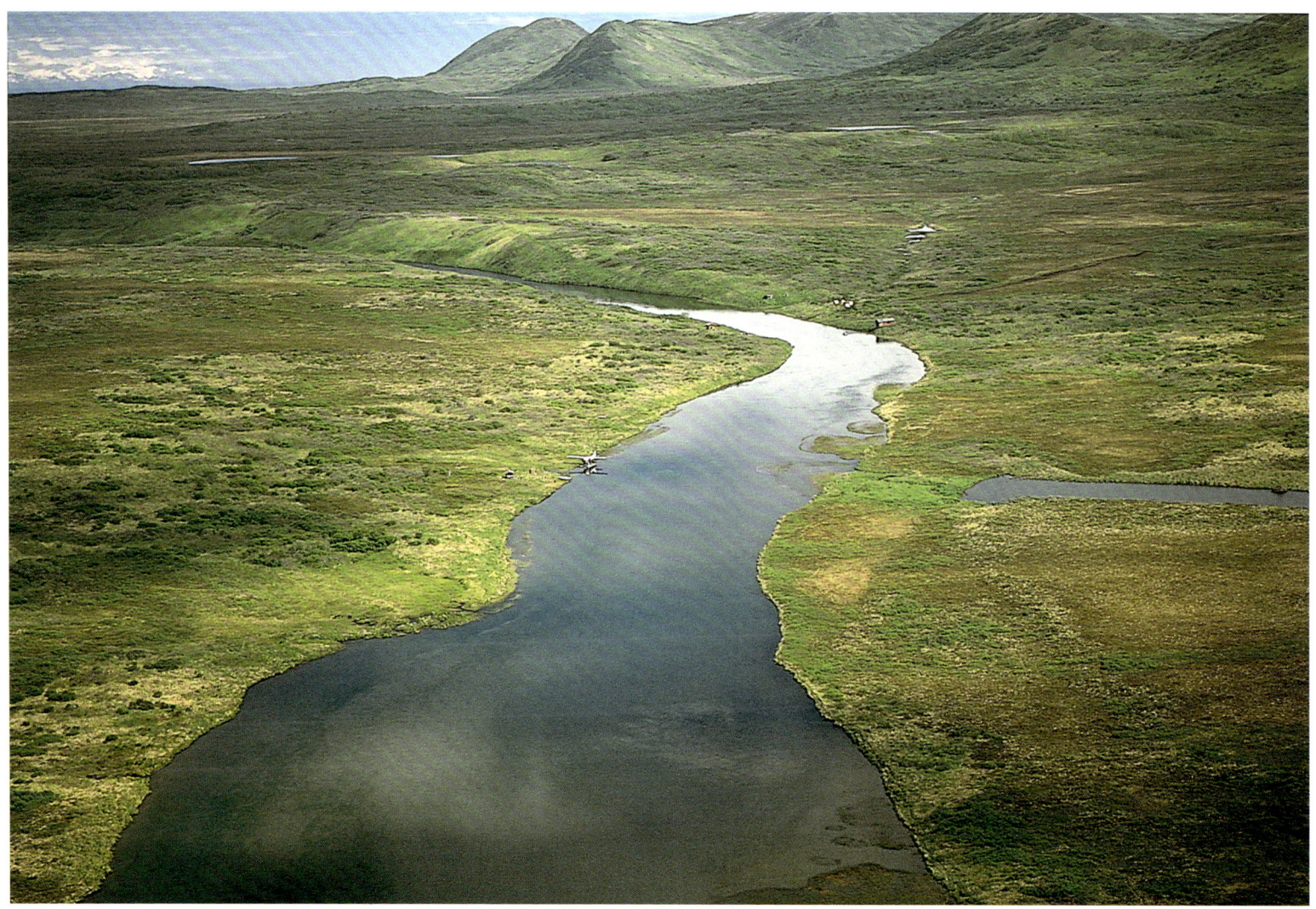

above Floatplanes provide access to great fishing on the Karluk River. (Calvin Hall)

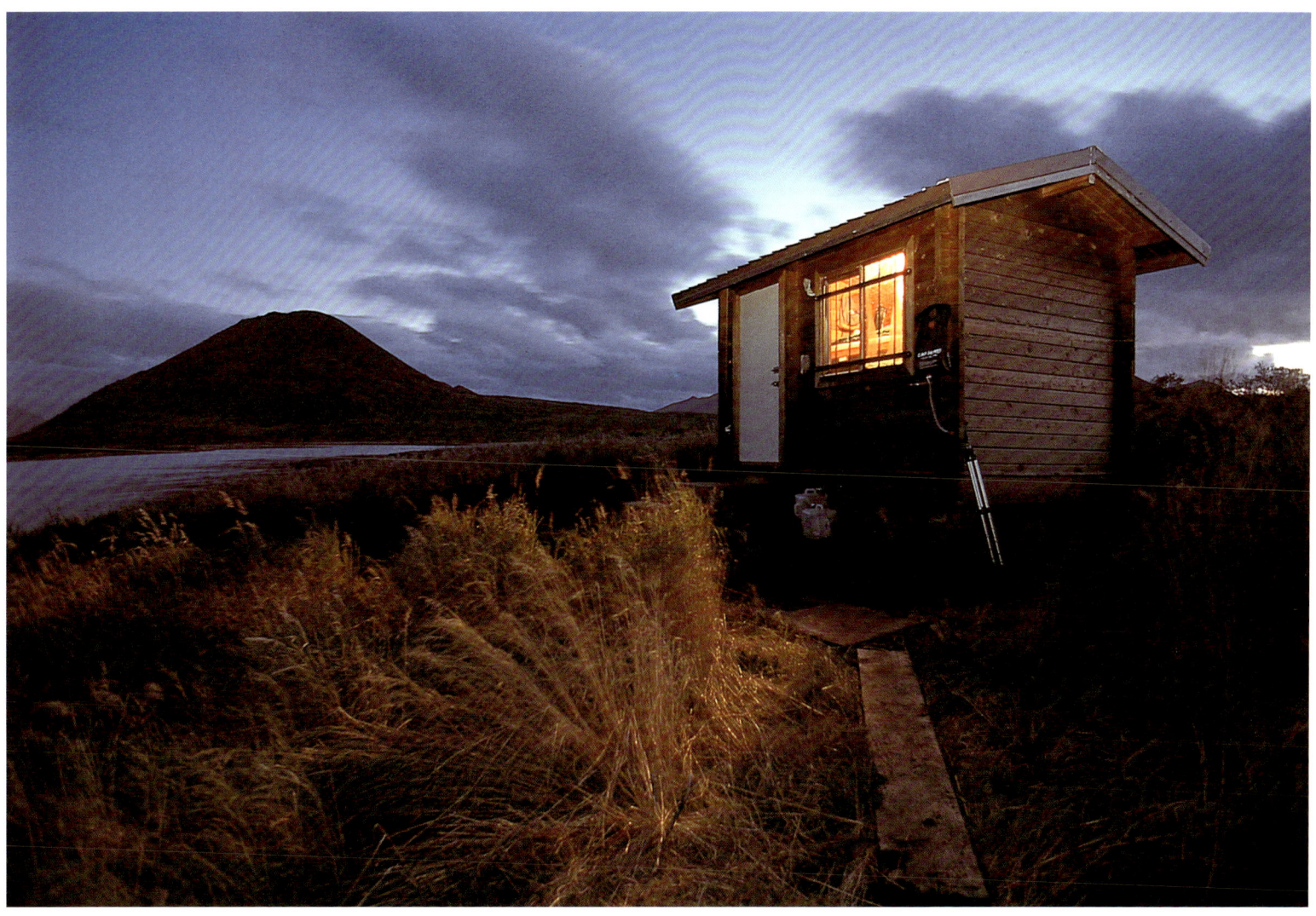

above Public use cabins and private camps are found across Kodiak. (Tom Evans)

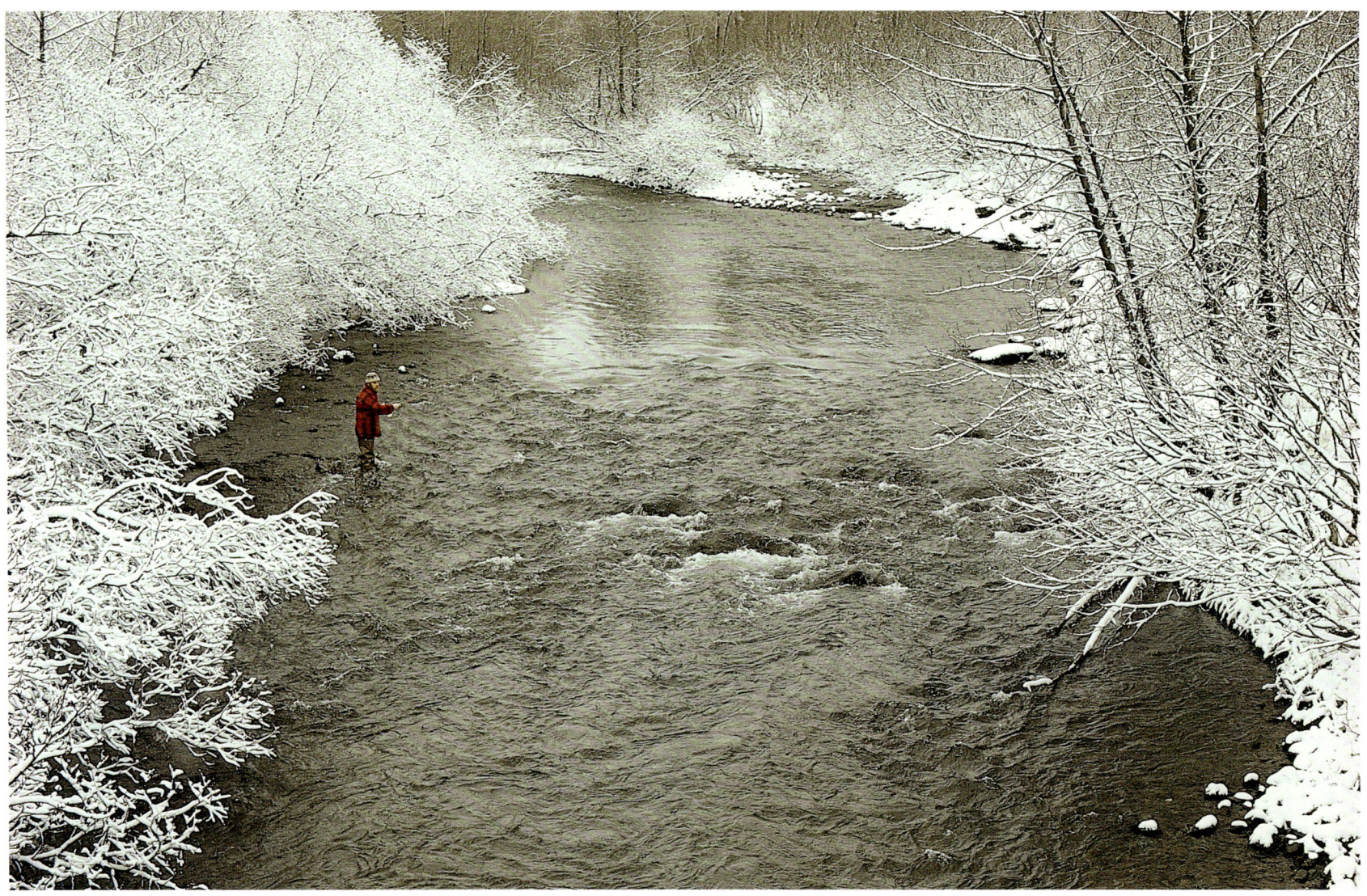

above Fly fishing for
Dolly Varden in March
on the Buskin River.
(Marion Owen)

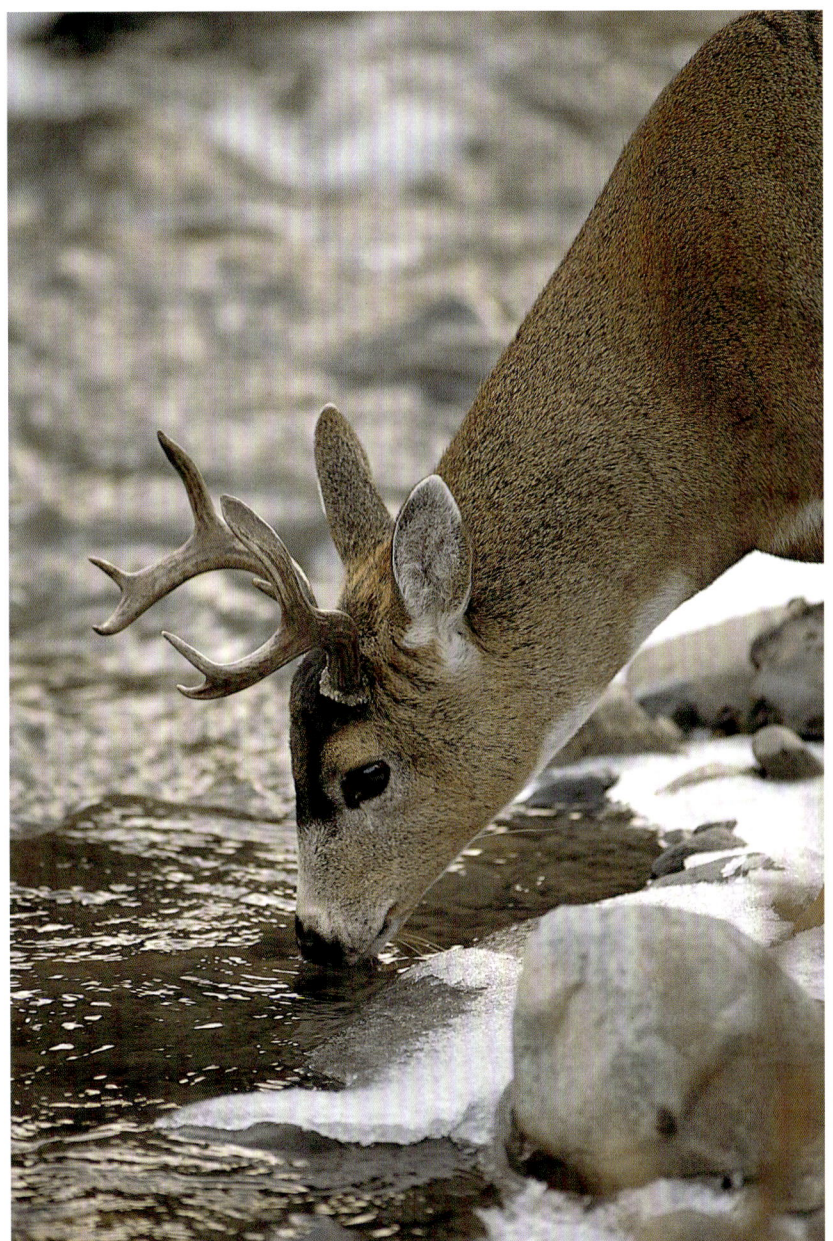

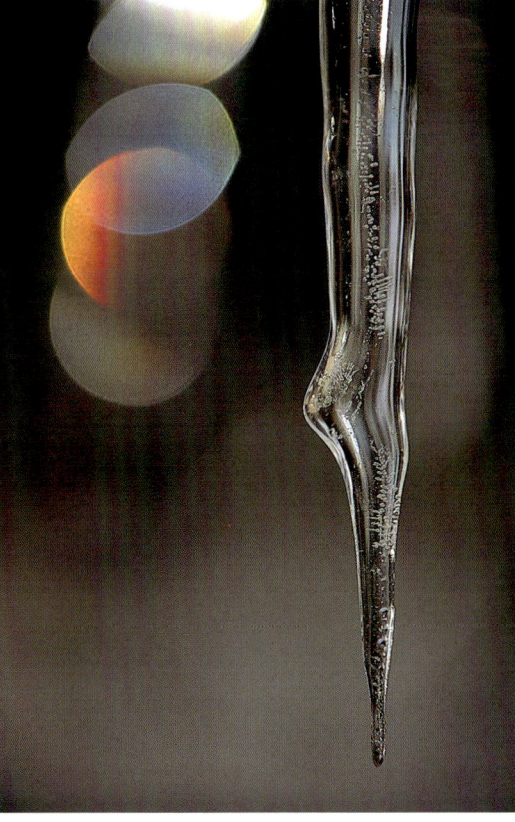

left A rainbow prism is formed on an out-of-focus icicle. (Marion Owen)

left Sitka black-tailed deer often come down to beaches and the forest's edge in winter to seek food. (Lon Lauber)

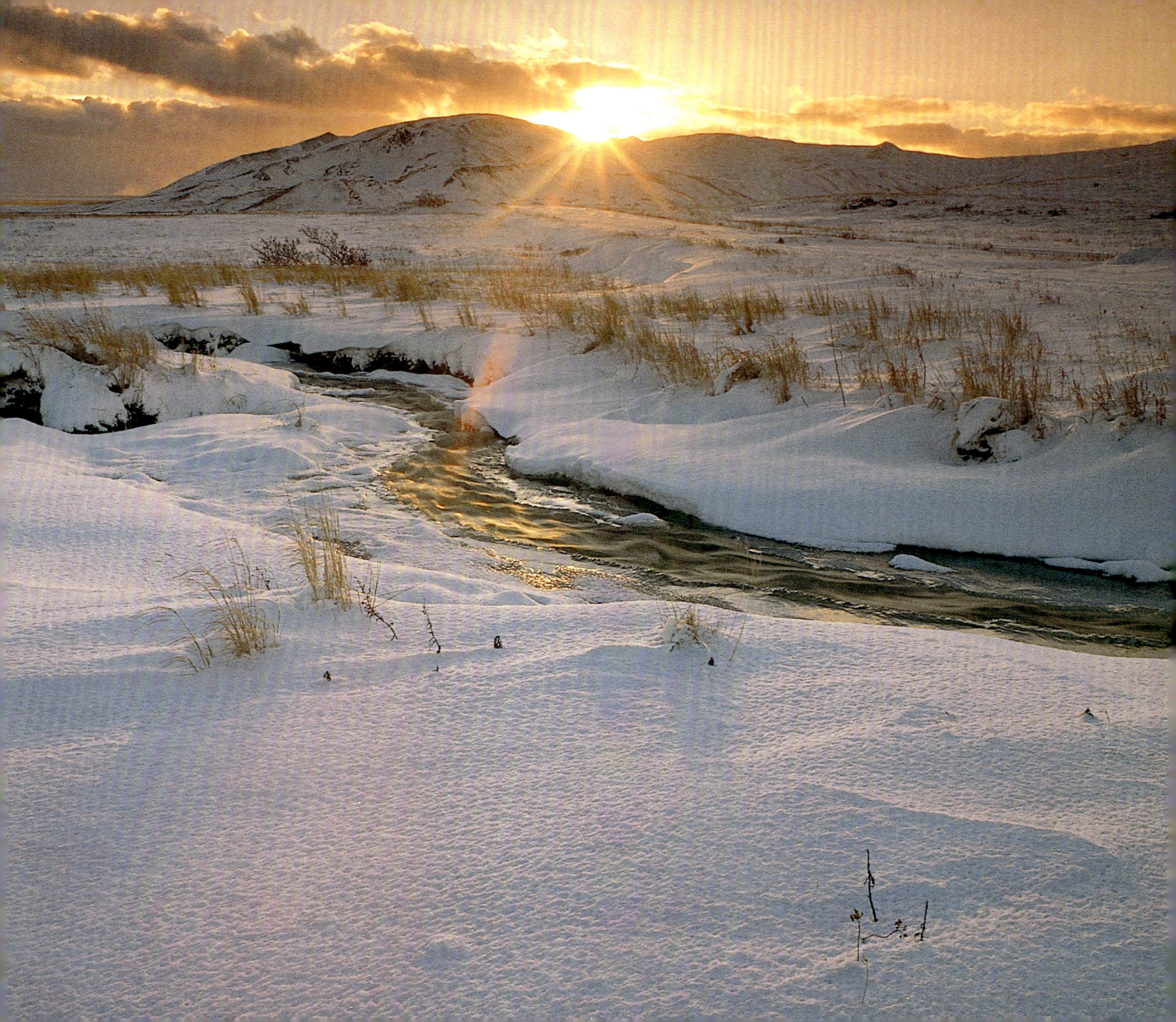

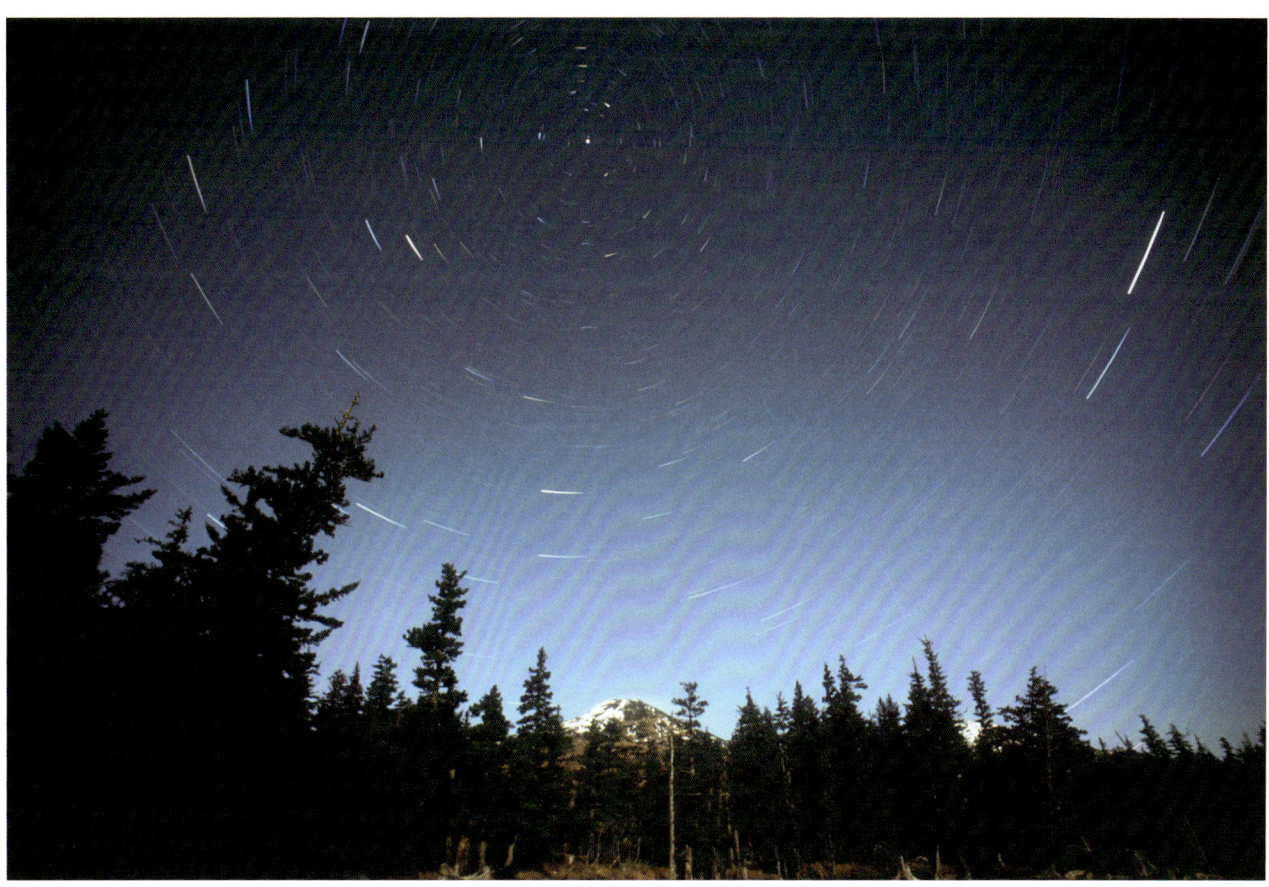

left Sunrise in January on
Sitkinak Island, south of
Kodiak Island.
(Marion Owen)

above 30-minute night
exposure from Afognak
Island in November. The
North Star (Polaris) is in
the center. (Marion Owen)

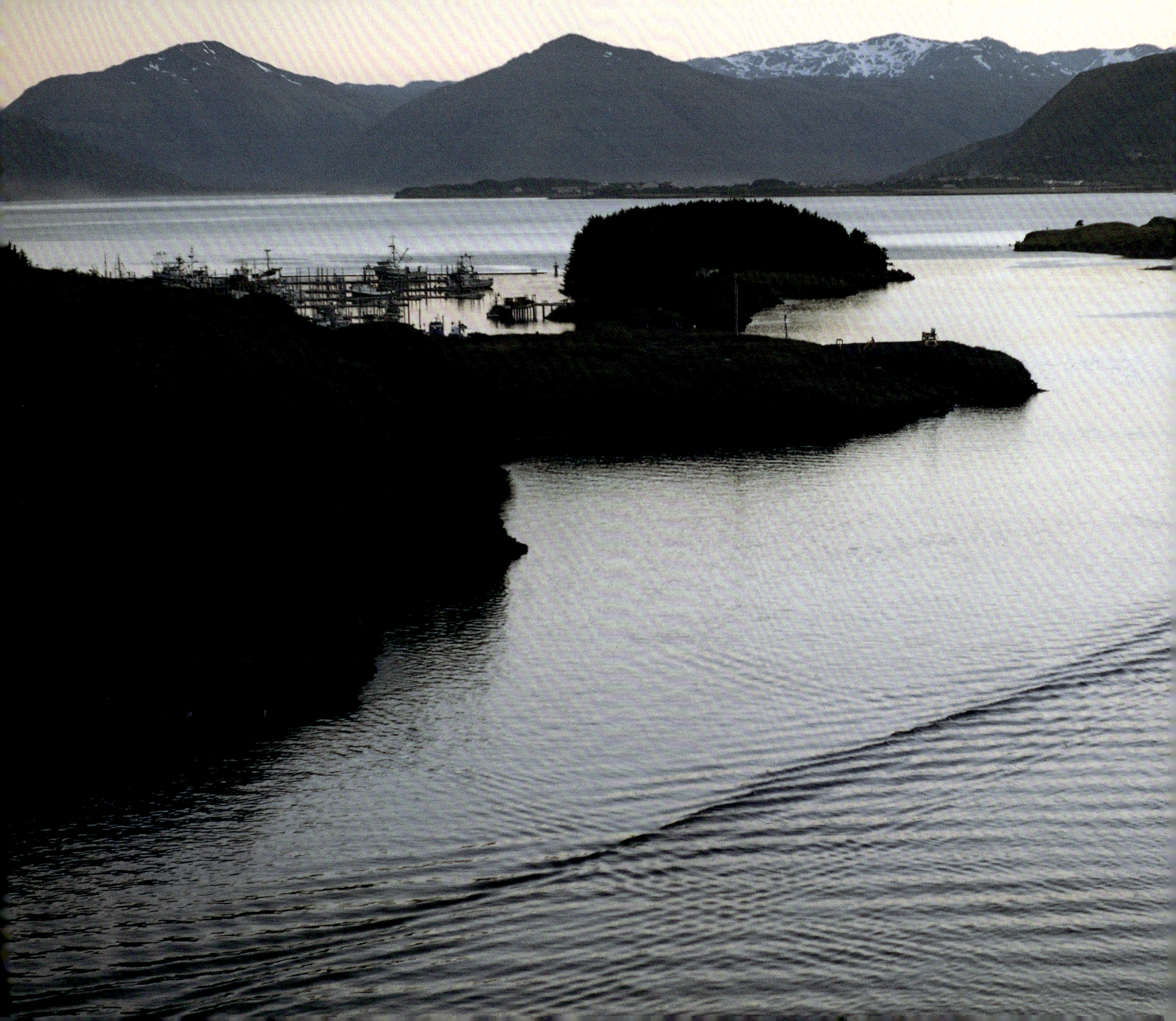

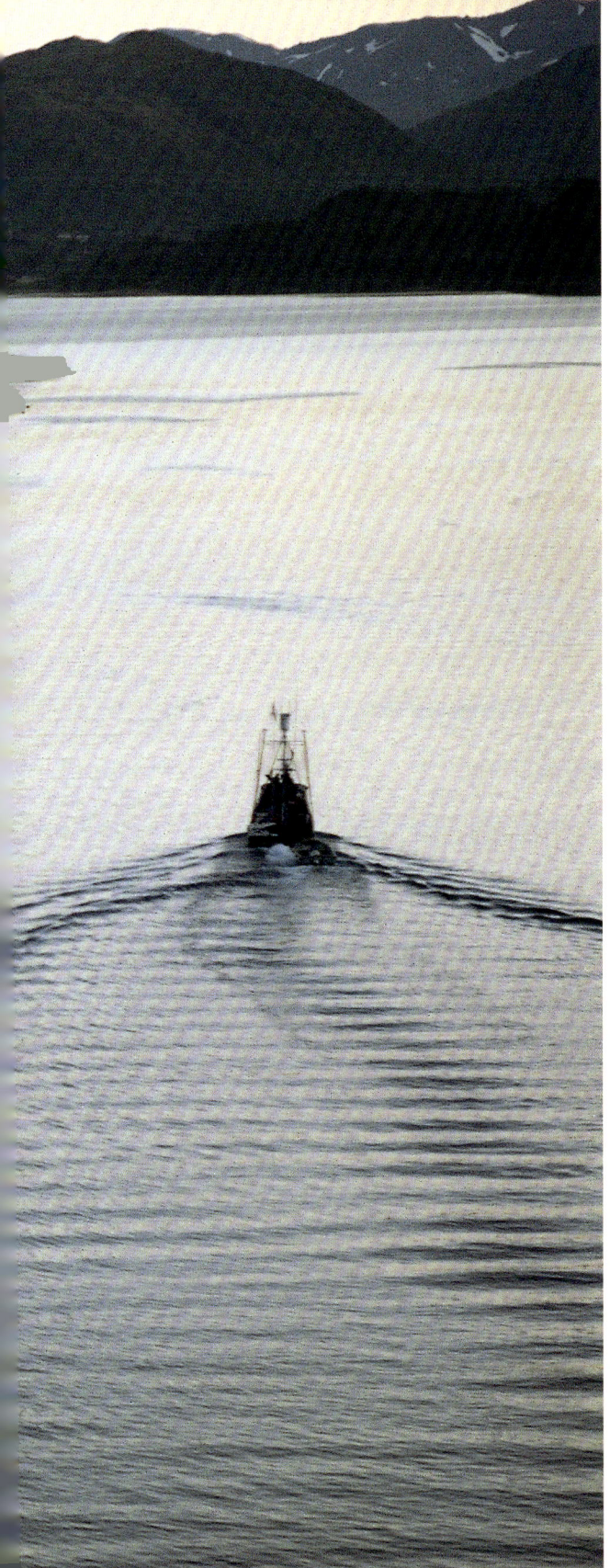

The 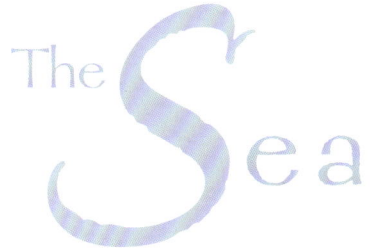 ea

THE SCENT, THE SOUND, AND THE SIGHT OF THE OCEAN ARE EVERYWHERE ON KODIAK. NO POINT ON THE ISLAND IS MORE THAN 15 MILES FROM THE EMBRACING SEA.

There are times when being this close to the ocean frightens, when anxious ears listen to howling winds and crashing surf, and eyes strain to spot a familiar vessel battling into port. Once a year, the bell tolls at the Fishermen's Memorial, numbering the souls lost to the sea.

But those who love this part of Alaska can't hold grudges. The sea takes much, but it also gives. It gave birth to these islands. Uplifted from the sea floor by tectonic forces. they rise unexpectedly from the watery horizon, a welcome haven for sailors and sea creatures alike.

The sea feeds Kodiak. Where freshwater streams meet salty waters, marine creatures find food aplenty. When the first people discovered the abundant wildlife, they made their home in these islands. Well-fed by the sea, the Alutiit had leisure time to build a rich and varied culture. Their skin boats, cradled close to the sea, are designs still envied today. Their food, clothing, ornaments, building materials—even their spirit world—was fed by the ocean.

The sea's generosity fed others, too. The Alutiit of the 1760s saw foreign men come in large ships, hunting for sea otter and seal. Those lush pelts clothed kings and tycoons in Europe and Asia, and built fortunes for Russia. When the sea otter was hunted to near-extinction,

previous page A fishing boat heads through the Near Island Channel at sunset. (Clark James Mishler/Alaska Stock)

below Commercially caught Dungeness crabs. (Marion Owen)

right The *F/V Jeanoah* underway in the Gulf of Alaska during Tanner crab fishing. (Marion Owen)

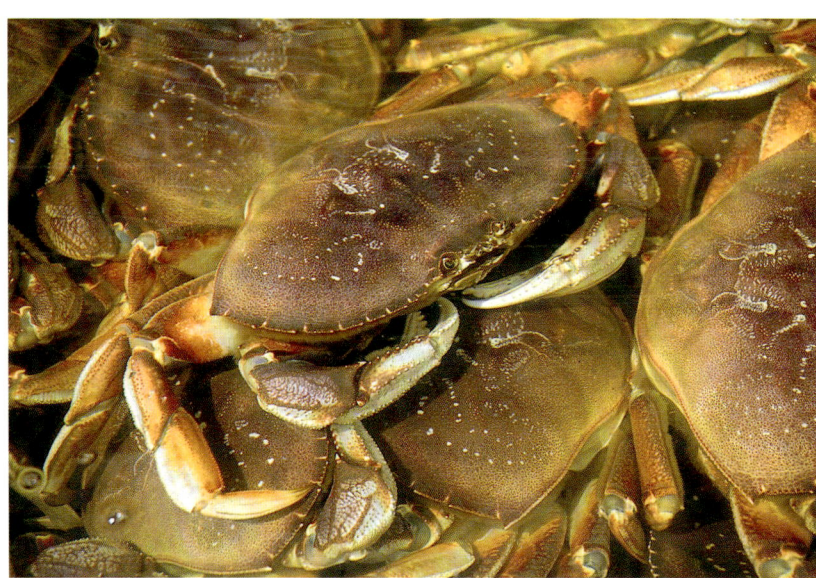

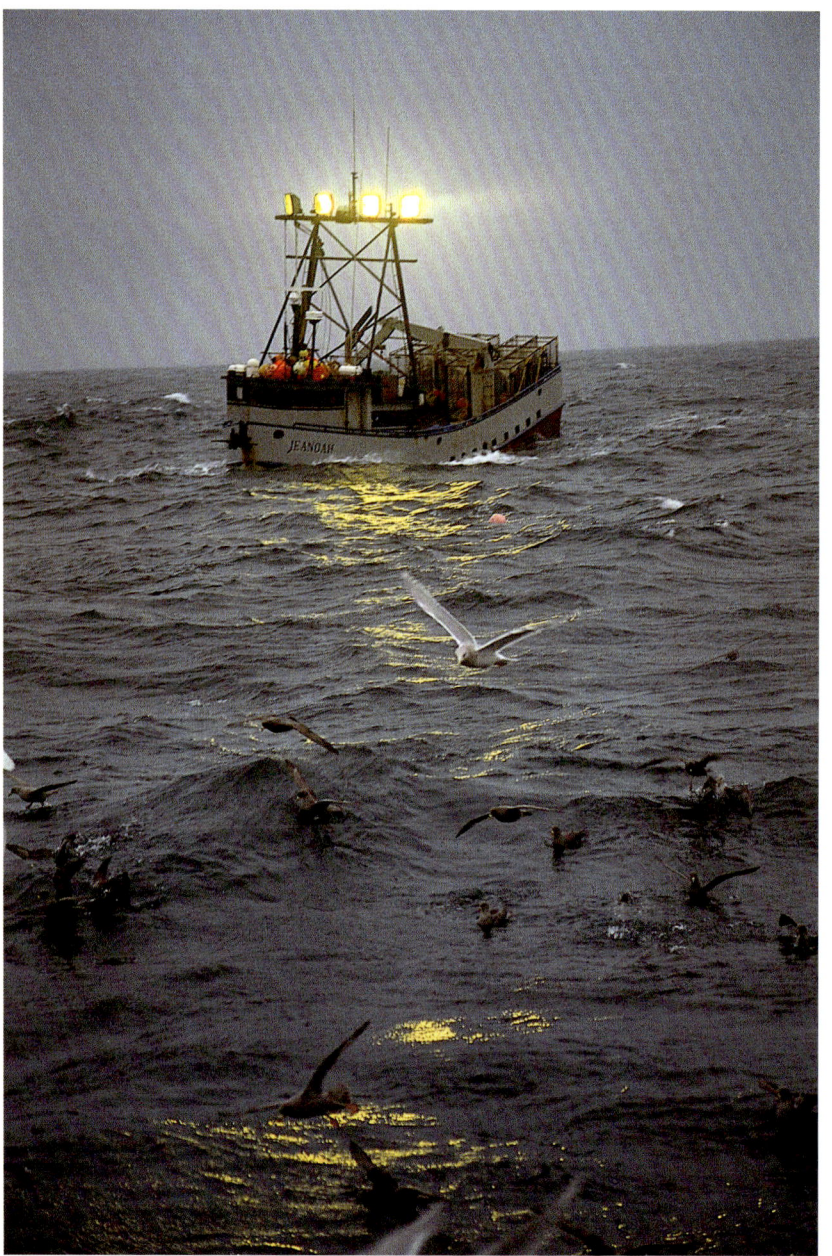

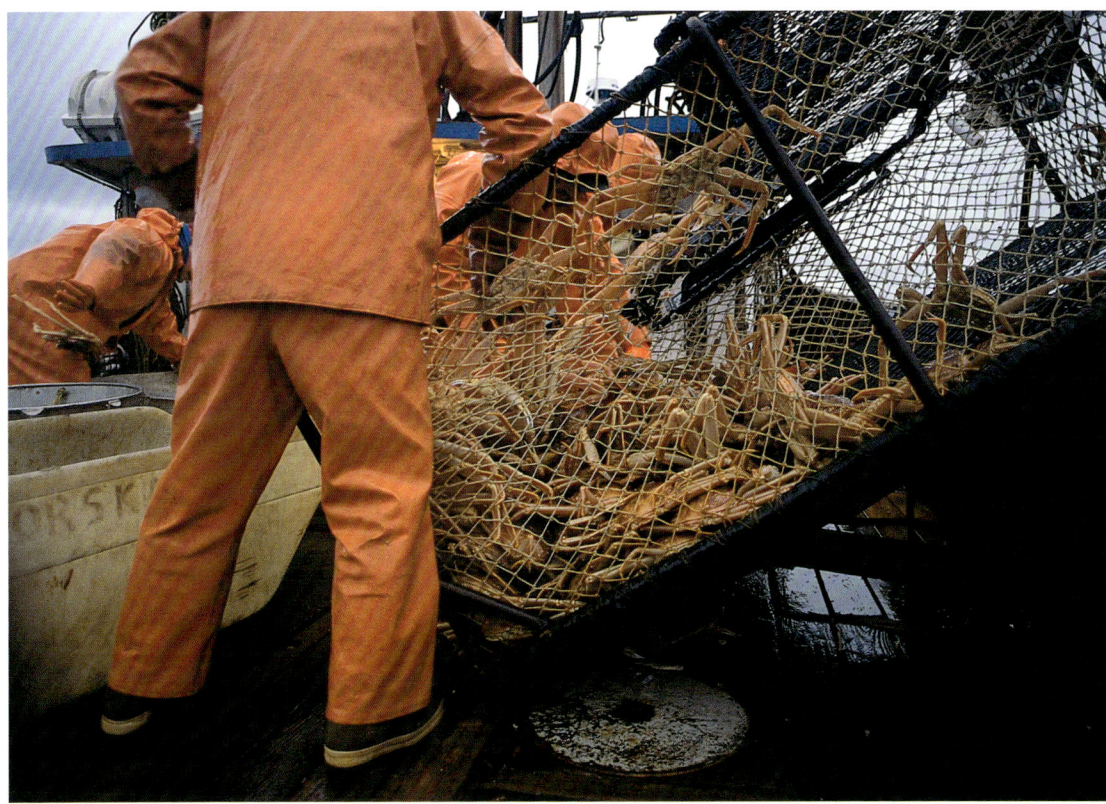

above Pulling Tanner crabs out of a pot on the *F/V Ruff 'n Reddy*. Kodiak is the only port in Alaska where all commercial fishing species—including salmon, crab, halibut, herring, cod, pollock and rockfish—are processed onshore. It is the only port with a large resident fleet of all gear types—trawl, longline, pot, net and jig. (Marion Owen)

harvesters turned to salmon. The Karluk River became famous in the 1890s as the richest red salmon stream in the world. Thousands of cannery workers came to catch and pack another fortune in silver.

Even in times when the ocean's cycle or man's poor planning weakened the salmon runs, the sea had new riches to offer: halibut, herring, shrimp, scallops. In the 1960s, "Kodiak" meant "king crab." More fortunes were won and lost as fishing crews battled storms, fatigue and luck itself to bring home the prized seafood.

Today, pollock and other groundfish are king here; Kodiak is consistently one of the top fishing ports in the United States. Processing plants use high technology to utilize all they can of their catch, from fish fillets for the restaurant trade, to fish meal fertilizer. "That's what money smells like," mothers say, walking their children past the waterfront.

The children here learn early about the sea. Kindergarten classes memorize the life cycle of the salmon. Older children tour the Kodiak Fisheries Research Facility Center, tickling sea

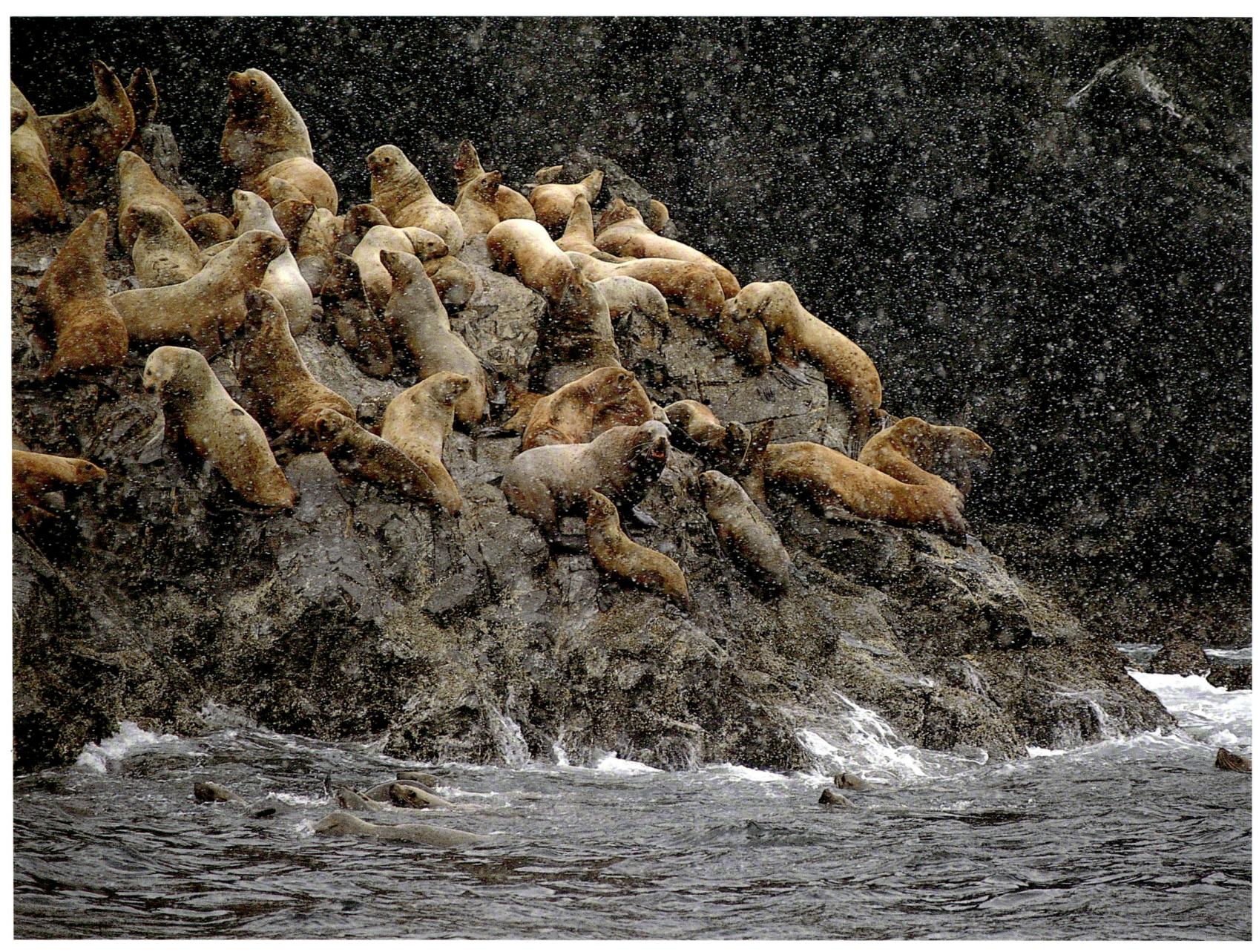

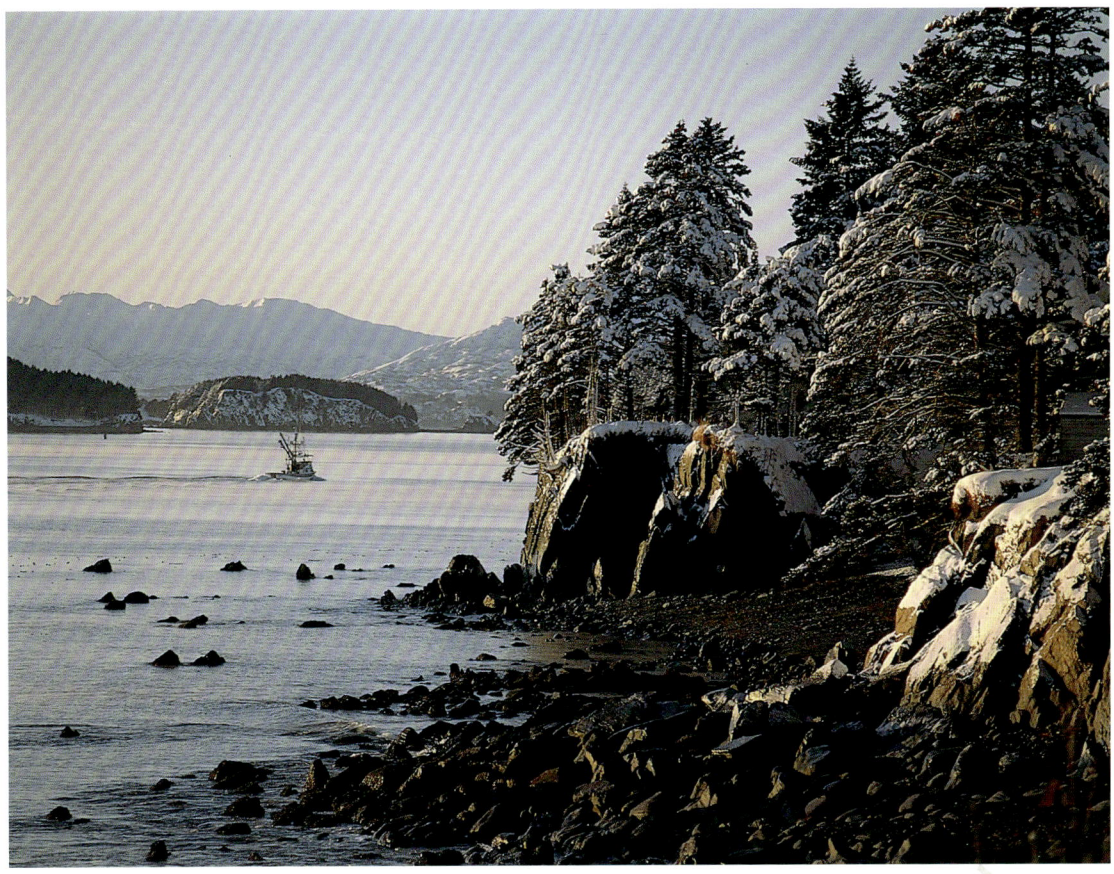

left Steller sea lions at haulout during a spring snowstorm in Chiniak Bay. (Marion Owen)

above North Chiniak Bay with a purse seiner. Kodiak's economy relies largely on the fishing industry. (Tom Watson)

cucumbers in the touch tank, and looking forward to Kodiak National Wildlife Refuge's summer "salmon camp." High school students take marine biology, learn cold-water survival skills and even set out on the high school's own fishing boat to learn skills at sea. University scholars study fisheries and marine mammals hands-on.

In state and federal research programs, Kodiak's marine specialists struggle with how to keep the sea in balance. The web that connects living things ripples whenever one strand is touched. Is what we do with the pollock affecting the sea lions? Are there more halibut because there are less crab or less crab because there are more halibut? The sea teaches, but there are so many things we still struggle to understand. In Kodiak's research laboratories, class-rooms and offices, the mysteries are explored.

As the sea feeds the mind and the bankbook, it also feeds the spirit. Kodiak waters teem with constant reminders of the living force of the ocean. Fat sea lions in velvet suits roar at passing

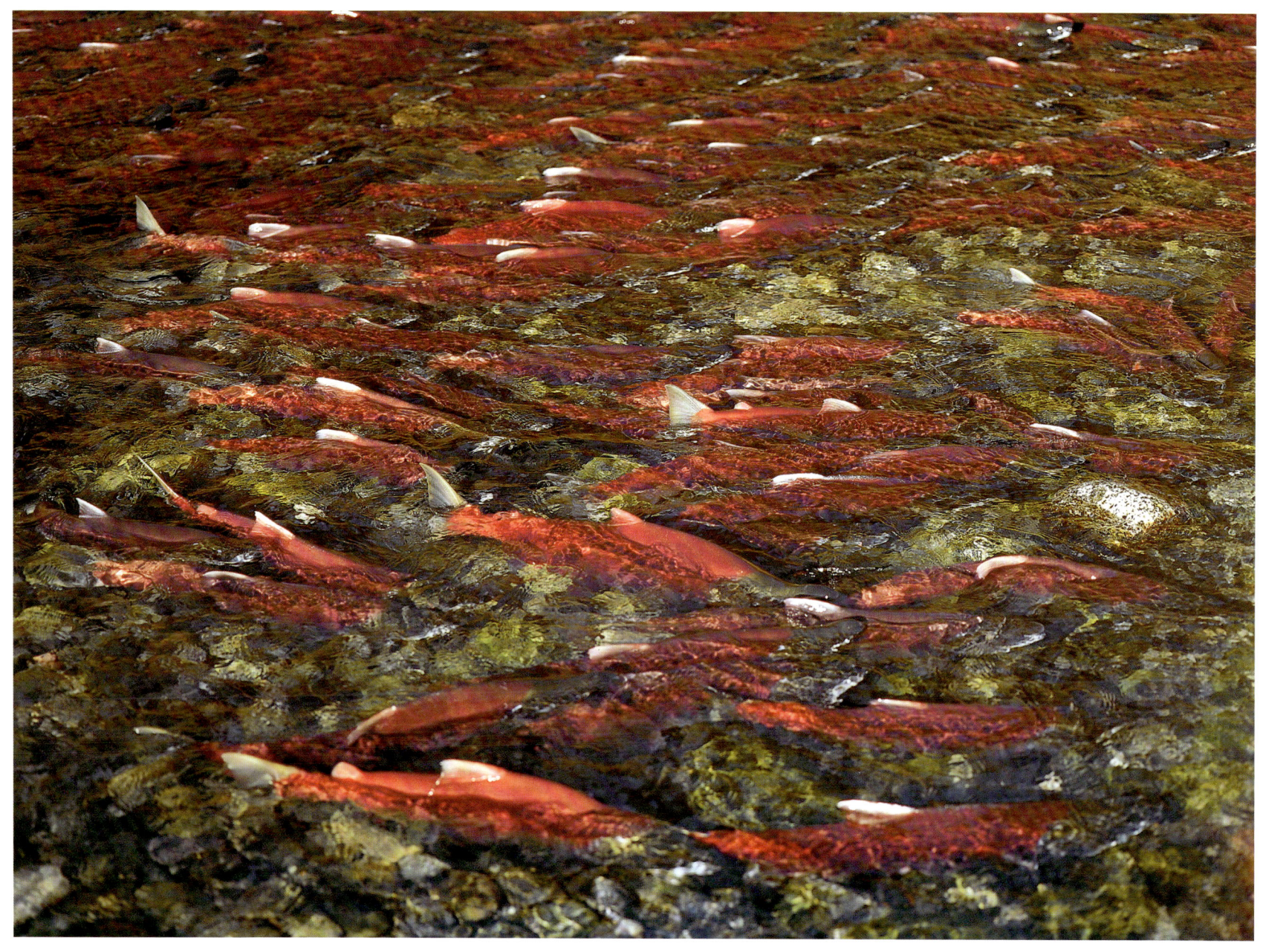

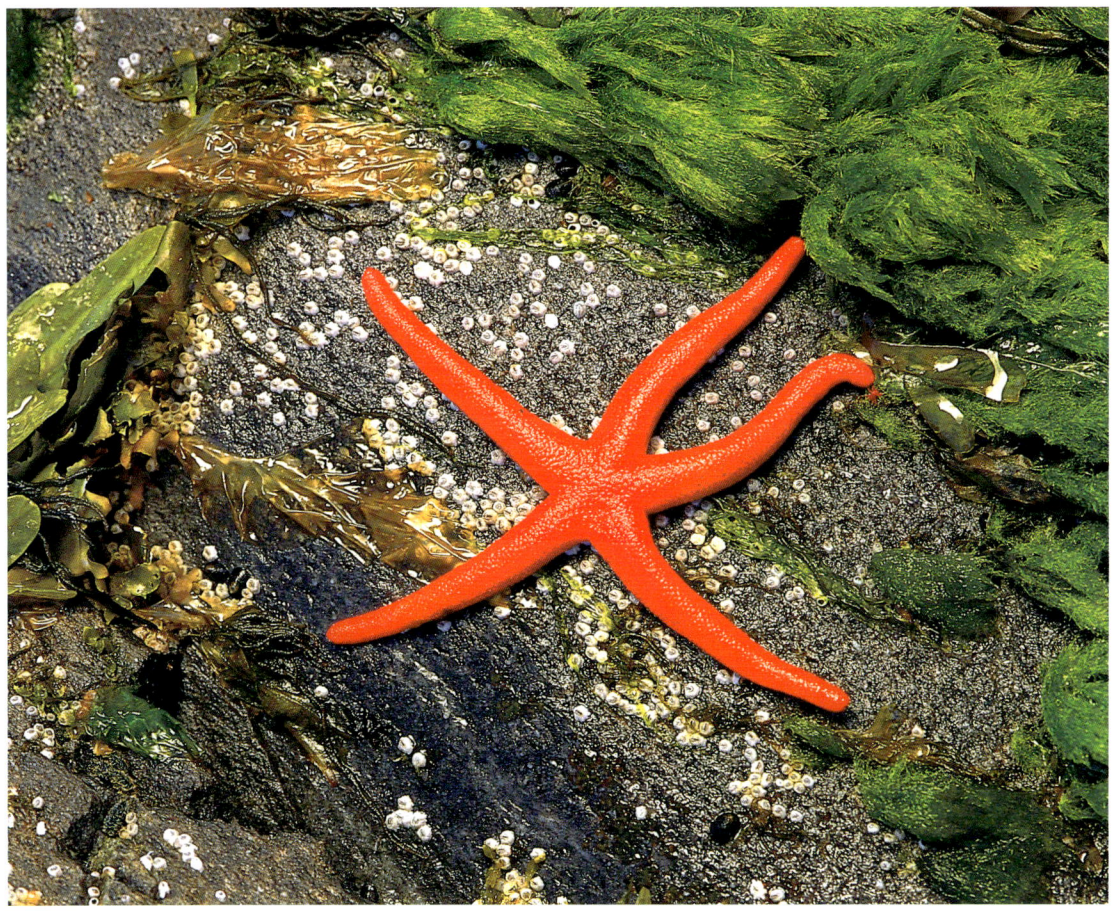

left Sockeye salmon return to spawn. More than 800 streams in the Kodiak area are home to spawning stocks of wild salmon. (Gary Schultz)

above Blood sea star and seaweed. Minus tides reveal the unique and colorful world of the intertidal zone. (Cathy Hart)

vessels in the harbor. Bewhiskered sea otters float on their backs eating a fresh crab lunch as awed kayakers paddle past. Every spring gray whales form a stately parade on their path north to the Beaufort Sea. Stout puffins, long-necked cormorants and some 200 other bird species entertain birdwatchers and photographers.

Nearly year-round, locals and tourists alike hope for a chance at pulling up a halibut so big it's labeled a "barn door." Dolly Varden, rainbow and steelhead trout dance in freshwater streams in summer, winter and fall. Salmon fishermen set their calendars by the fish. The early kings come in spring, followed by the flavorful red salmon. By mid-summer, children thrill to the easy catch of pinks and chums, while die-hard fishermen chase the fierce-fighting silver salmon. Subsistence fishers set their nets as the scent of wood-smoked fish perfumes the beaches. Even in midwinter, that rich, oily fragrance brings back visions of summer's harvest, and the gift of the sea.

In an added act of generosity, the sea adorns Kodiak. Beaches are arrayed in a

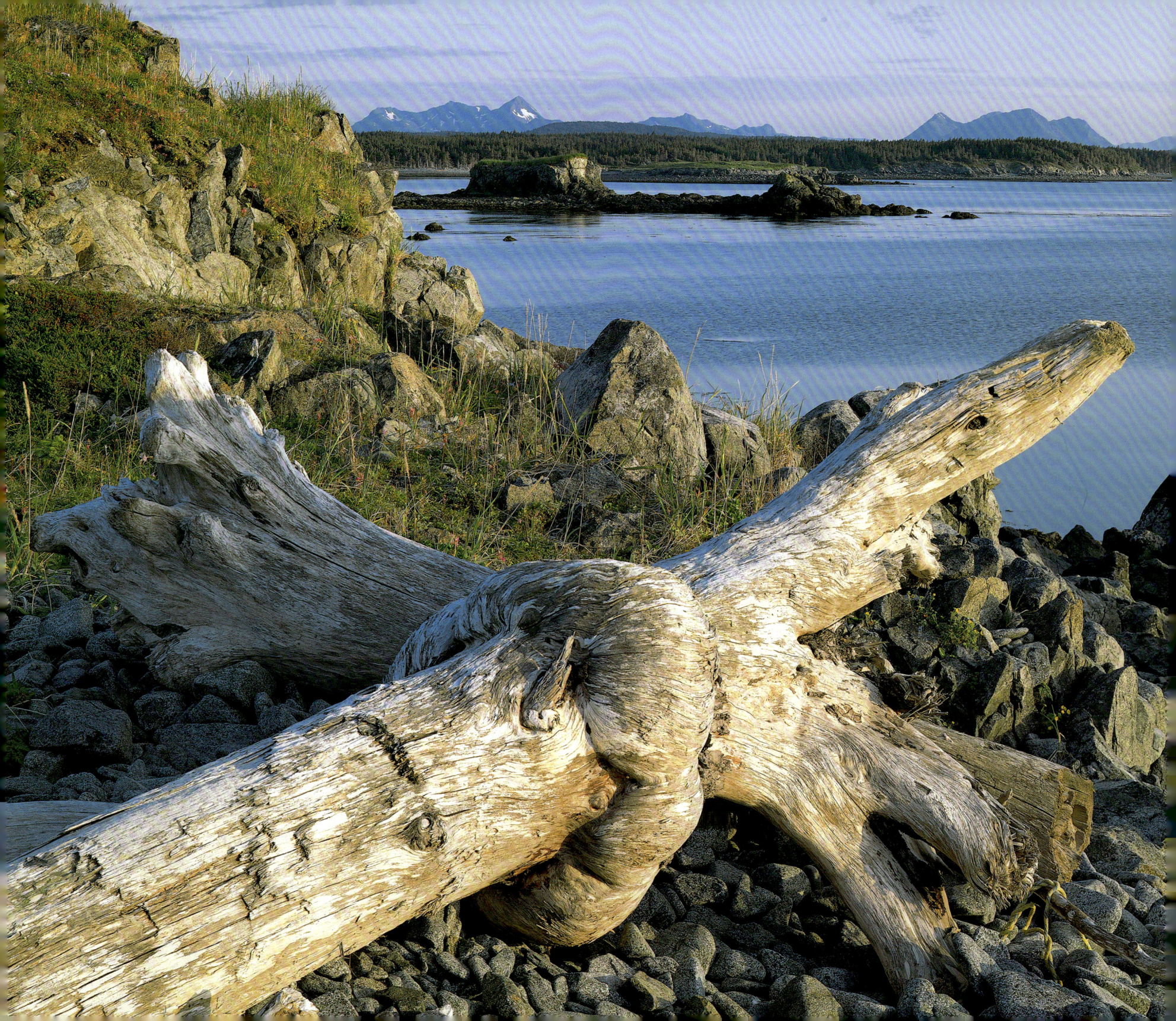

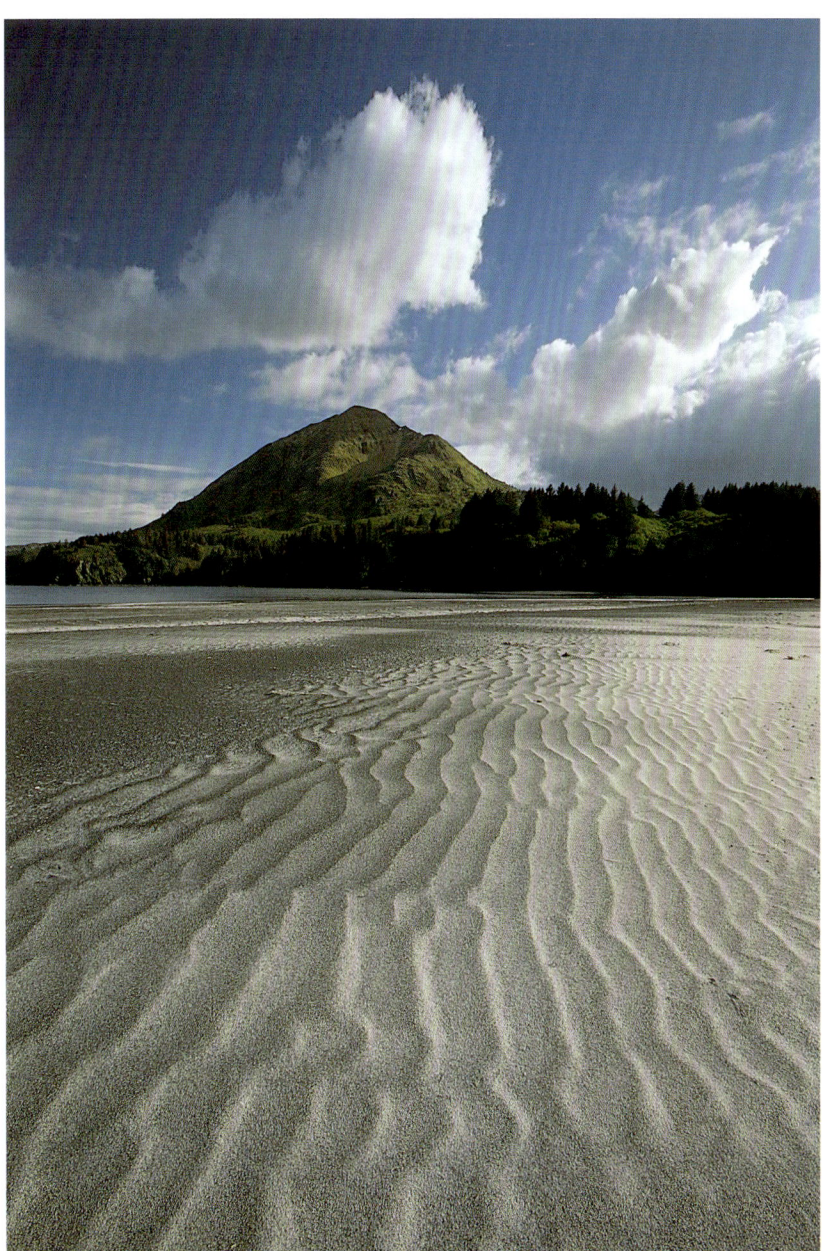

bright mosaic of brilliant sea stars, long-armed anemones and carved driftwood. Chiming buoys and murmuring waves create an ever-present symphony. The ocean whittles at sharp cliffs, polishes rock-strewn beaches, and scours the sand dunes of the southwest shore.

Generous Nature is constantly replenishing her gifts.

far left Driftwood on an island north of Carry Inlet, Shuyak Island State Park. The park is a favorite kayaking destination with sheltered bays and channels that offer unsurpassed opportunities for exploring. (Fred Hirschmann)

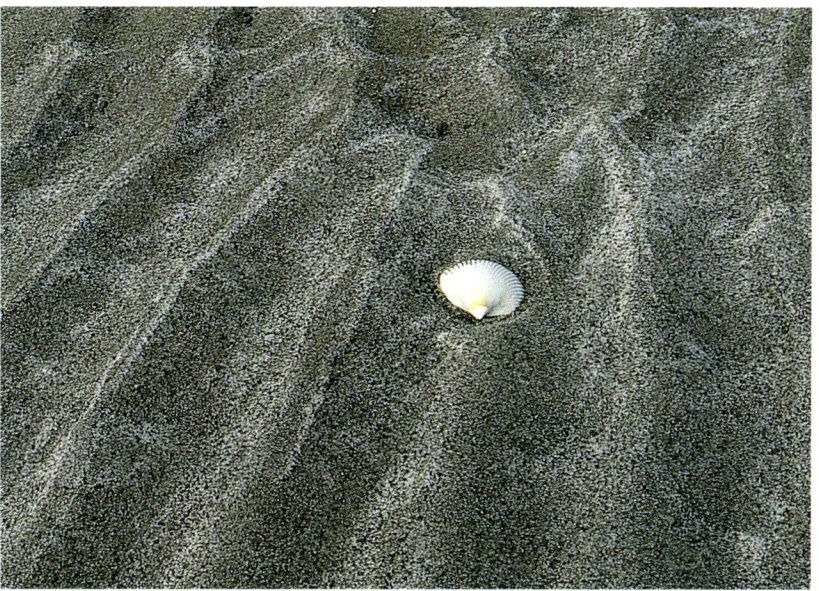

left and above Patterns from wave action on White Sand Beach at Monashka Bay, a popular recreation spot near the city of Kodiak. (Calvin Hall)

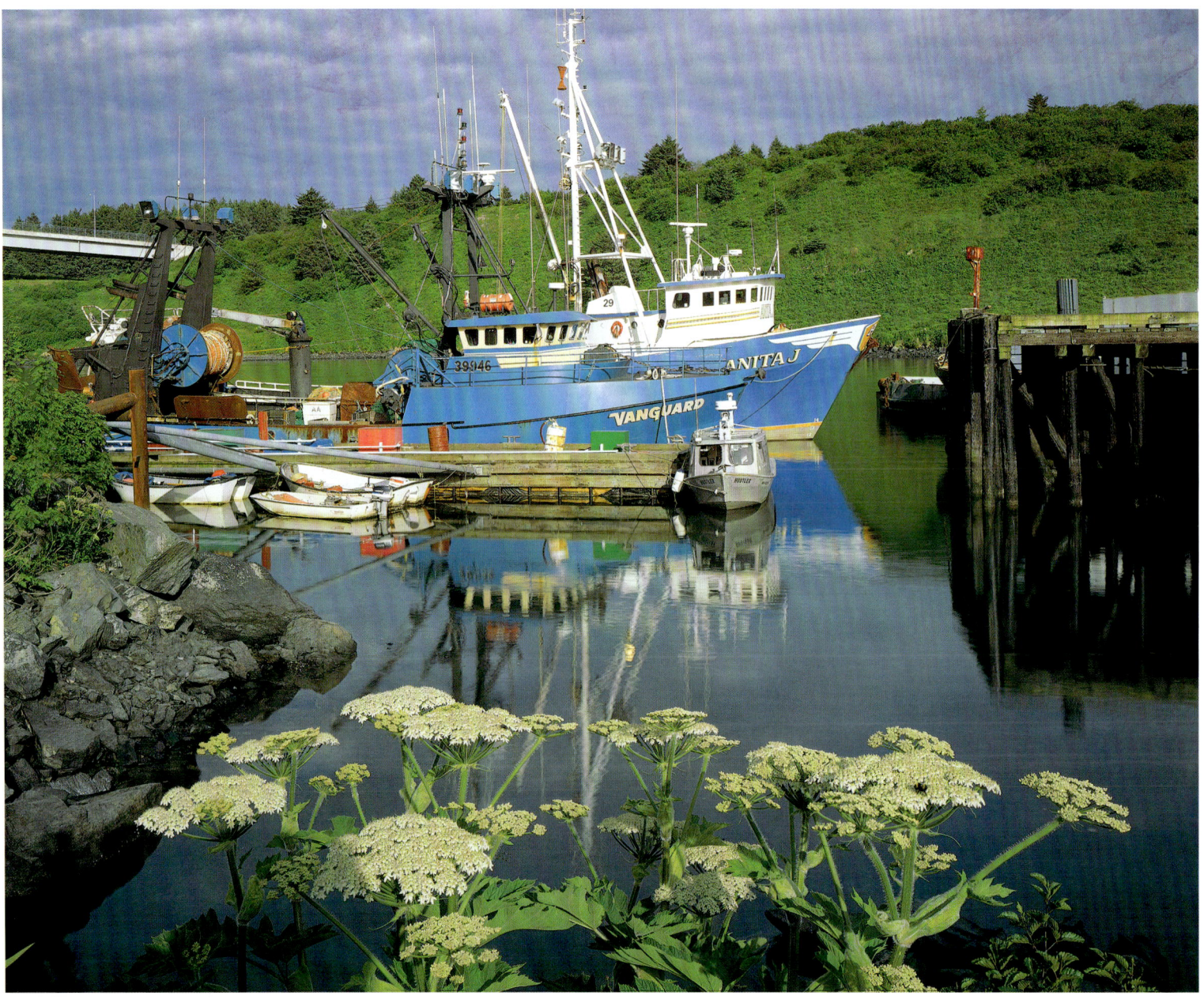

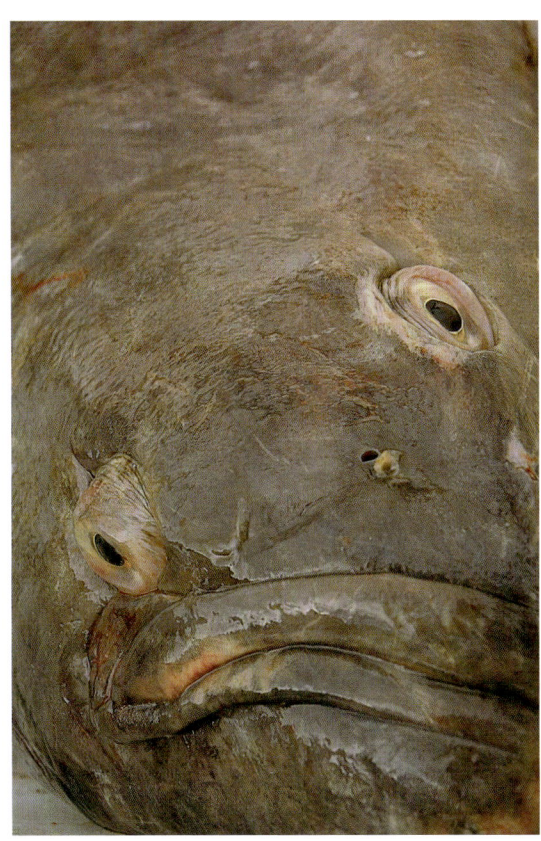

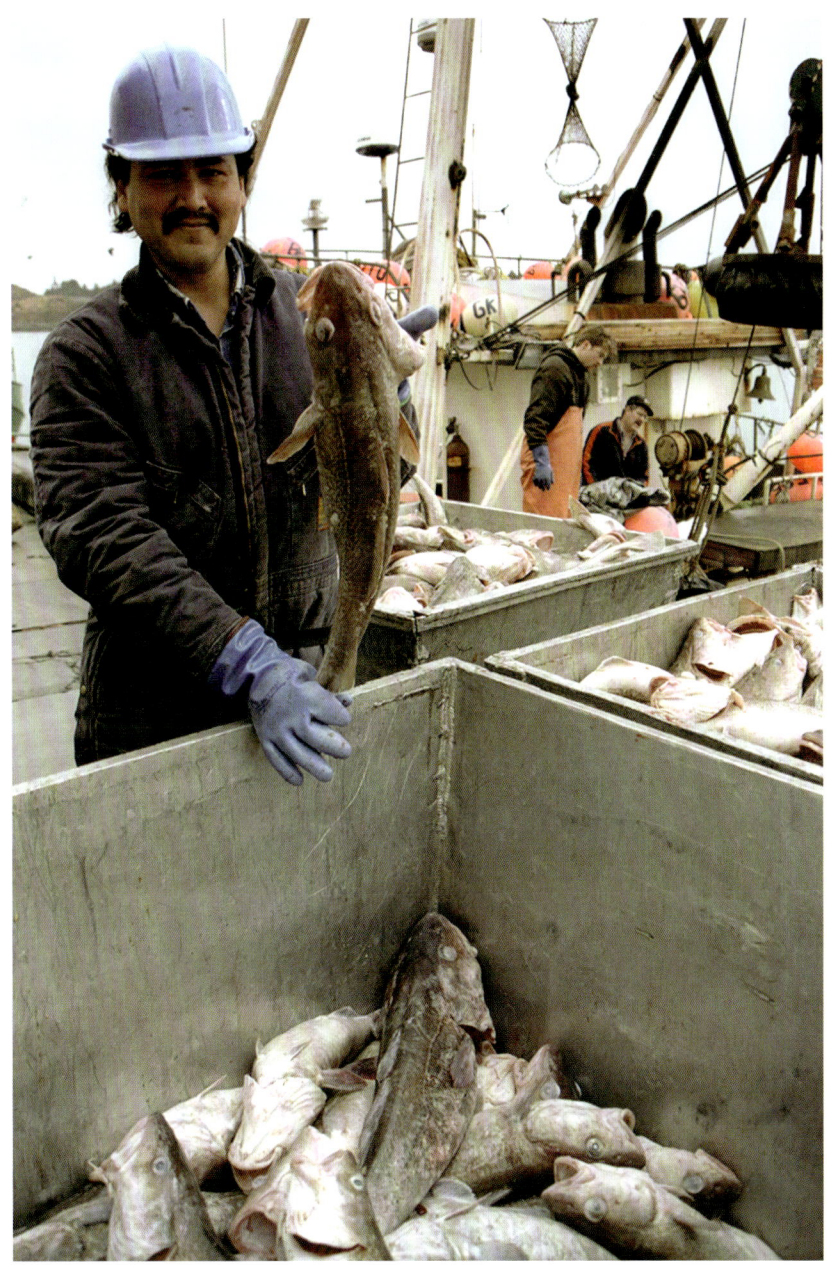

left Cow parsnip frames fishing boats docked in the Kodiak harbor. (Fred Hirschmann)

above Barn door-sized halibut are a sought-after catch, in Kodiak waters. (Alissa Crandall)

left A fish processor sorts Pacific cod. (Elysia Leake)

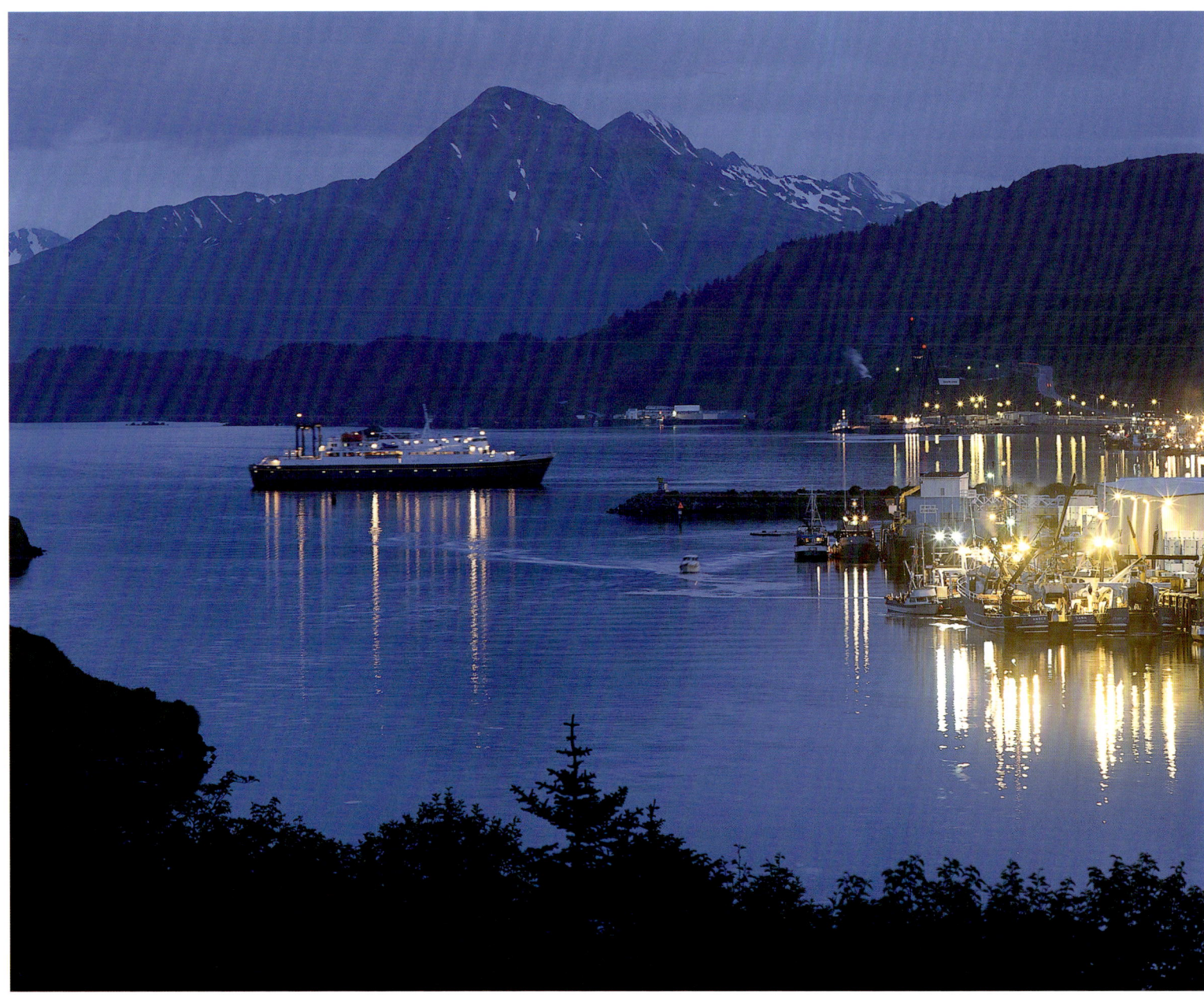

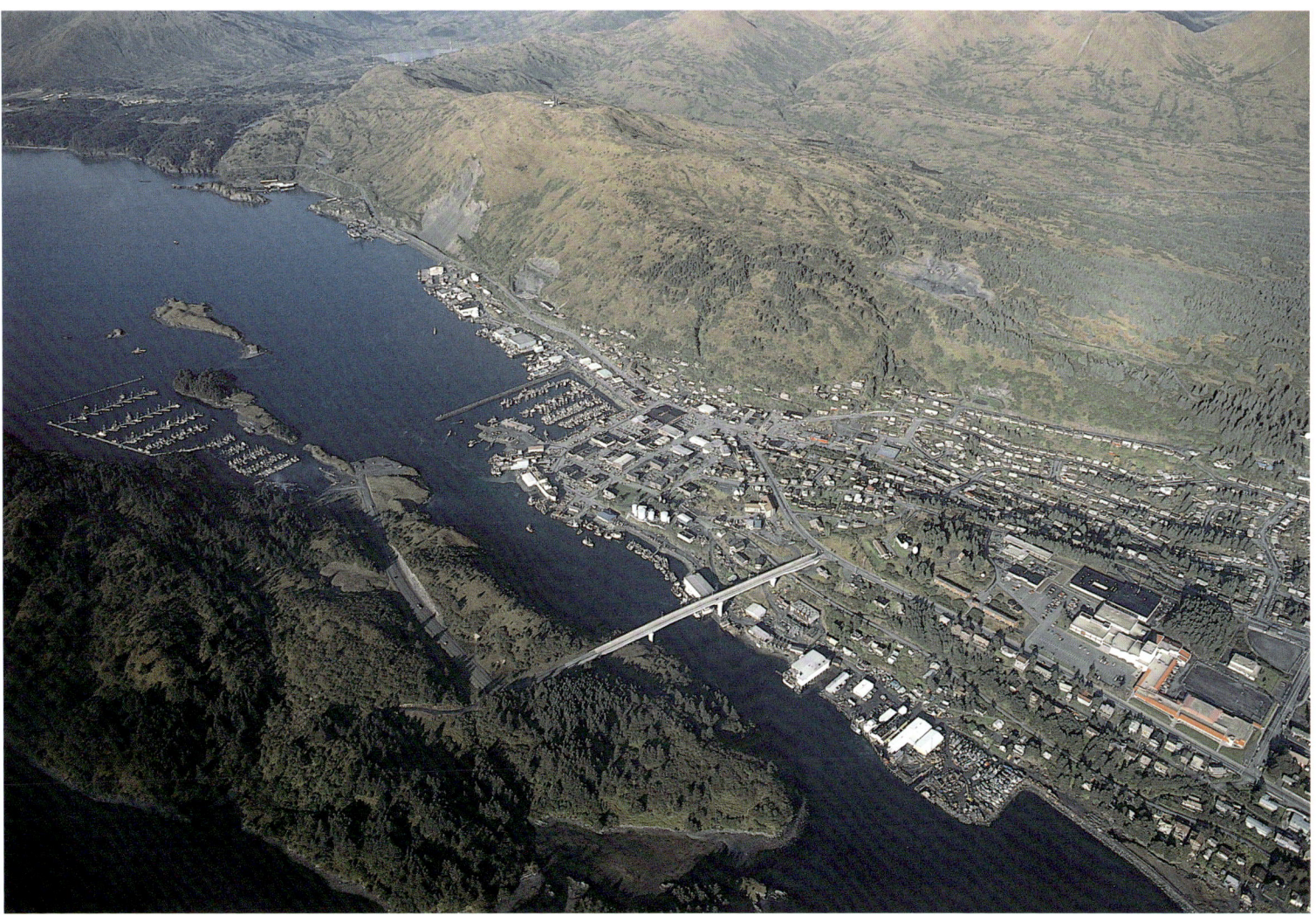

left The Alaska State
Ferry *M/V Tustumena*
turns in Kodiak Harbor
at dusk. (Jeff Gnass)

above An aerial view of
the Fred Zharoff Memorial
Bridge connecting Near
Island to Kodiak Island,
shortly after it opened in
1986. (Alissa Crandall)

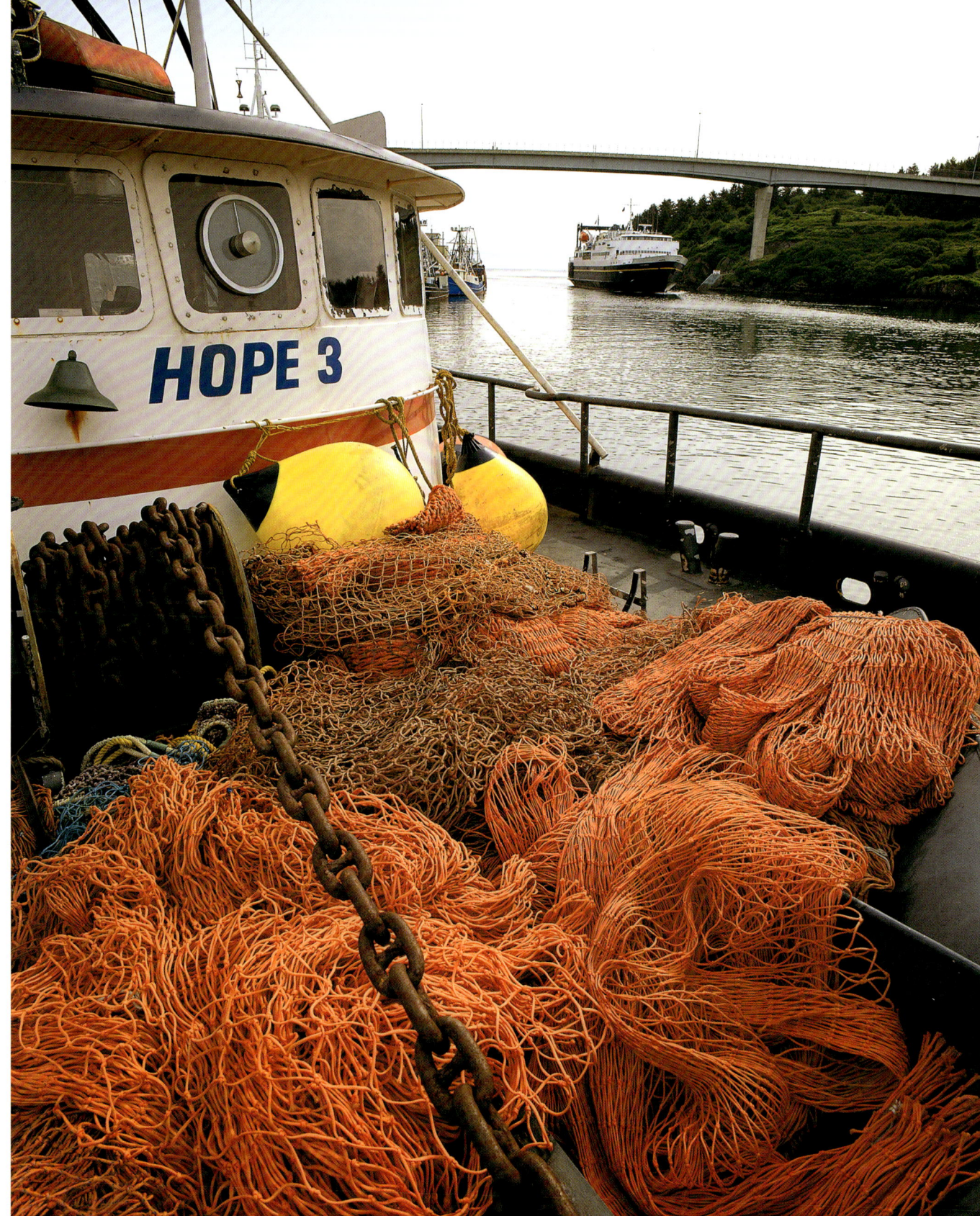

right Fish nets on the foredeck of the *F/V Ocean Hope 3* with the *M/V Tustumena* approaching under the bridge to Near Island. (Jeff Gnass) *right* Fishermen mend a seine net in the Kodiak boat harbor. (Patrick Endres)

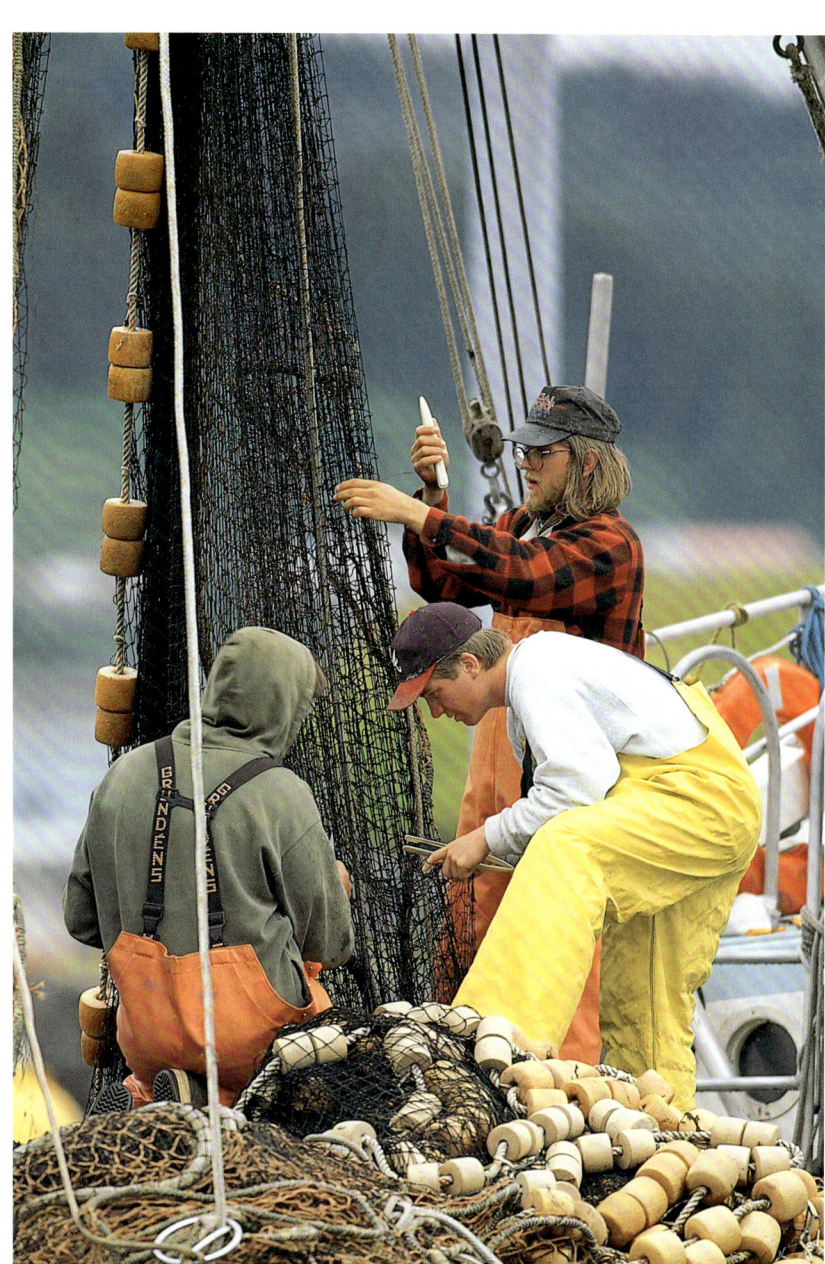

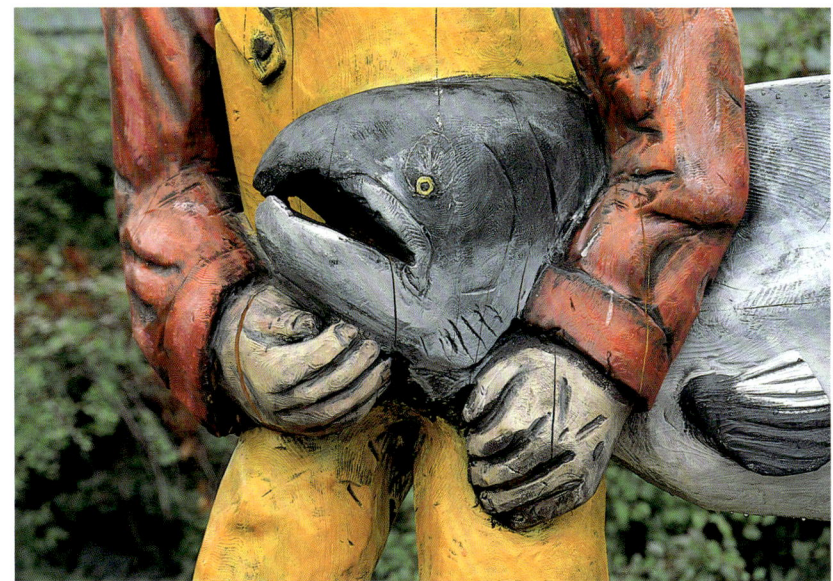

above Detail of a wooden sculpture of fishermen—a downtown Kodiak welcome sign. (Patrick Endres)

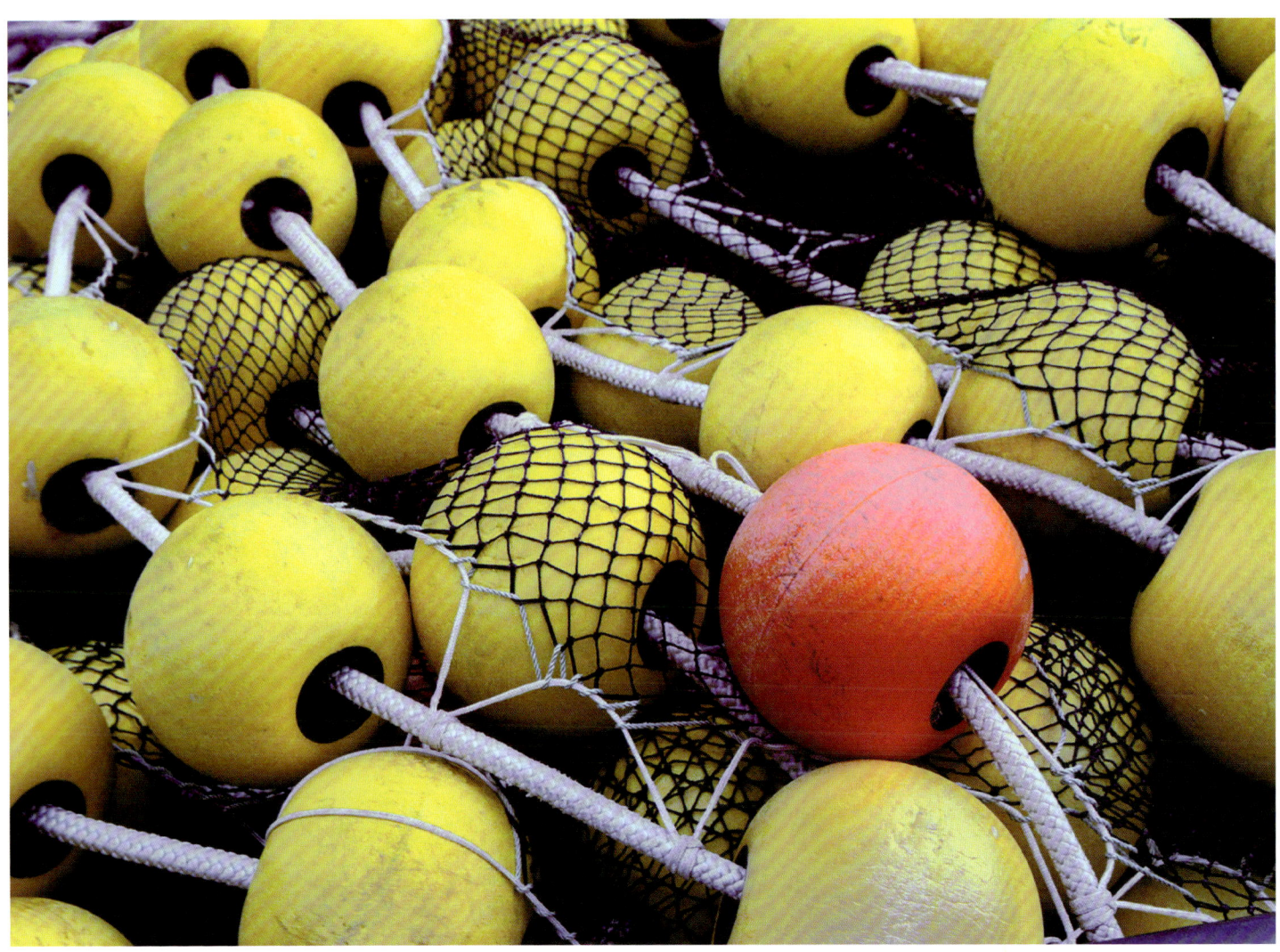

above Fish net and floats.
(Elysia Leake)

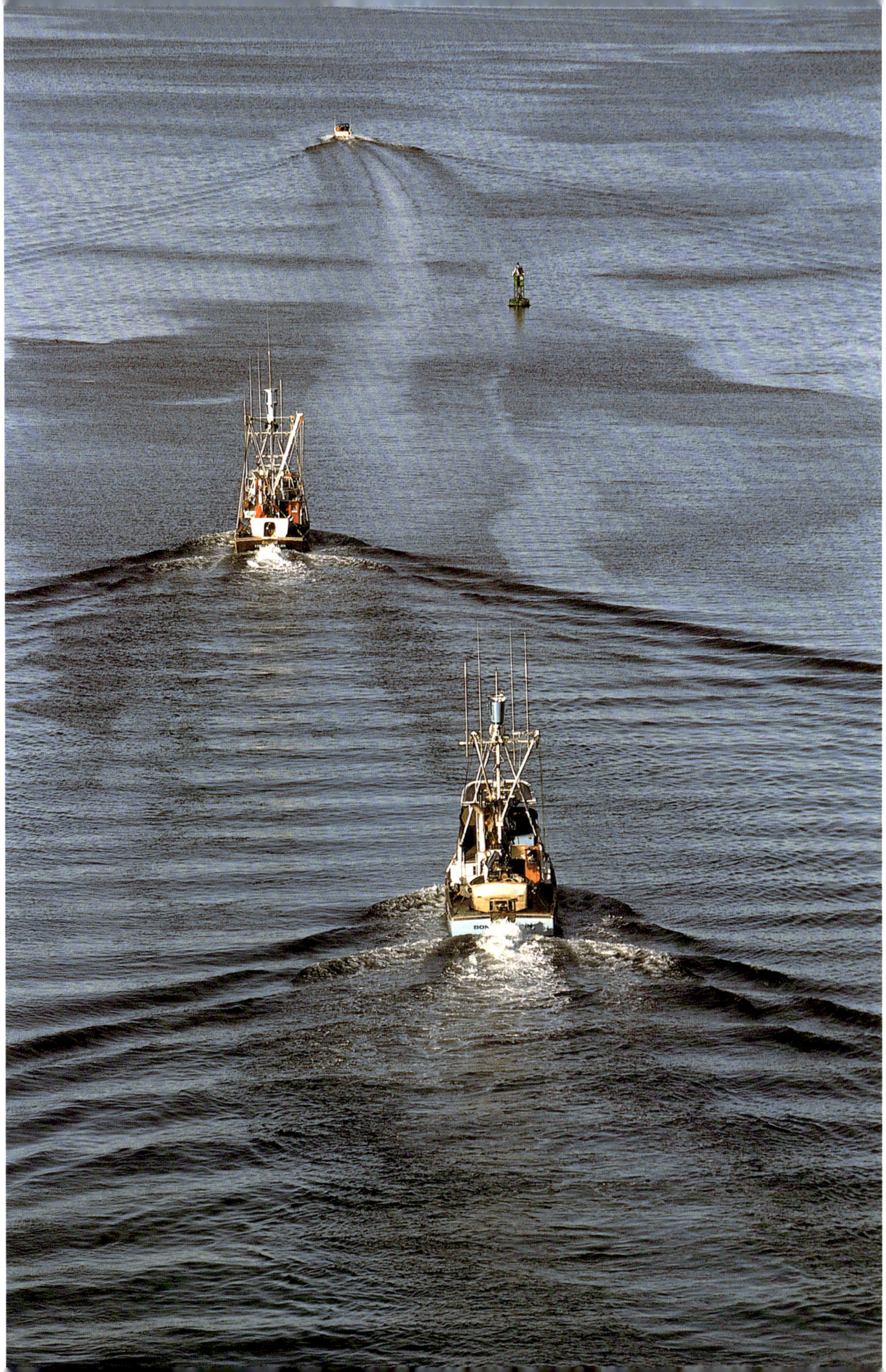

left Fishing boats head out of St. Paul Harbor in Kodiak. (Clark Mishler/ Alaska Stock)

below A fisherman mends a net aboard a trawler. (Elysia Leake)

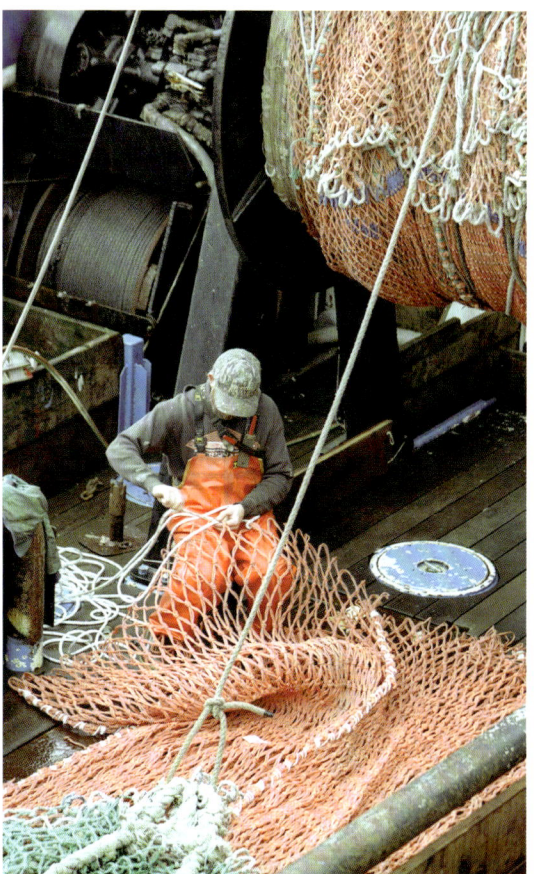

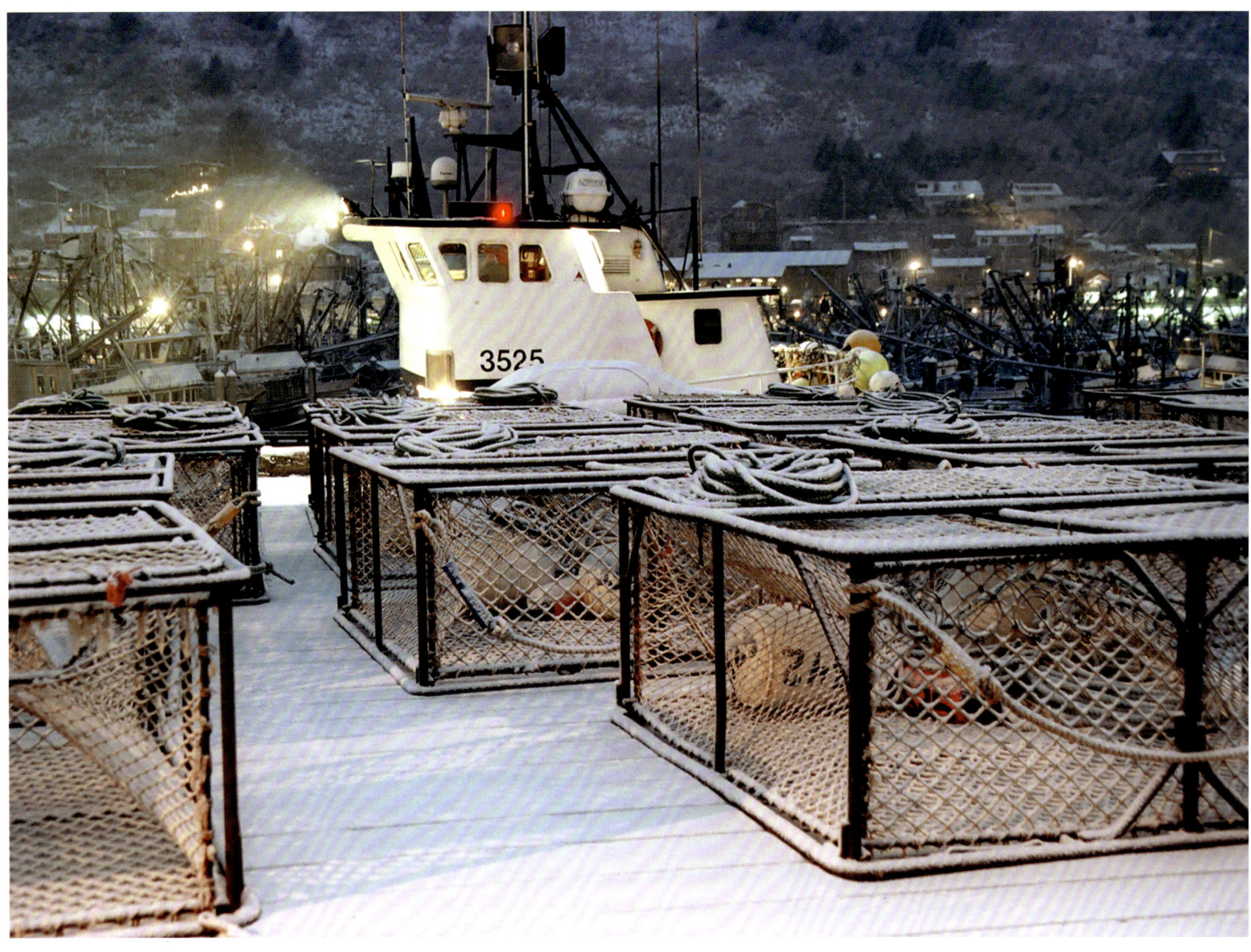

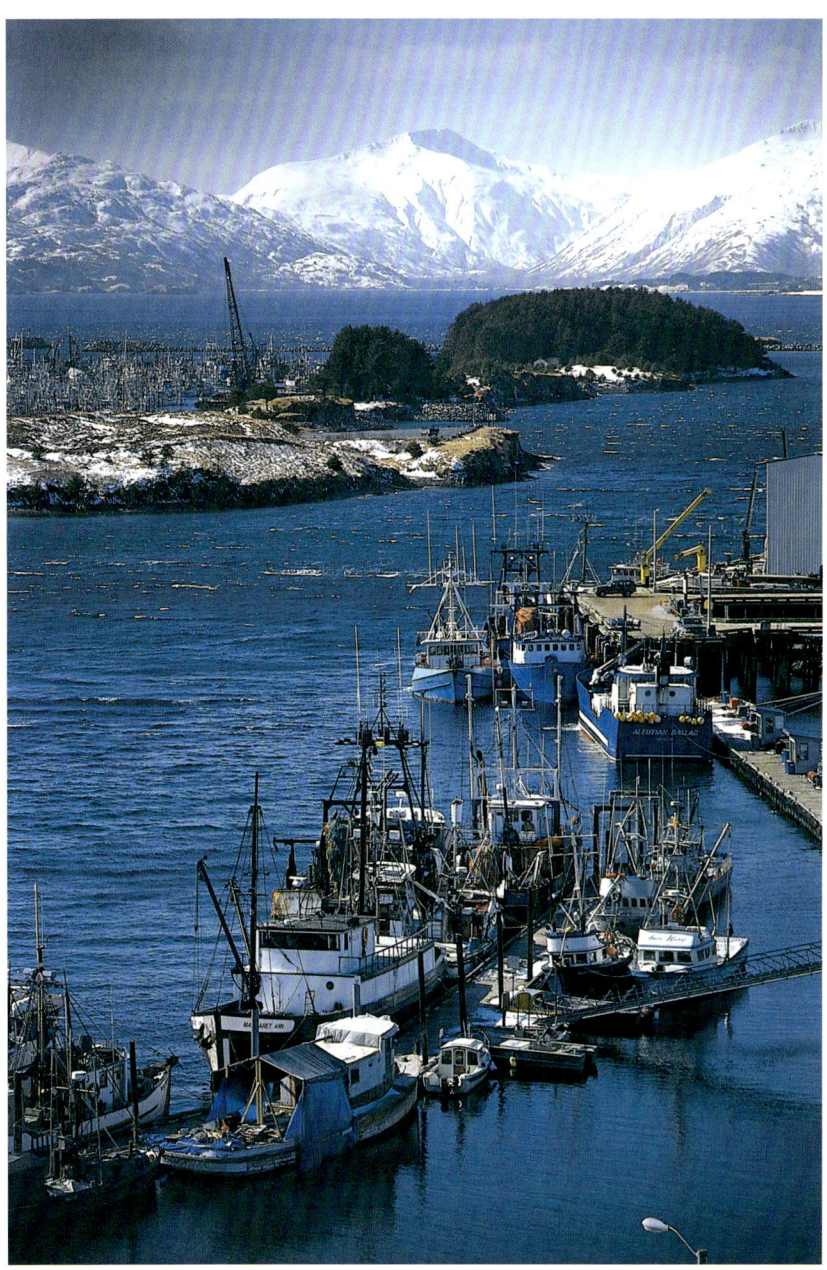

far left Crab pots at the boat harbor in winter. (Elysia Leake)

left Spring winds create chop in the Kodiak boat harbor. (Chris Arend/ Alaska Stock)

below Steller sea lions haul out on a breakwater at St. Herman Harbor minutes from downtown Kodiak. (Marion Owen)

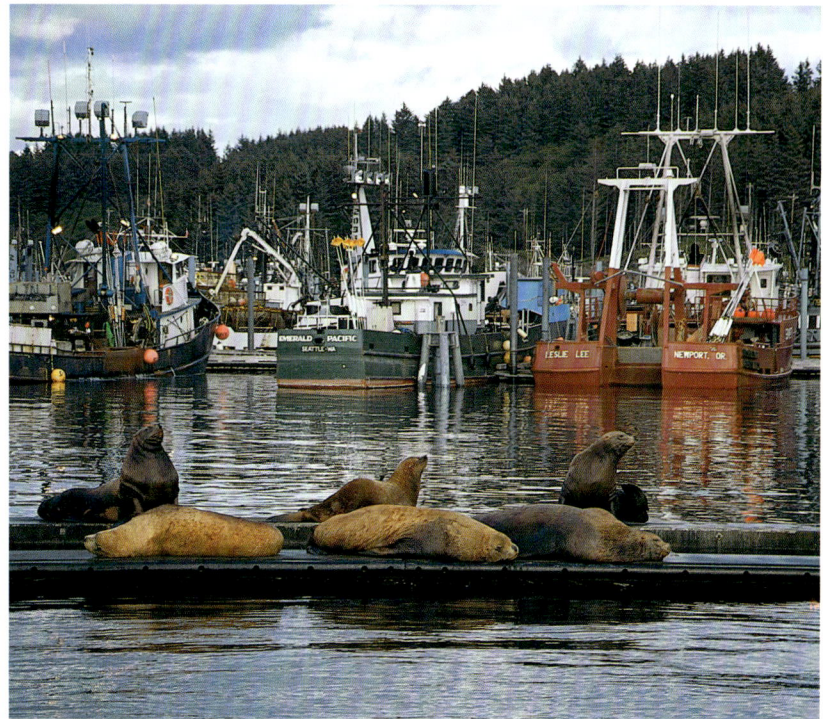

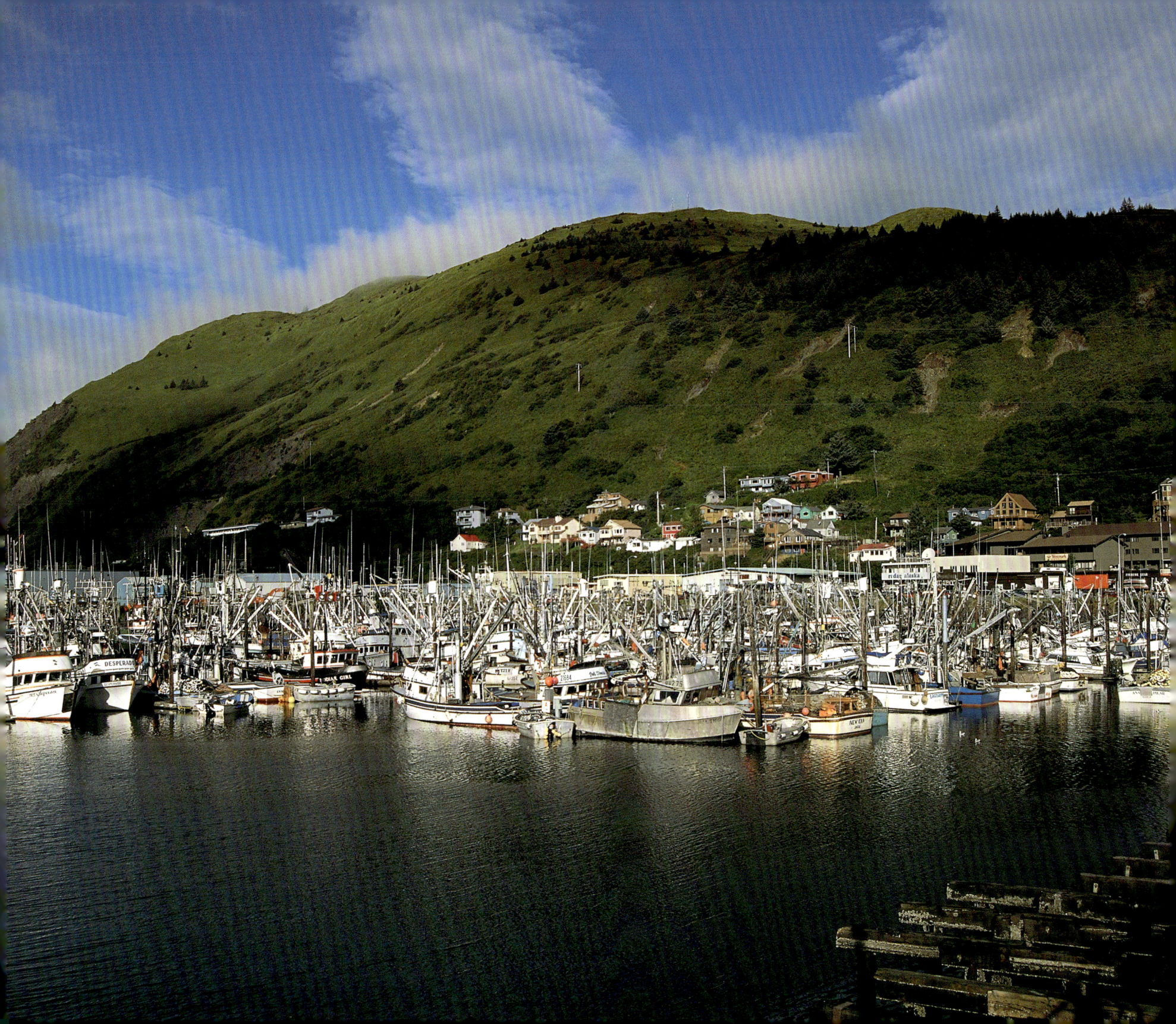

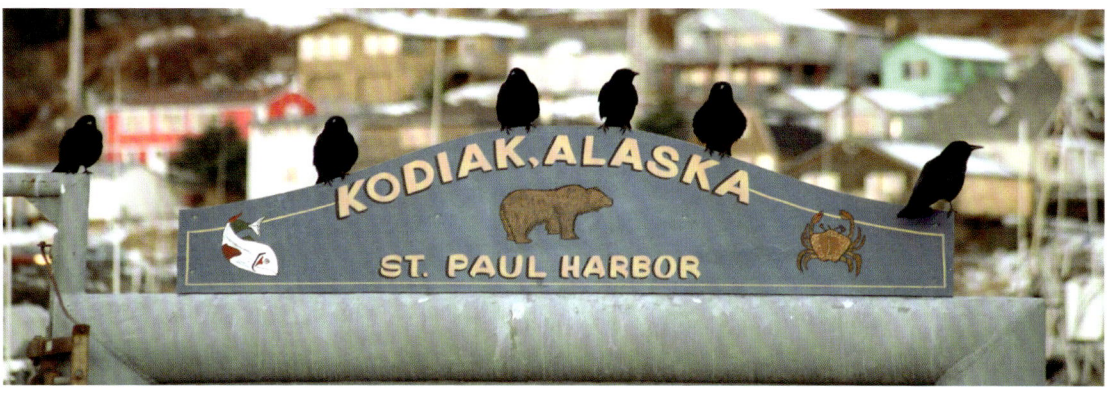

Kodiak's Seafaring Legacy

People on Kodiak have bonded with the sea for centuries, venturing out to harvest the ocean's bounty for more than 7,500 years. Those first fishermen used woven nets as well as hooks and harpoons that had barbed points made of bone or antler. Those tools are in museums now, replaced by modern fishing gear. Sleek, spare Native kayaks and high-masted sailing ships have given way to modern vessels.

Today's fishermen are not only masters of the ancient arts of navigation and seamanship, but also wizards of cutting-edge technology. Mariners mend nets by hand and plot their course with satellite telemetry. They pass secret fishing hotspots from parent to child, and search the depths with sonar. They craft bowlines and rolling hitches out of polyethlene line, blending the ancient traditions of fishing with these modern synthetics.

This combination of lore and technology has made Kodiak one of the country's top fishing ports. It is home to more than 1,000 fishing vessels and second in the nation in value of product landed and tonnage processed.

The vessels in the harbor are as diverse as the island's fisheries. Here is the entire range of Alaska's commercial fishing vessels, from massive, 150-foot crabbers to pint-sized 32-foot gillnetters and smaller pleasure boats that can double as halibut longliners. These boats are a blend of form and function. Their designs have been refined by hard-earned experience as fishermen challenge the towering waves, fierce currents and tempestuous moods of the sea.

Why do people live and work in such a place? It's the ancient lure of the sea, the passion for life on the open ocean. Although the tools of the fisheries have changed, the sea still beckons those who thrive on the challenge of wresting a living from these cold, dark waters.

The joy of the open sea and hard work with a hardy team has always been the lure of ocean fishing. Mysterious to some, it is Kodiak's pride.

left Kodiak frames St. Paul Harbor. (Tom Watson)

above St. Paul Harbor. (Elysia Leake)

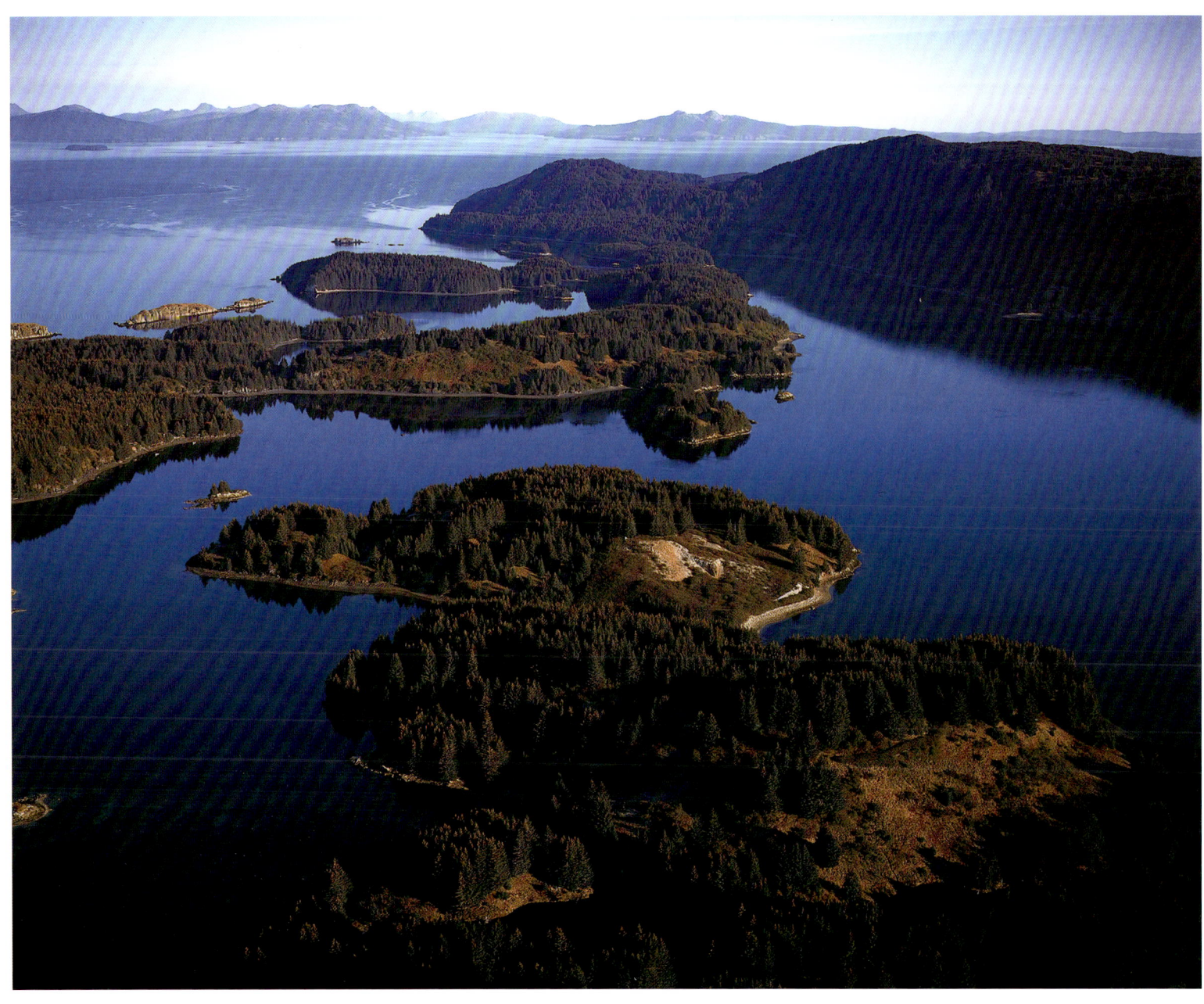

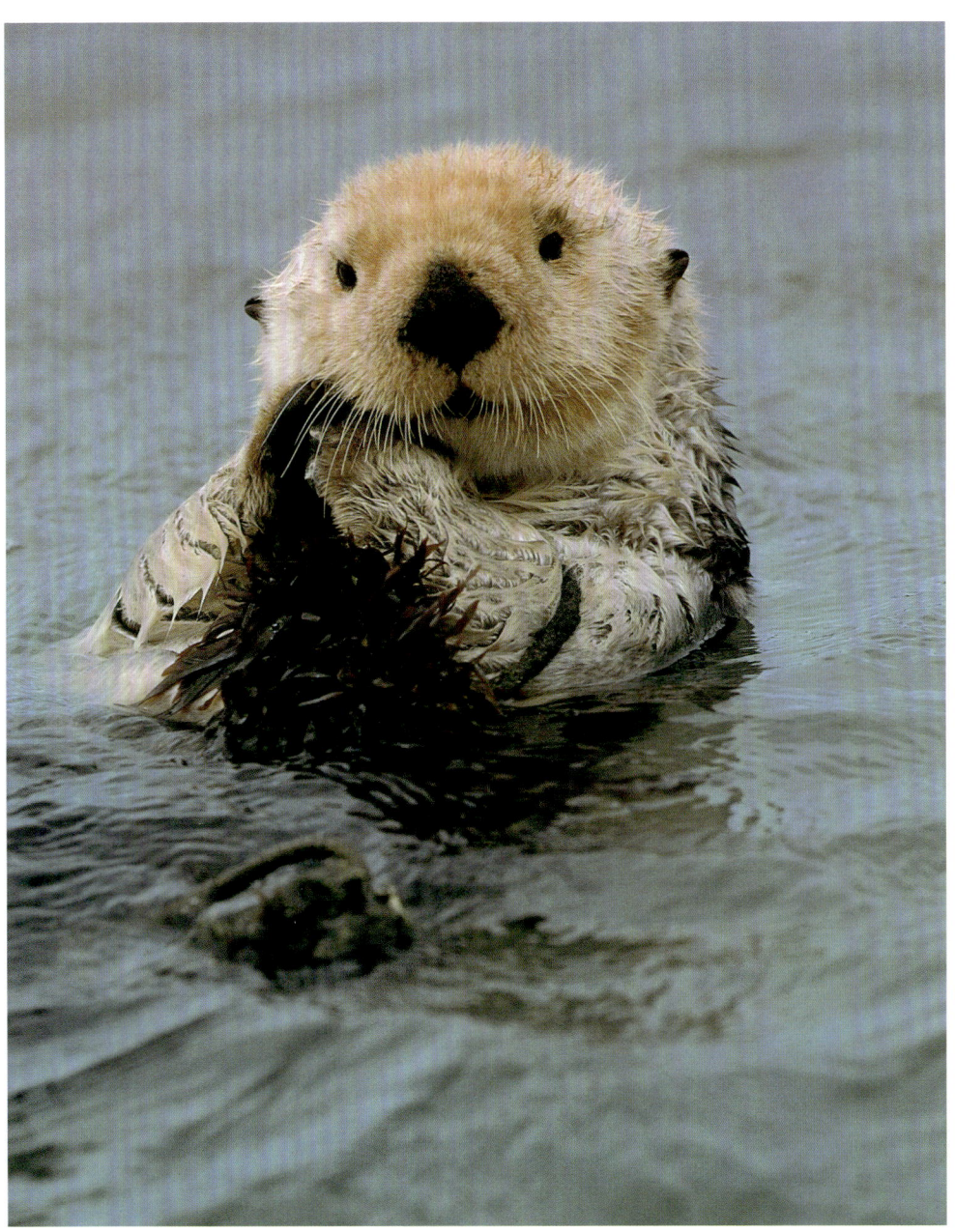

far left Aerial view of
Anton Larsen Bay. Once
cloaked in grinding ice,
Kodiak Island emerged
15,000 years ago. When
the ice retreated, it left not
only chiseled mountain
peaks, but also fjord-like
bays, rocky islets and
wide valleys.
(Fred Hirschmann)

left The sea otter's fine,
dense fur traps air, helping
to maintain its body
temperature in Alaska's
chilly waters.
(Robin Brandt)

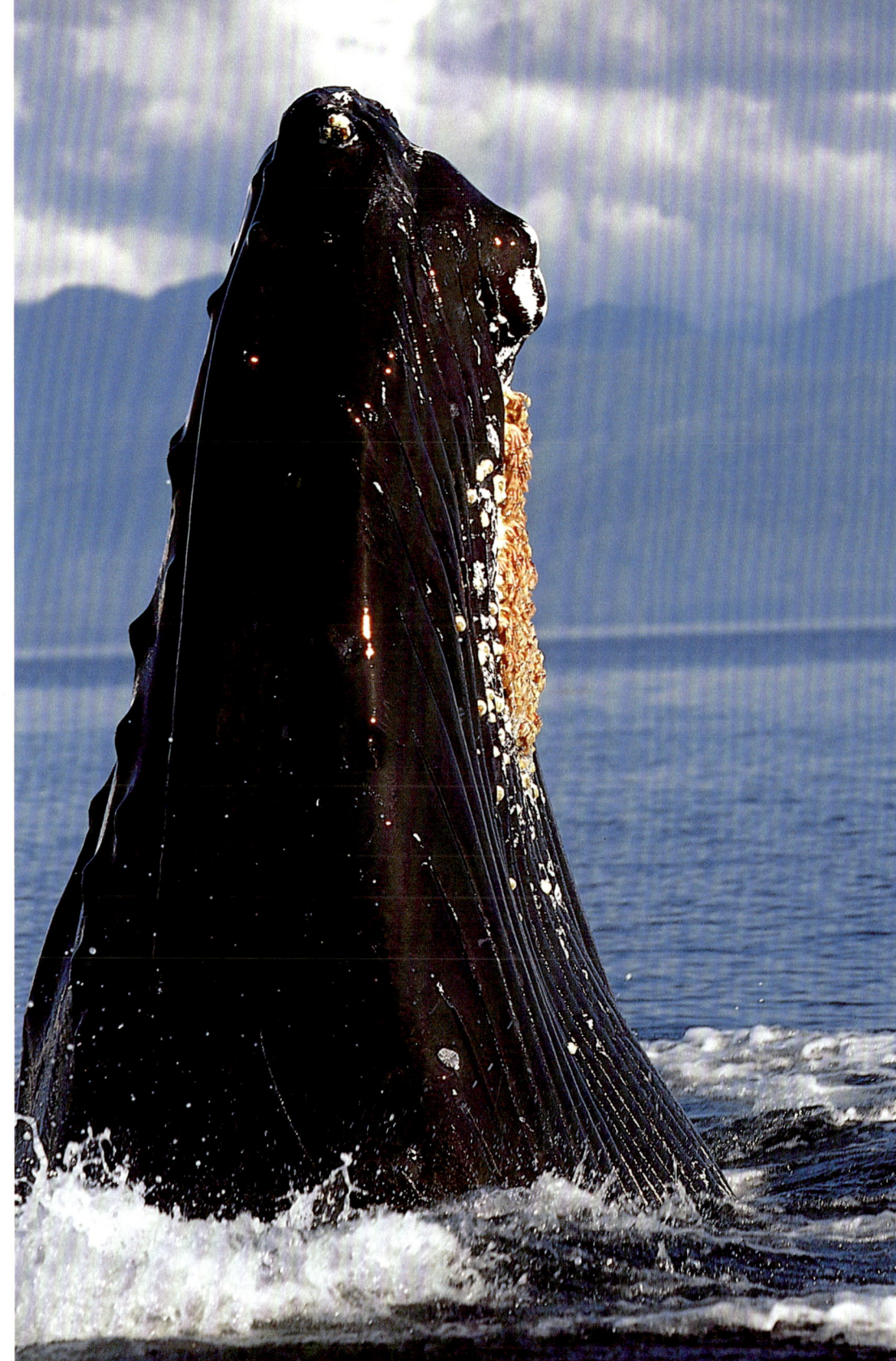

right A spy-hopping humpback whale. Six types of whales are found in Kodiak waters—fin, sei, minke, humpback, killer and gray whales. (Barbara Brundege)

far right Killer whales, also known as orcas, are common in the spring and summer. (John Hyde)

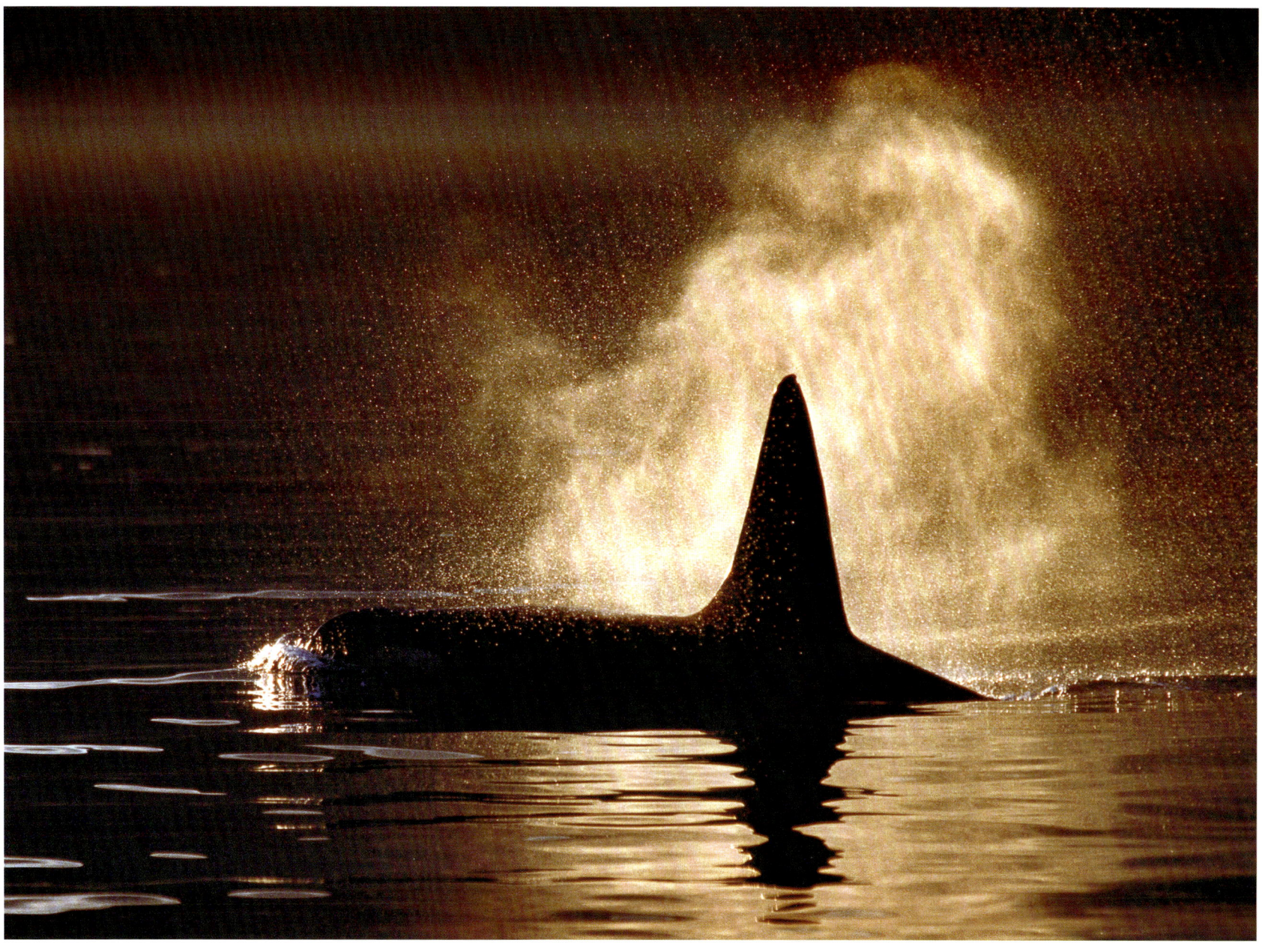

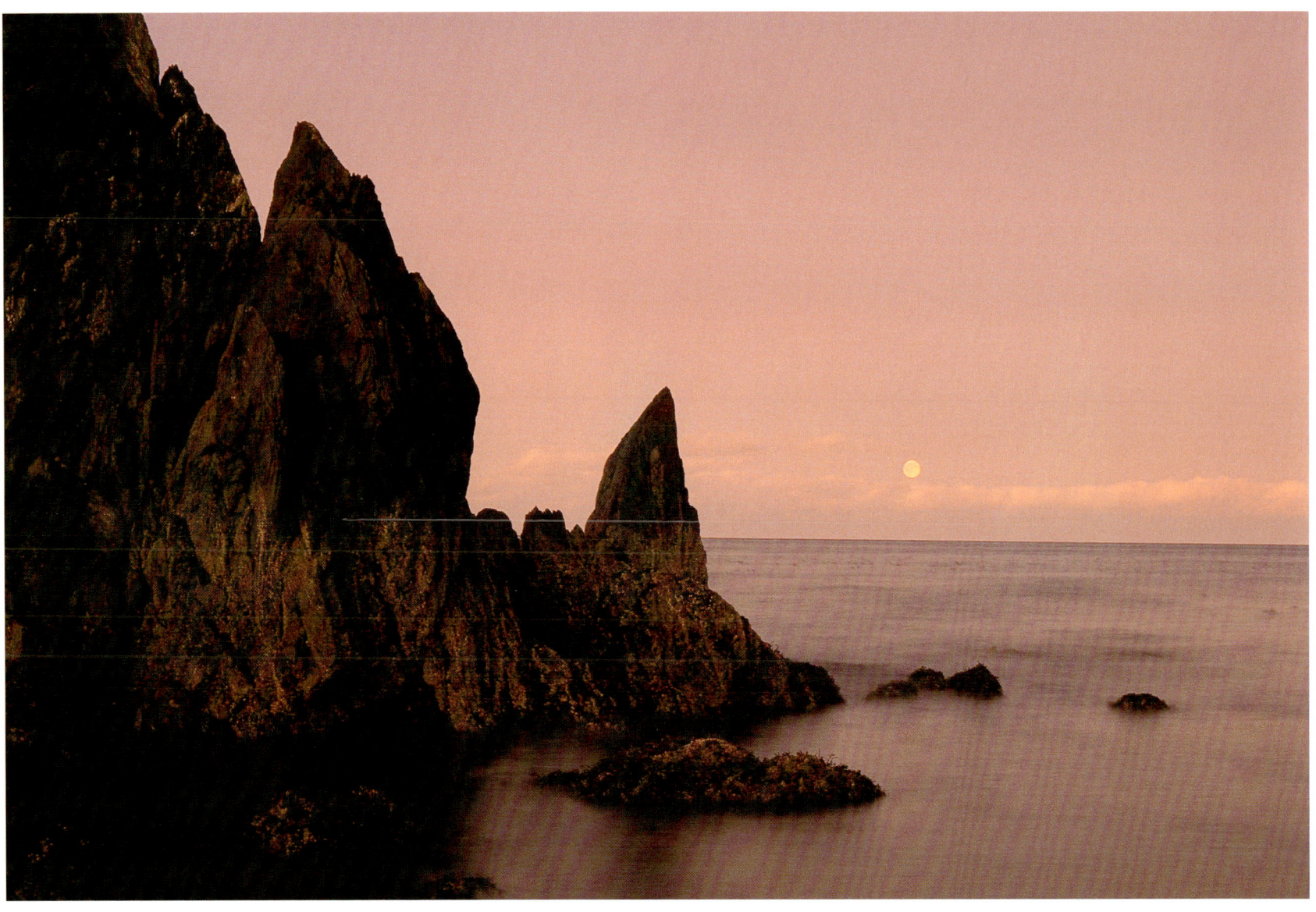

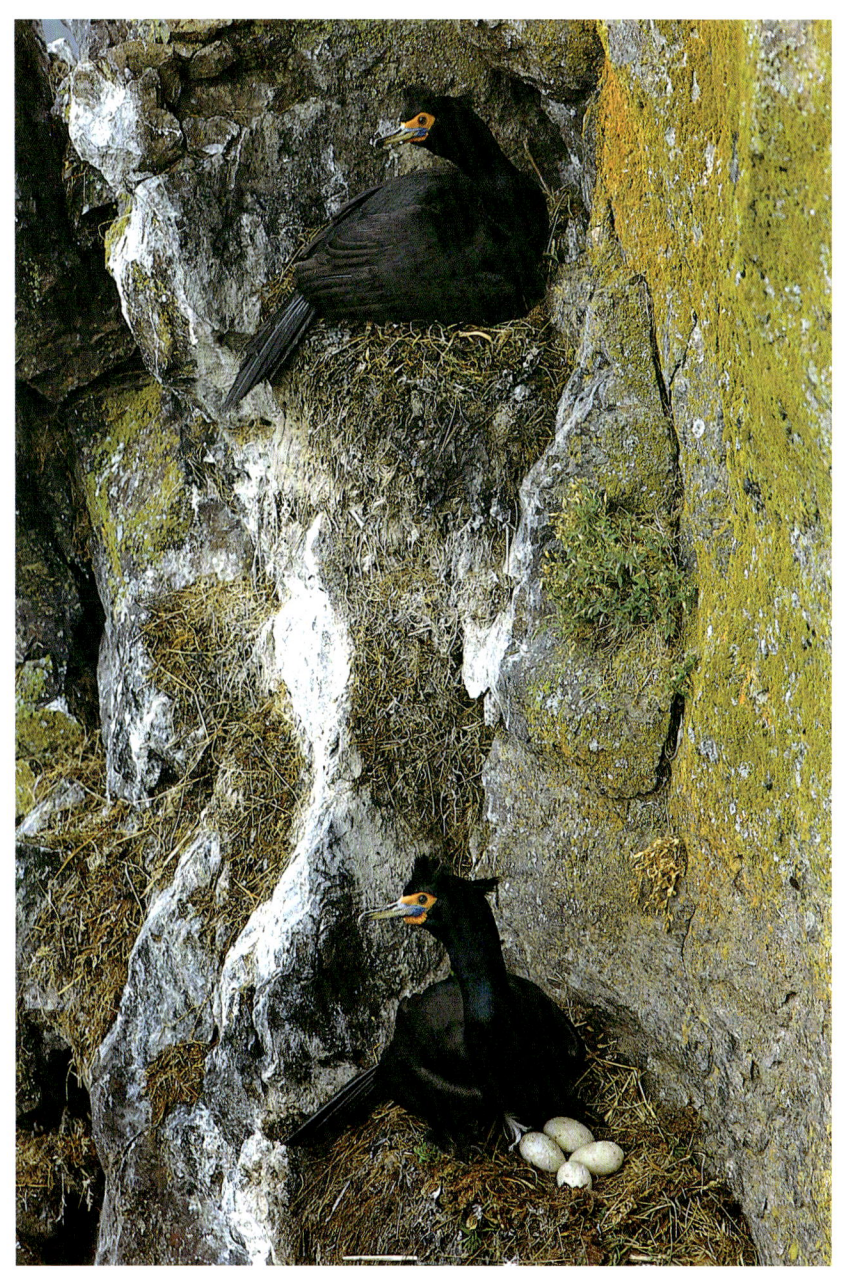

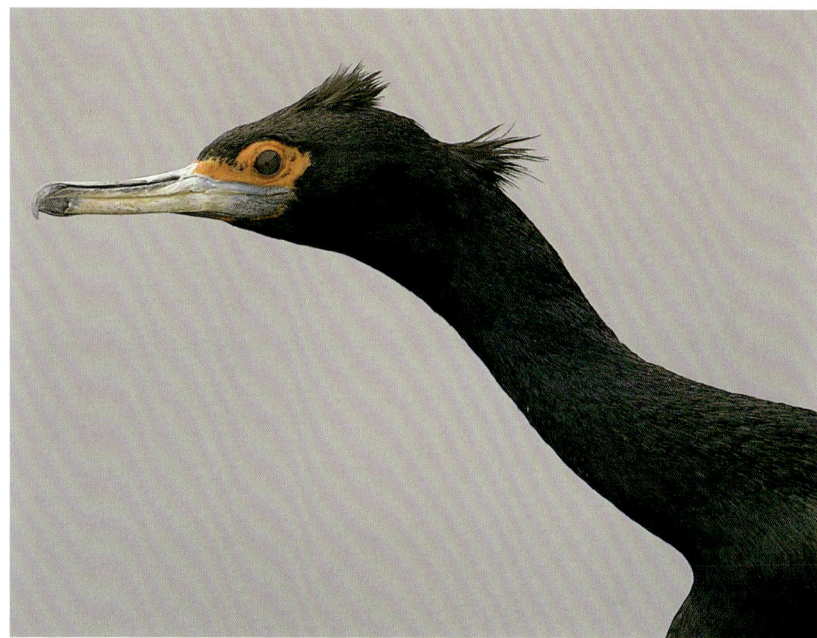

far left Moonrise over
Spruce Cape. (Marion
Owen/Alaska Stock)

left Red-faced cormorants
are one of the many
seabirds which nest on
cliffs in the Kodiak
archipelago.
(Heather L. Johnson)

above Red-faced
cormorant.
(Alissa Crandall)

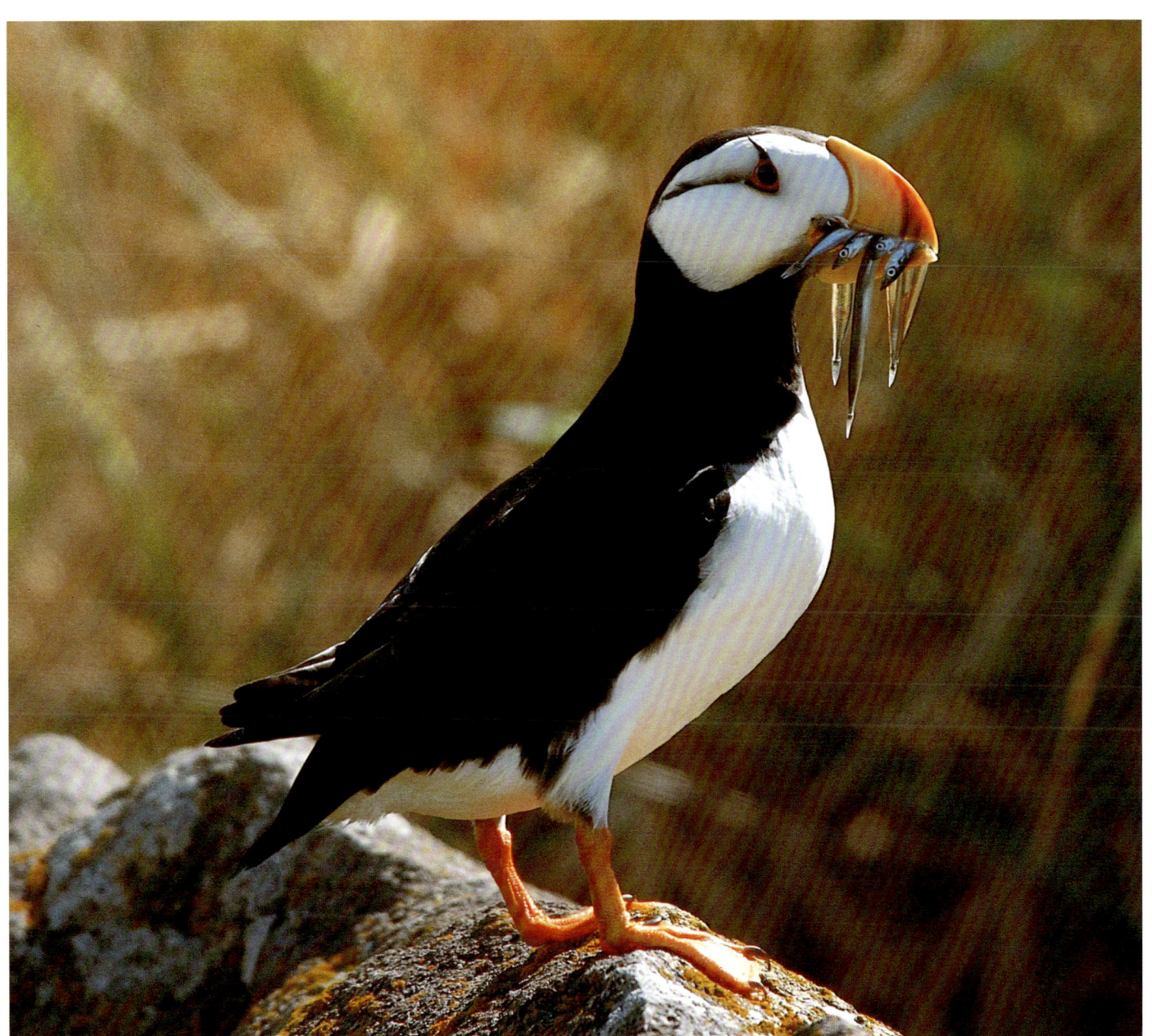

right Horned puffin with fish at Halo Bay on the Katmai coast. Puffins' serrated bills allow them to hold their catch while continuing to fish for more. (Robin Brandt)

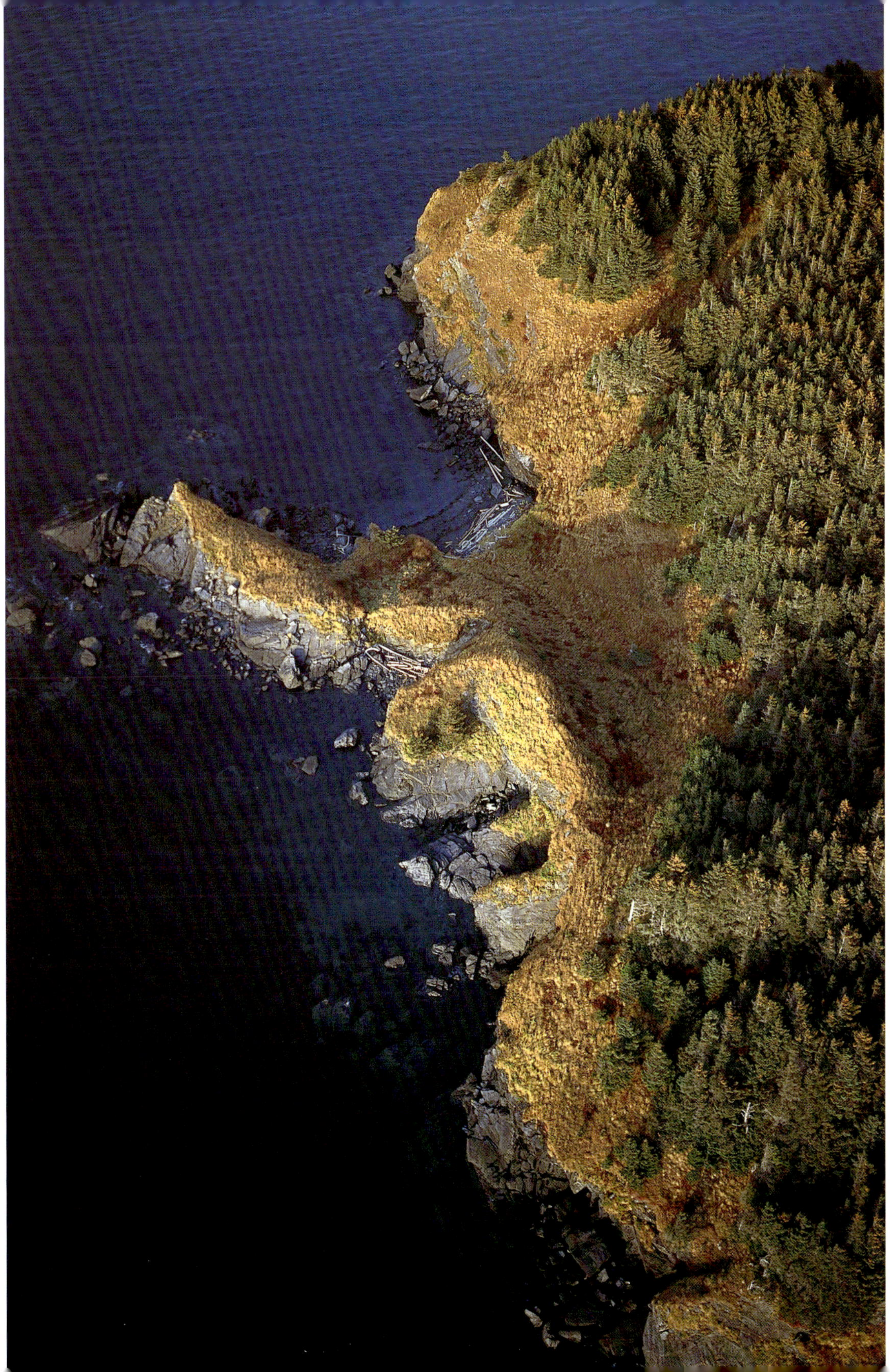

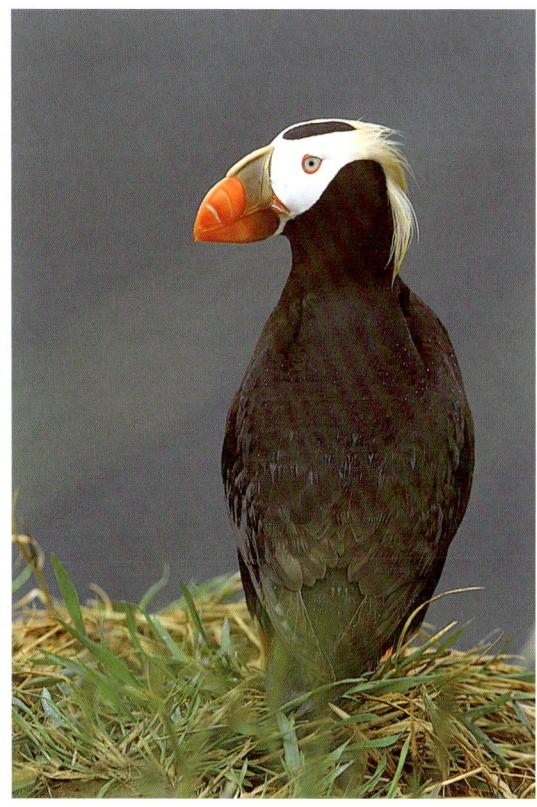

left Aerial view of the
coast of Afognak Island.
(Fred Hirschmann)

above Tufted puffin,
Kodiak. Puffins spend most
of their lives on the sea
and only visit land to
breed and raise their
young in the summer.
(Heather L. Johnson)

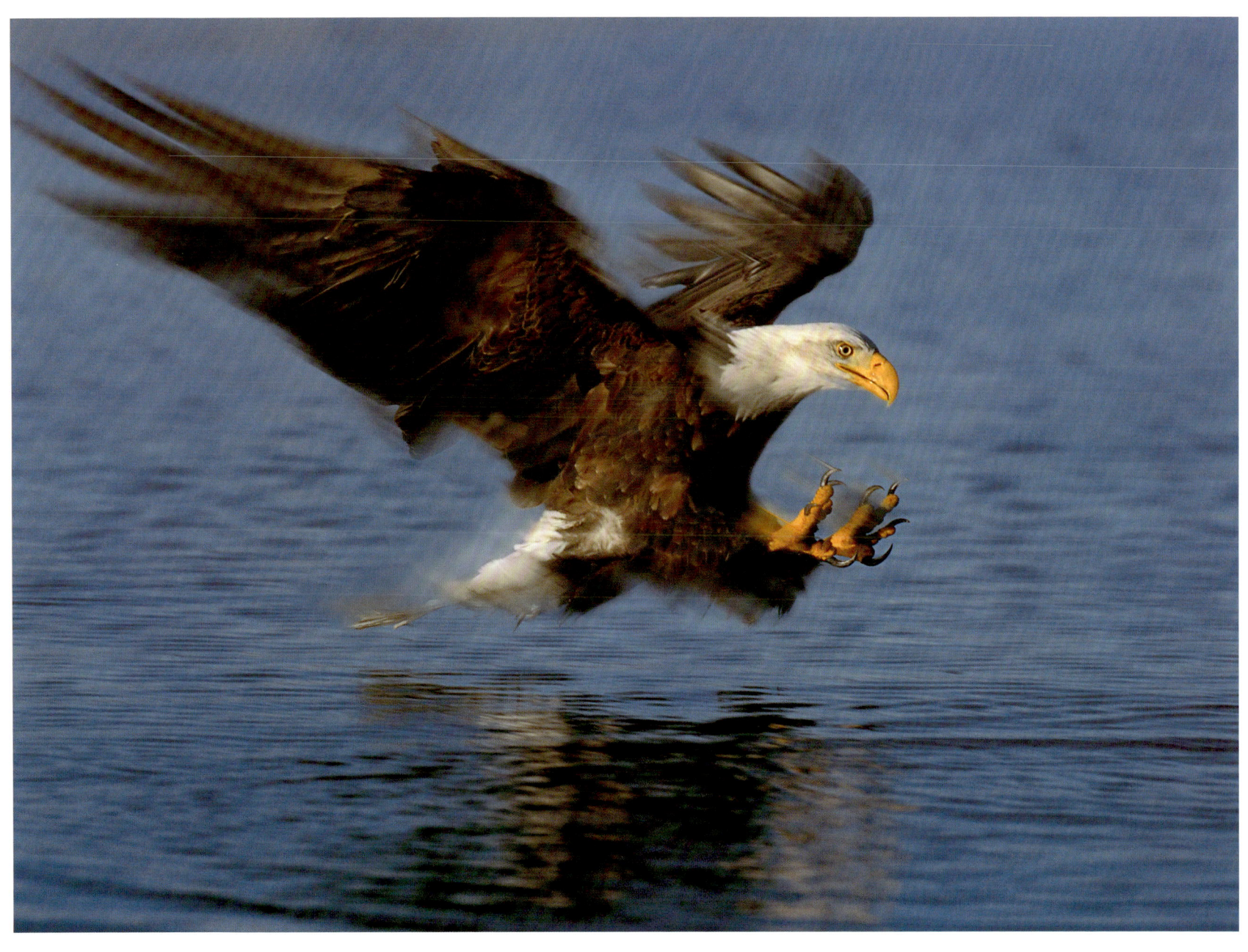

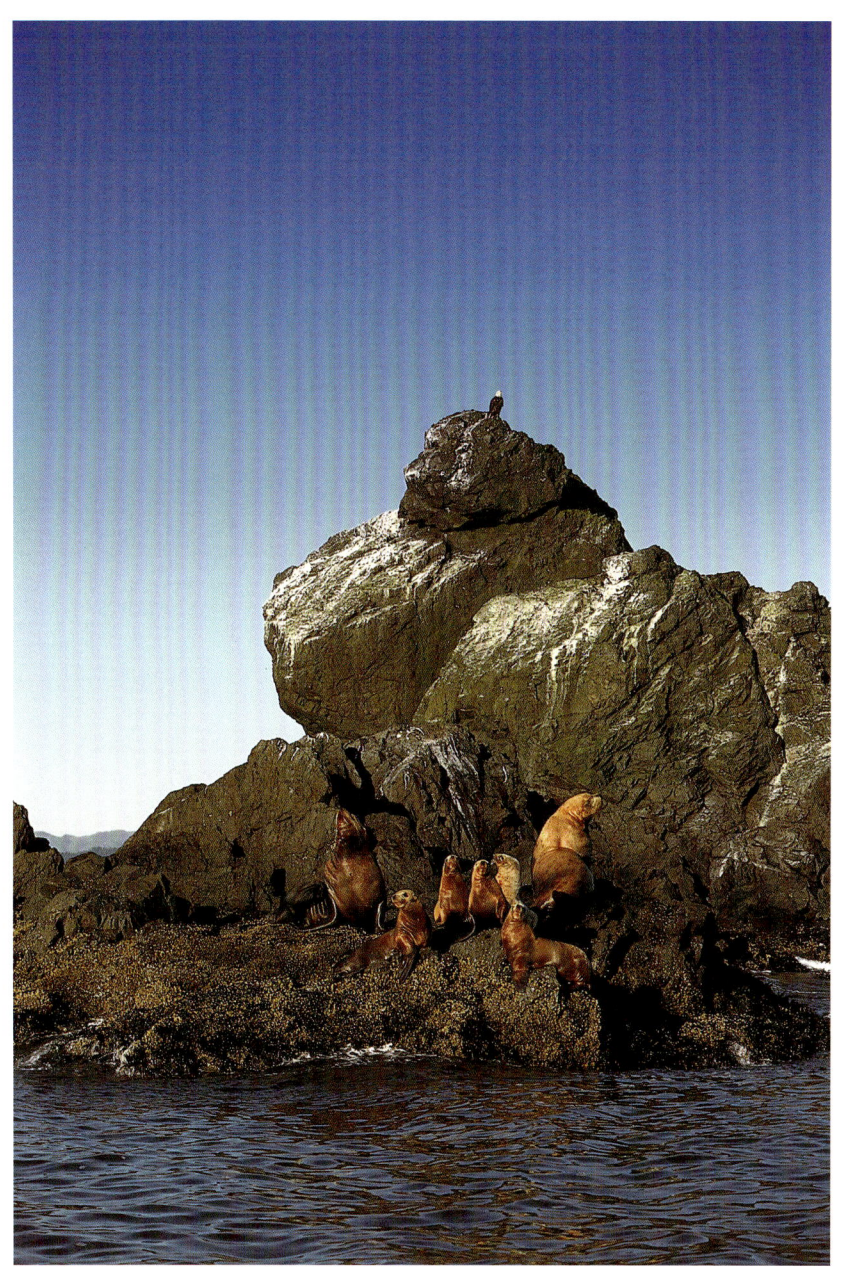

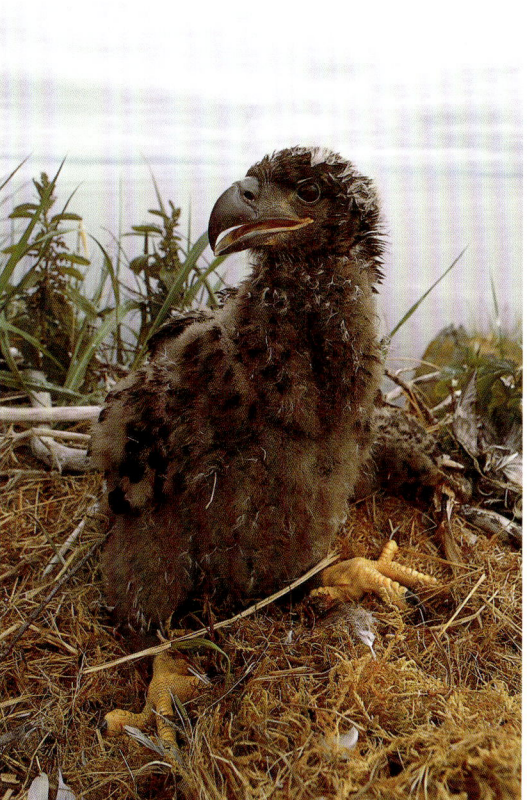

left Juvenile bald eagle in nest on Ayakulik Island. More than 2,000 bald eagles reside in the Kodiak Island Archipelago. (William H. Mullins)

far left Bald eagles are efficient fishermen and are found in abundance throughout the area. (John Hyde)

left Steller sea lions haul out on a rock below a bald eagle. Sea lions are marine carnivores, eating a wide variety of fish. (Michael DeYoung)

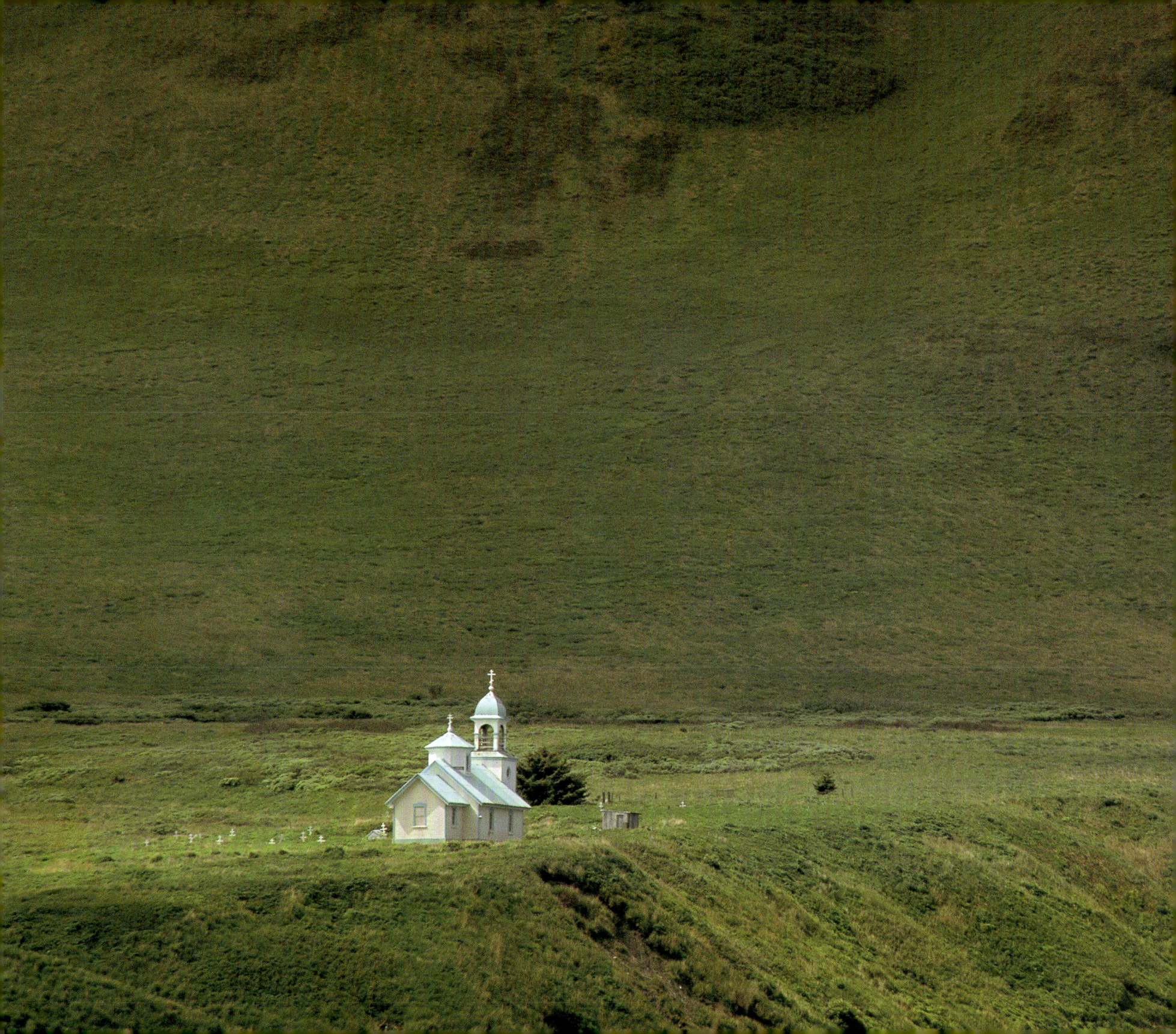

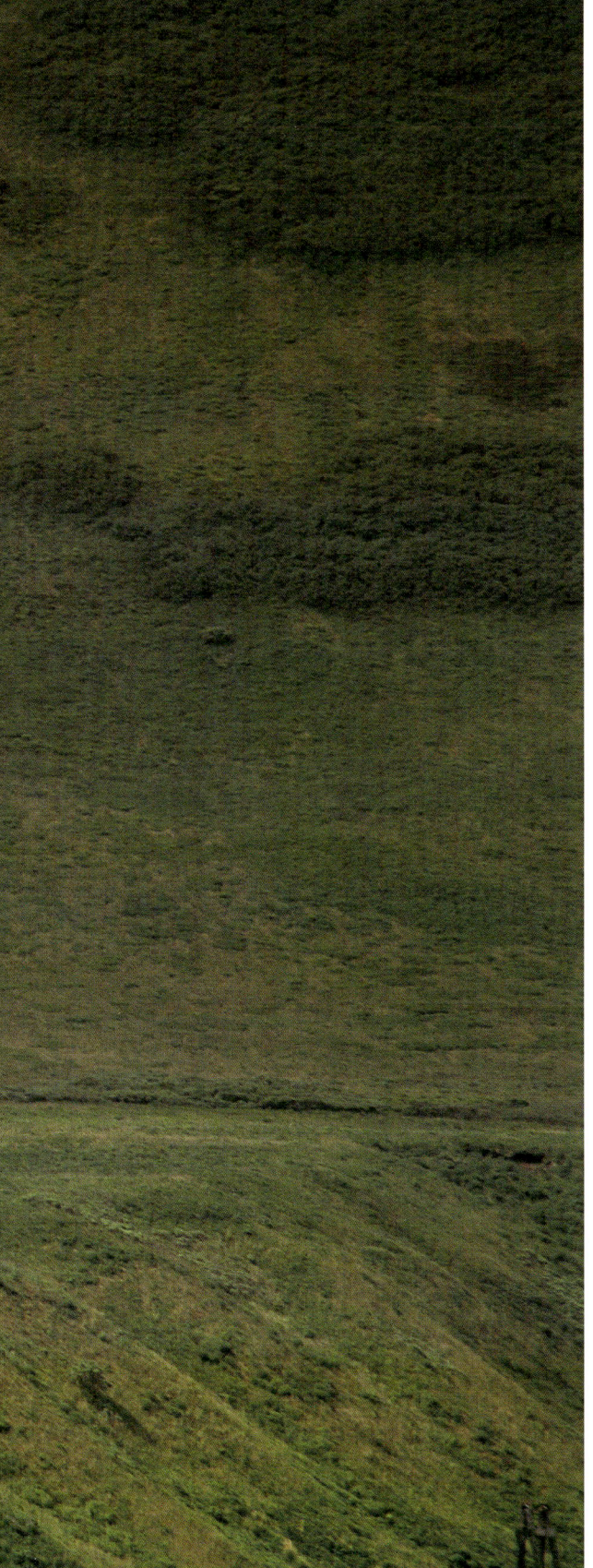

The People

Kodiak has always been a meeting place of cultures. For more than 7,500 years, the richness of land and sea has drawn people to these shores.

Distant tales and worn petroglyphs remind us of the earliest peoples. The forerunners of today's Alutiit were related to Yupiit and Inupiat people from the north, and to the Unangan (Aleut) of the west. Using the wealth of their maritime world, they crafted seaworthy skin boats and sturdy waterproof clothing, tightly woven baskets and ornate spirit masks. Theirs was a culture of great artistic and spiritual complexity, interwoven with goods and ideas from neighboring cultures. Kodiak's place in the Gulf of Alaska made it a favored trading point among the Chugach, Yupiit and Unangan, as well as the Tlingit and Haida to the southeast. People came together on these shores to trade, to fight, to intermarry.

In 1763, new faces came. Spanish, English and American explorers charted the waters surrounding Kodiak, but it was the Russians who came first, and the Russians who stayed. Hungry for the feast of furs that Alaska promised, traders crossed the Bering Sea, following the Aleutian Islands into the Gulf of Alaska. Kodiak became the first capitol of Russian America. But the lush pelts of sea otter and seals that the newcomers sought came with a price. Bloodshed, slavery, disease and

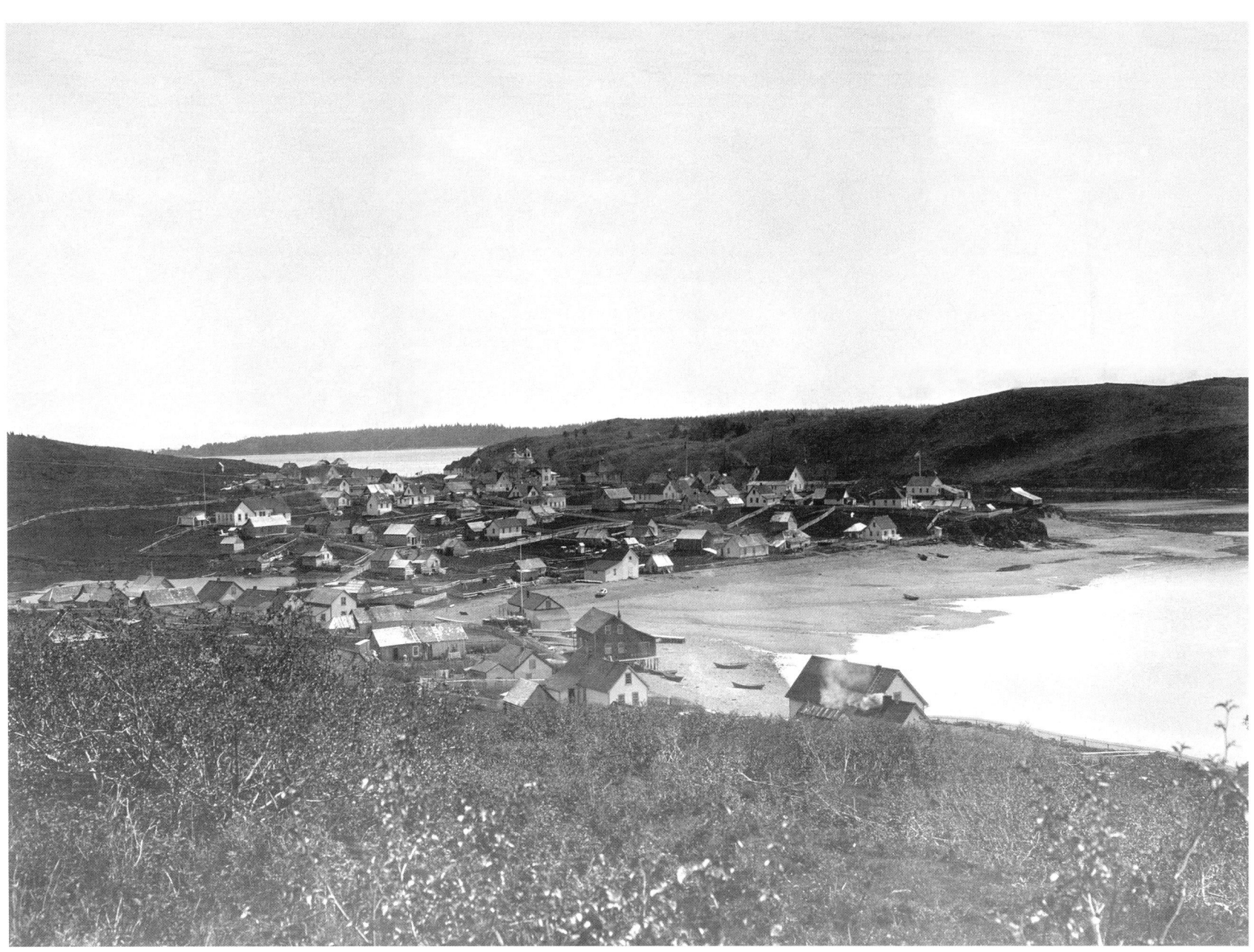

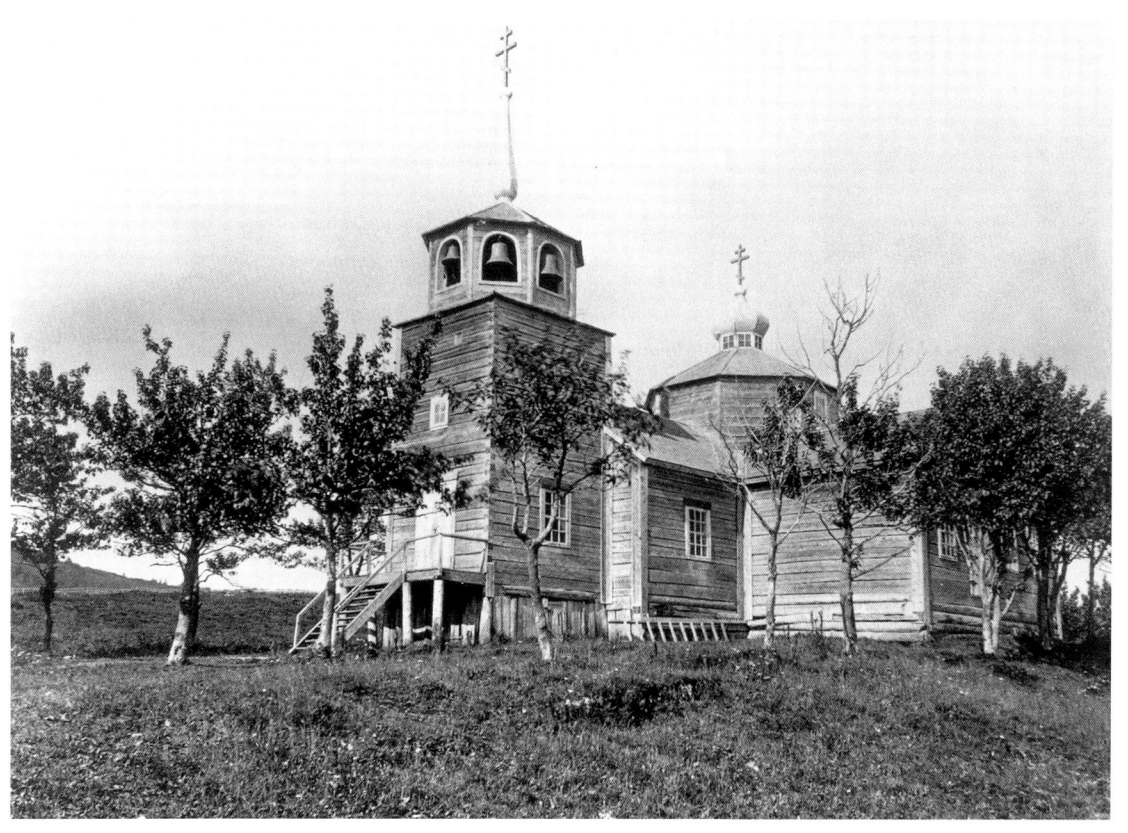

assimilation wore away the Native population, until only six Alutiiq villages now remain of the hundreds from past centuries.

A new flag came to Kodiak in 1867, the year Alaska was sold to the United States. American soldiers and bureaucrats arrived only to find that many Russians were happily settled, married into local families, and with no interest in returning to their homeland. The Russian Orthodox faith was deeply engrained in the island people, inspired by charismatic leaders like Saints Veniaminoff and Herman. That Russian influence remains strong today, present in everything from the onion domes of island churches to holiday customs and cooking to the Slavonic names of Russian descendants.

When Alaskan gold fever broke out in the 1890s, Kodiak again became a crossroads. Ships on their way from the Pacific Northwest to the golden sands of Nome stopped here to refuel. Some folks went no further than the cozy fishing village. Scandinavians in particular found a familiar haven in northern island fjords. And when cannery workers

previous double page
The Ascension of Our Lord Russian Orthodox chapel, built in Karluk in 1888, is the oldest remaining Russian Orthodox church in Alaska and is on the National Register of Historic Places. Tiny Karluk was once known for having the largest salmon cannery and the greatest red salmon stream in the world. (Marion Owen)

left Kodiak town site, 1908. The lake to the left was filled in by ashfall from the 1912 Novarupta eruption. (MSCUA, University of Washington Libraries, Cobb 2614)

above Three churches have stood on the site of the Holy Resurrection Russian Orthodox Church near downtown Kodiak's waterfront. The second church, shown here in 1888 or 1889, burned in 1943. (Anchorage Museum of History and Art, B91.43.13)

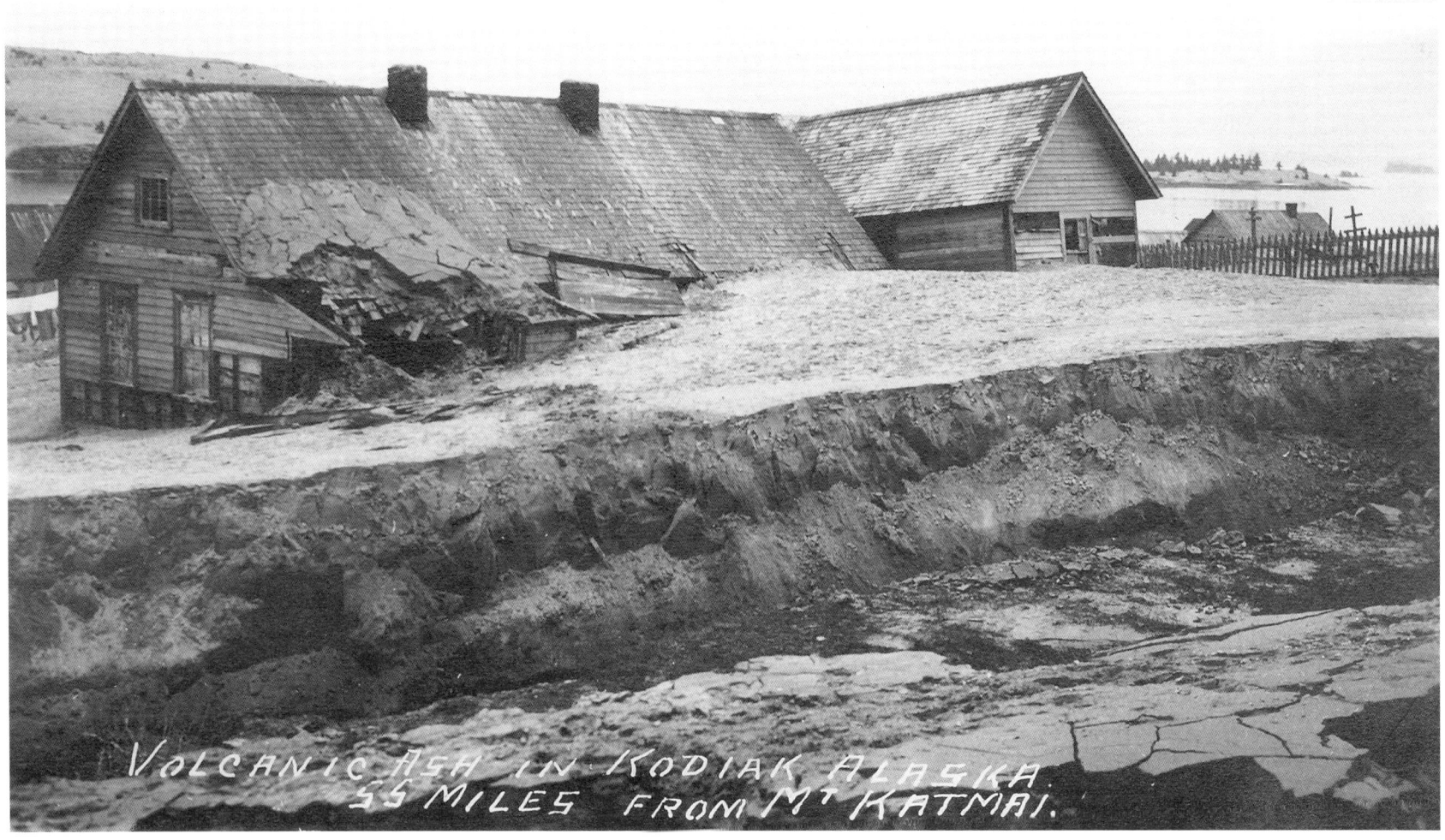

VOLCANIC ASH IN KODIAK ALASKA
55 MILES FROM Mt KATMAI.

above Kodiak after the Novarupta eruption, 1912. (Anchorage Museum of History and Art, B63.16.43)

"About 5 pm on Thursday, June 6, the sky suddenly darkened and heavy ash began to fall on Kodiak. By 6:30 that night, the thick ash blotted out all daylight... By the time the ashfall finally dwindled out on the morning of June 9th, Kodiak had experienced two days and three nights of nearly unbroken darkness. The land was cloaked under gray drifts several feet high and porches and roofs lay crushed under mounds of the fine grit."

(excerpted from *Katmai*, by Jean Bodeau)

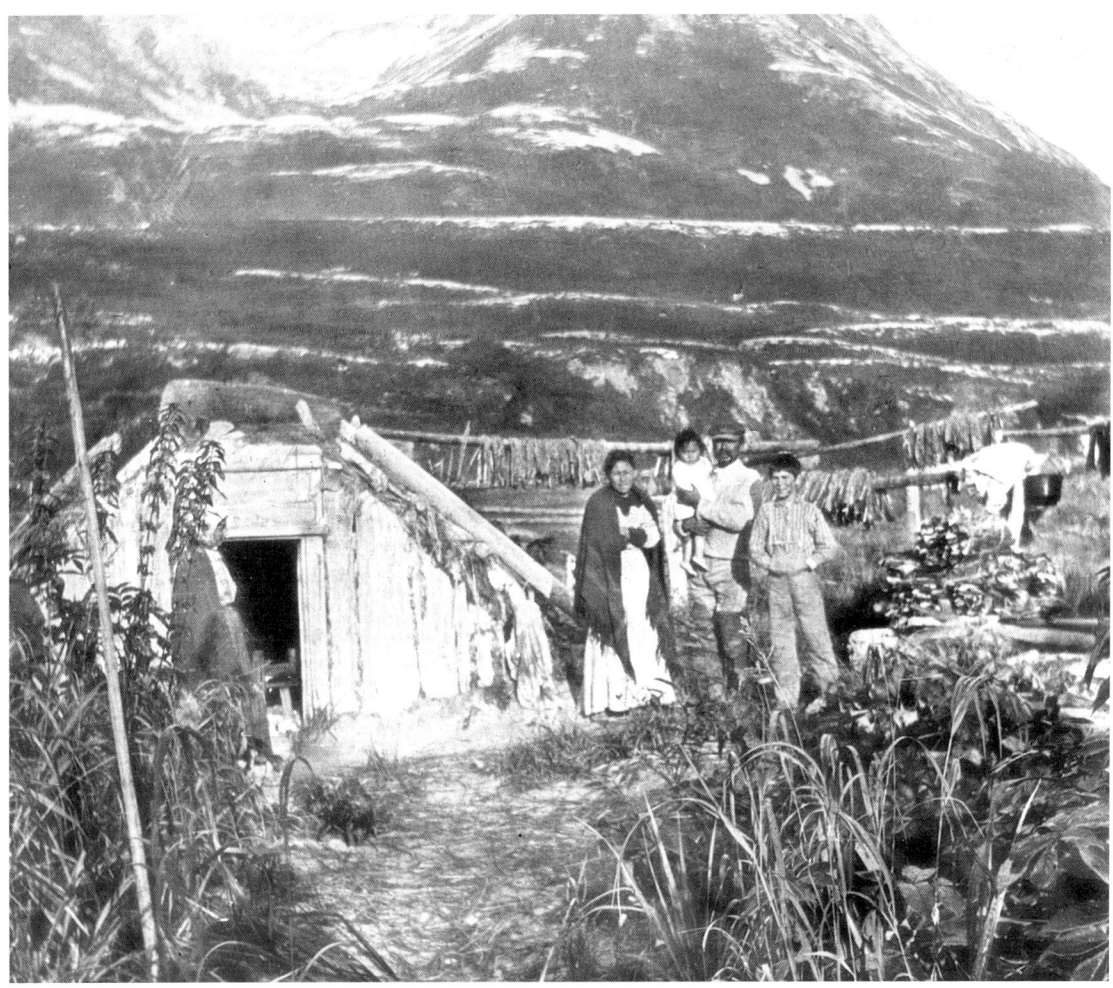

above A family outside their ciqluaq, an Alutiiq home. (Kodiak Historical Society)

from the Philippines came to harvest the salmon-thick waters at the century's turn, they too found a place here.

Some 50 years later, the world's eyes again turned to Kodiak. With the advent of World War II, the United States needed a strong defense system in the Pacific. A submarine base, air station and army outpost brought massive construction and thousands of men to safeguard the Gulf of Alaska and the Aleutian Islands. Japanese forces bombed Dutch Harbor and occupied Kiska and Attu in the Aleutian Islands, but were turned back by American and Canadian forces.

After the war, Kodiak kept its role as a protector of the North Pacific. The one-time World War II base is now the largest U.S. Coast Guard base in the country, a hub for fisheries enforcement and search and rescue operations.

Like the island tides, Kodiak's history is marked by the ebb and flow of good times and hardship. Prosperity has come in many guises, from fur bonanzas and gold strikes, to military construction and fishing booms. Then there are times when the community staggers to its knees. When Novarupta volcano erupted

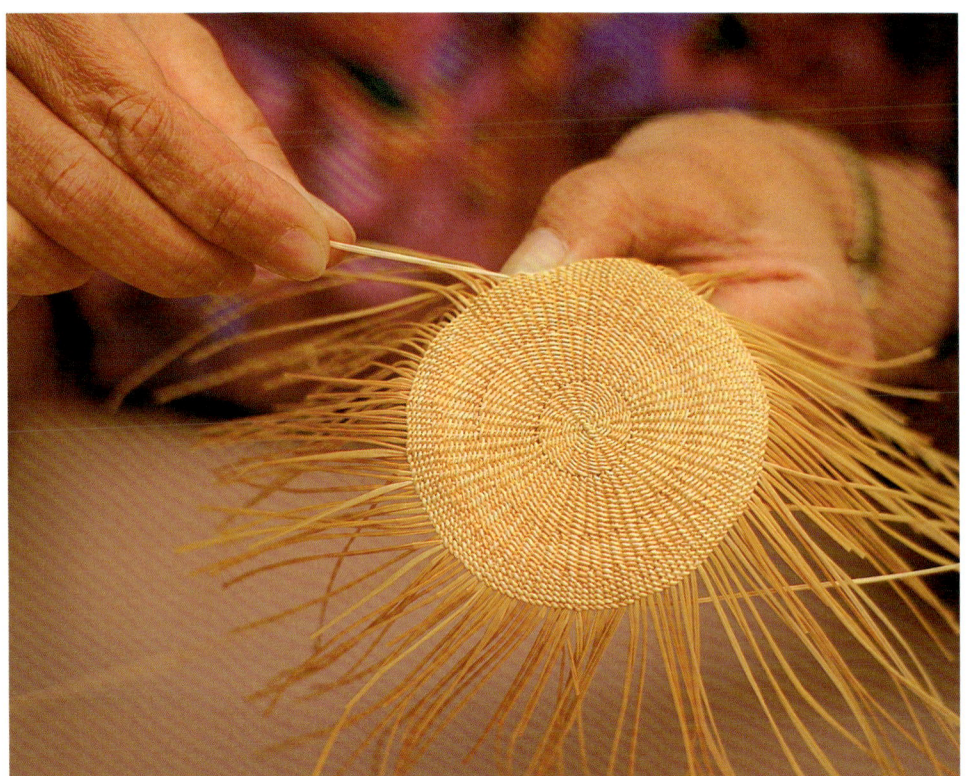

above Weaving the base of an Aleut-style basket. Local artisans practice ancient crafts passed down through generations. (Marion Owen)

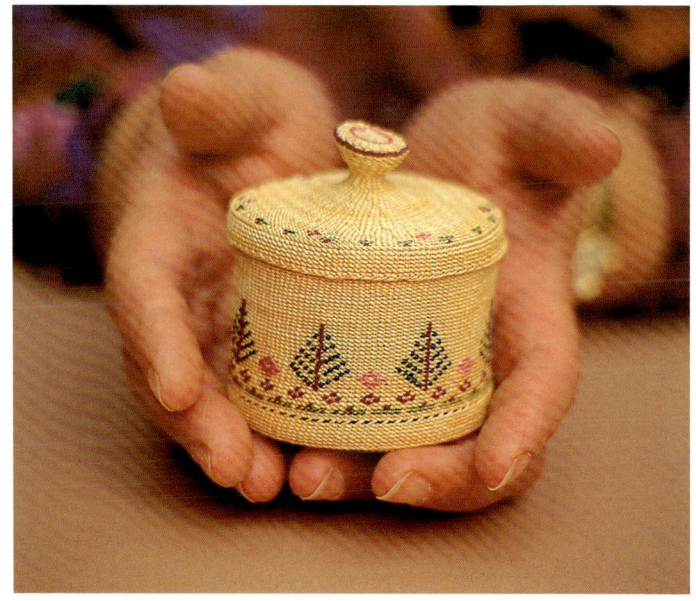

above Aleut-style basket made from beach rye grass by Arlene Skinner. (Marion Owen)

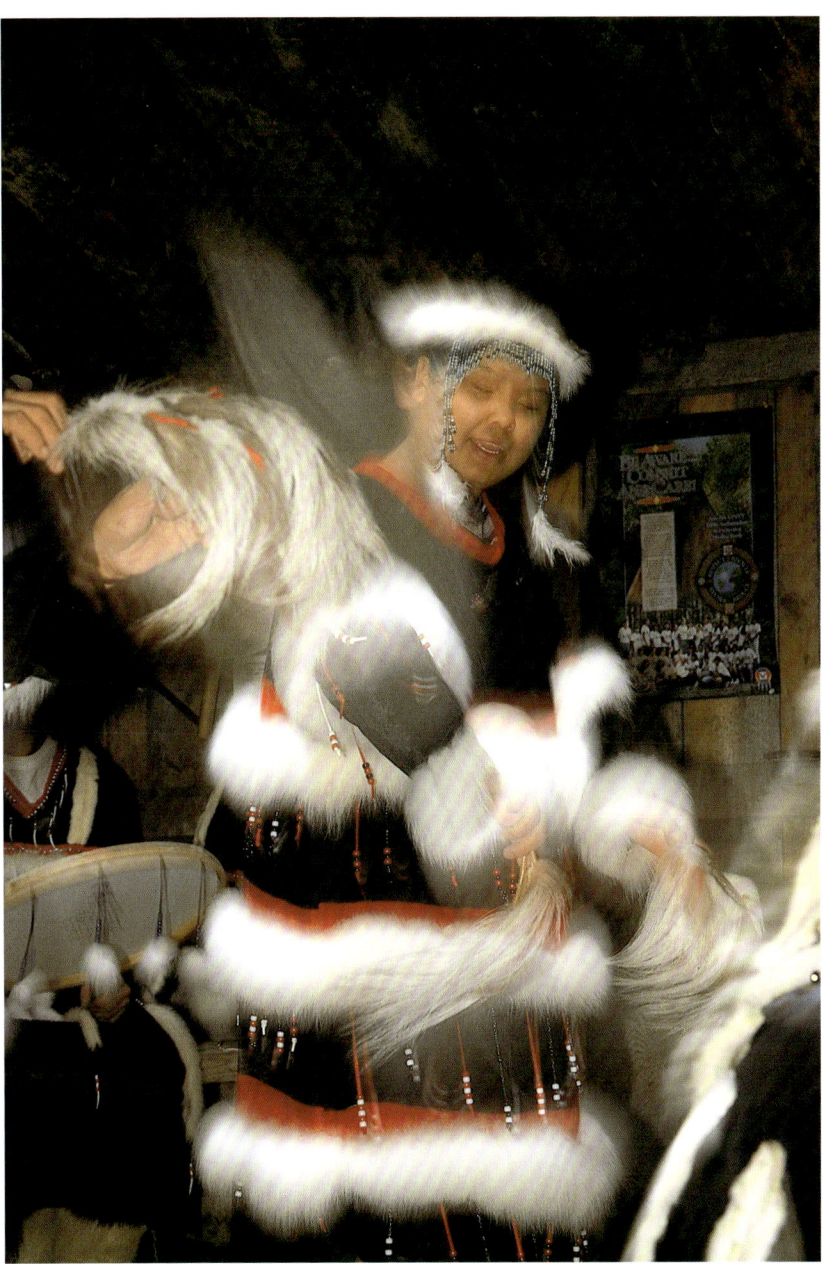

left Alutiiq dancer performs. The Kodiak Alutiiq Dancers preserve their heritage through song and dance. Their garments are replicas of traditional clothing, bead and ermine headdresses, and spruce root hats. The dances incorporate both traditional and contemporary stories. (Michael DeYoung/ Alaska Stock)

in 1912 on the Alaska Peninsula, cloaking Kodiak in three days of choking, ash-filled darkness, people stayed. When the great Alaska earthquake of 1964 sent tsunami waves sweeping over downtown Kodiak and island villages, people rebuilt. When black muck from the 1989 Exxon Valdez oil spill drifted into the region's pure waters, people cleaned it up. Generation after generation has stood strong against adversity.

Today, the wealth of the sea continues to draw people to Kodiak from around the world. The island is a kaleidoscope of cultures. At the park, a Russian Orthodox priest in his long, black cassock strolls past Filipino teenagers playing basketball and Nicaraguan men on the soccer field. At work, voices from Costa Rica, Samoa and El Salvador chatter over the hum of high-tech fish processing machinery. At the grocery store, bearded Russian Old Believers in embroidered shirts and hand-woven belts pass Coast Guardsmen in crew cuts and crisp blue uniforms. In the harbor, tired Japanese and Korean sailors pause on the long

right The Baranov
Museum, also known as
the Erskine House, was
built in 1793 as a
storehouse and
commissary. The oldest
Russian structure
remaining in Alaska, it
now displays artifacts
from Kodiak's past.
(Elysia Leake)

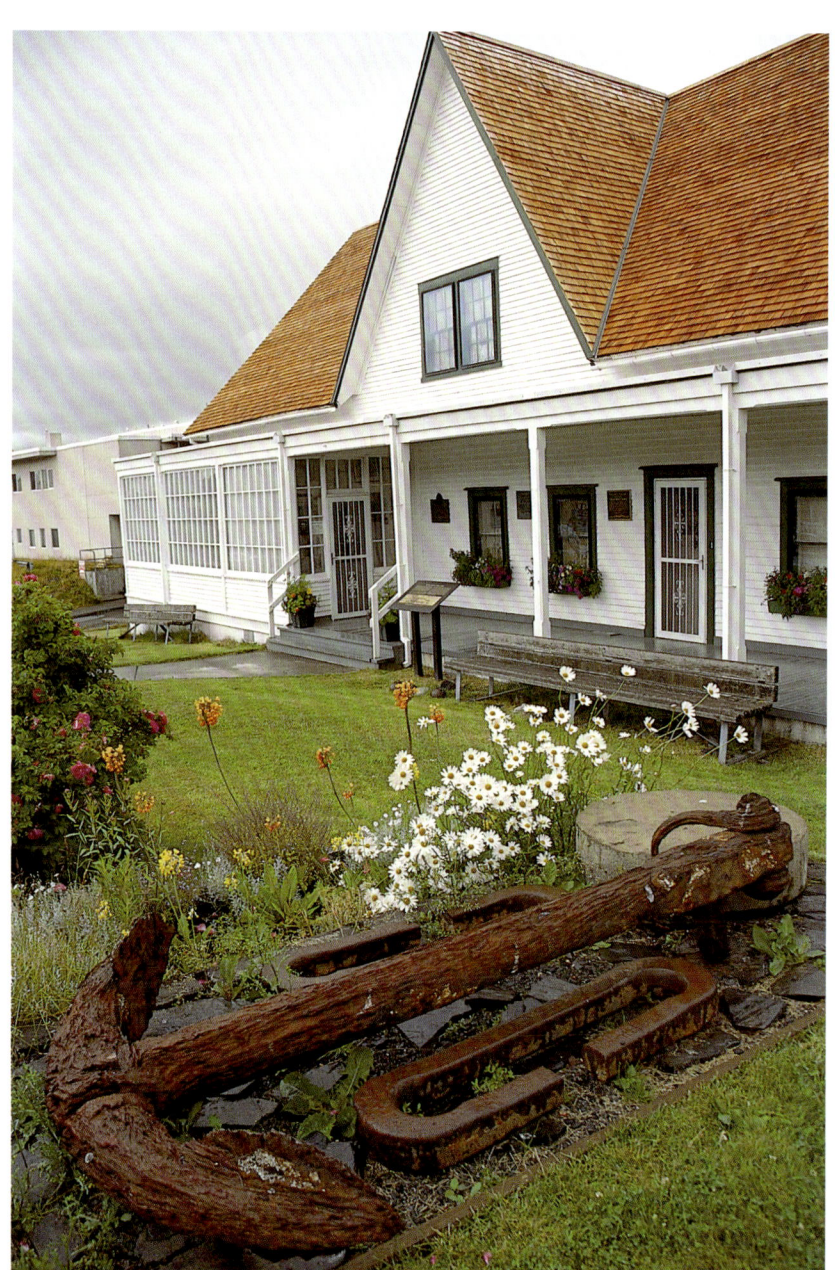

right The Alutiiq Museum
is the region's
headquarters for
preserving and sharing
Alutiiq heritage. The state-
of-the-art facility includes a
gallery, artifact repository
and research laboratory.
The museum has earned
national recognition for its
programs. (Elysia Leake)

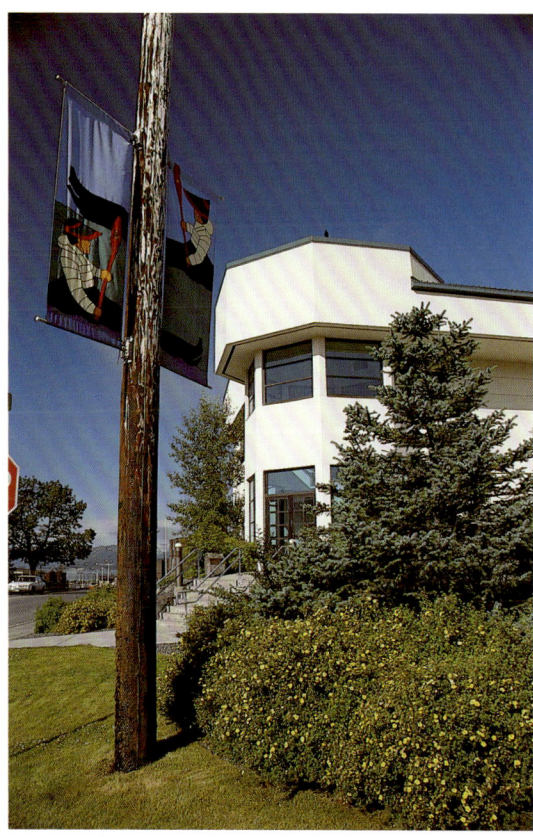

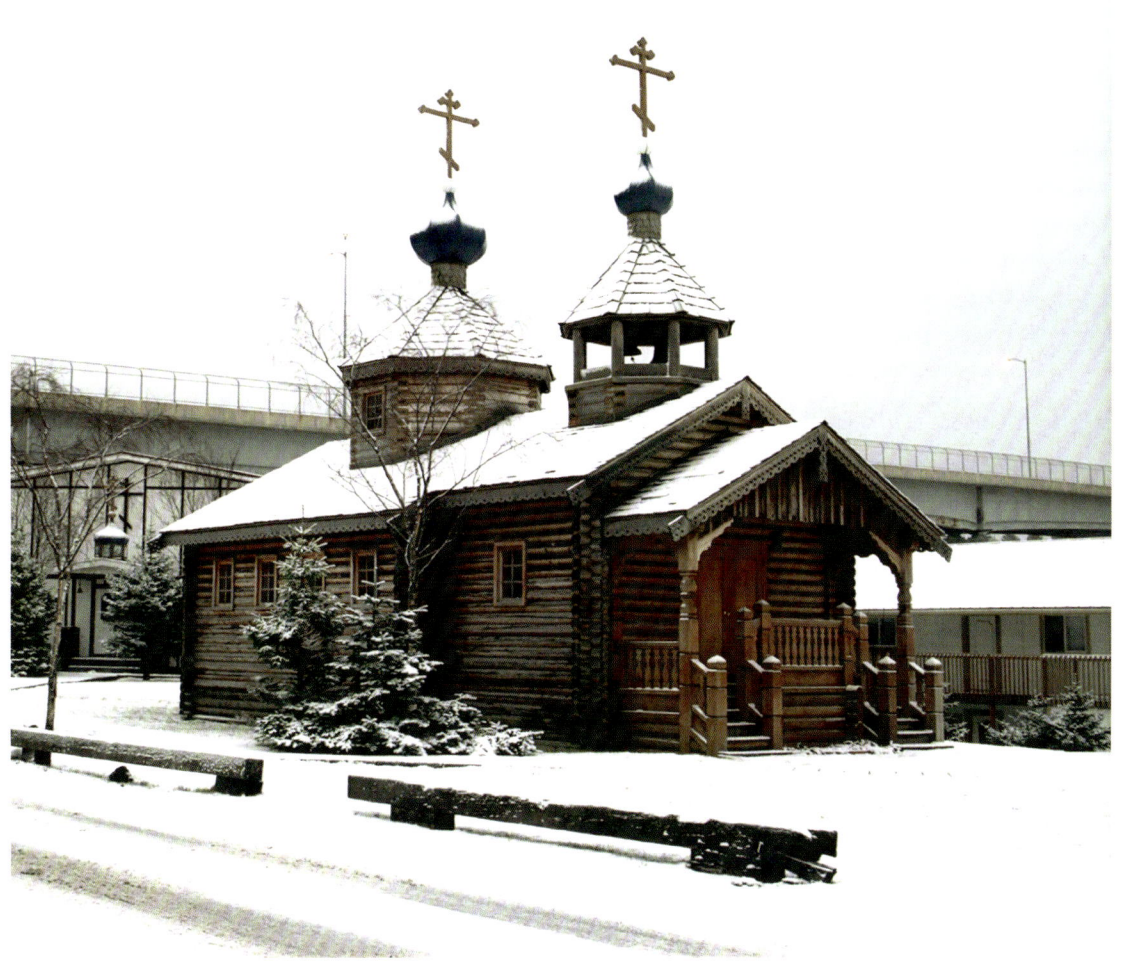

above The ornate chapel at St. Herman's Theological Seminary was built in 1995. It is a replica of the original Holy Resurrection Church built in the city of Kodiak in 1796, the first Russian Orthodox Church in the western hemisphere. The log building's style is from the Russian region of Valaam near Finland, home of the first Russian monks to come to Kodiak. (Elysia Leake)

journey home. And at a state-of-the-art satellite launch complex on Narrow Cape, U.S. military and civilian technicians hunch over computers charting the course of a new aerospace industry.

Amid the new faces, the past lives on. In a reconstructed ciqluaq or sod house, young Alutiiq dancers with beaded headdresses and ermine-trimmed robes drum and chant in the spirit of their forebears. Elders once forbidden to speak their native language are welcomed into schools to teach the young. Working archaeological sites are open to visitors and volunteers. Hikers wander the stark remains of gun emplacements at Fort Abercrombie and Chiniak, while the devout meditate amid the candle-lit splendor of Holy Resurrection Russian Orthodox Church.

Kodiak savors and saves the past— not only in museum showcases, but in the hearts of its people.

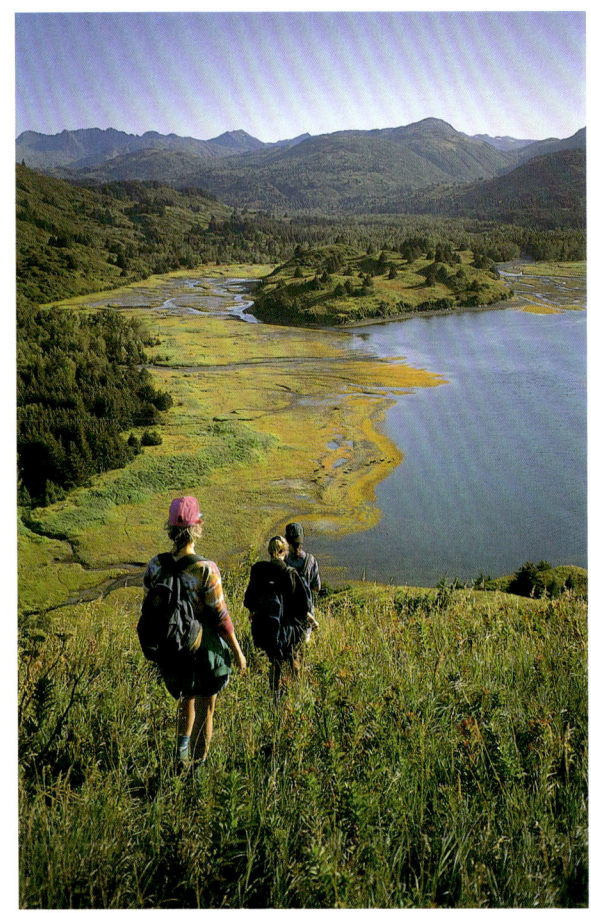

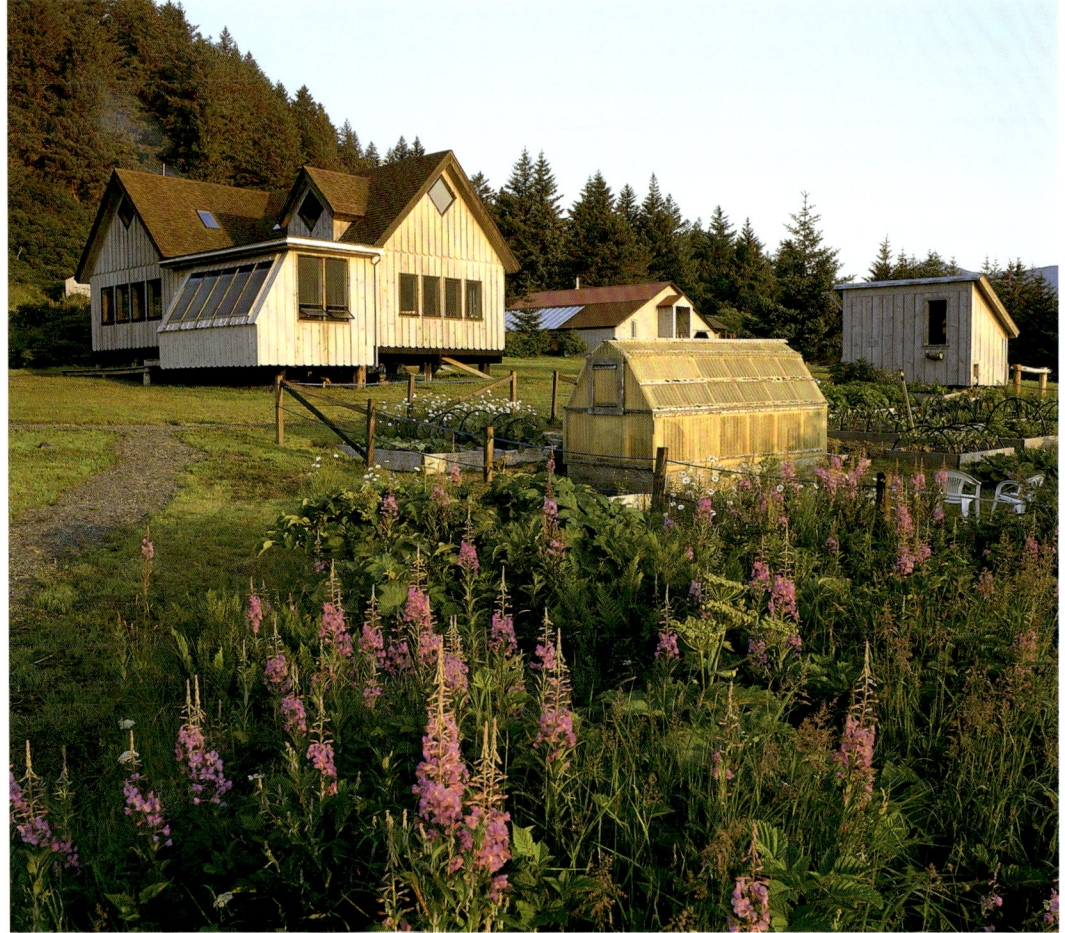

above Hiking at Anton Larsen Bay. Hikers on Kodiak Island will find a network of trails. (Tom Watson)

right Fireweed blooms at a lodge on Raspberry Island. (Fred Hirschmann)

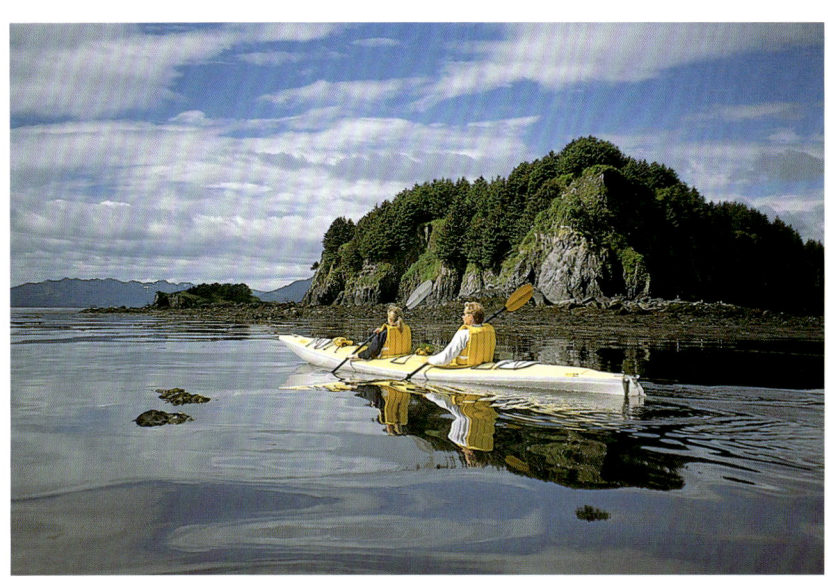

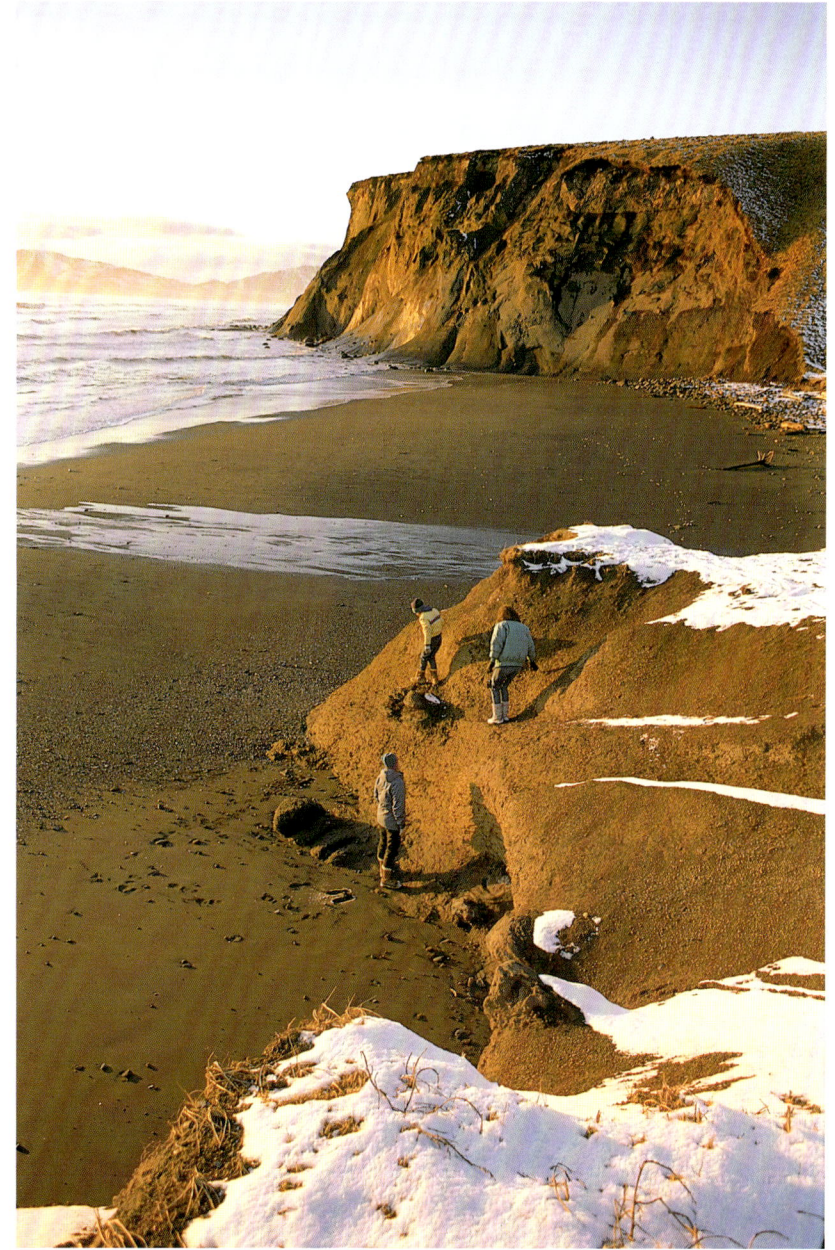

above Sea kayakers enjoy intimate views of Kodiak's rocky coastline at a leisurely pace. (Tom Watson)

right Fossil Beach at Narrow Cape offers year-round beachcombing. (Tom Watson)

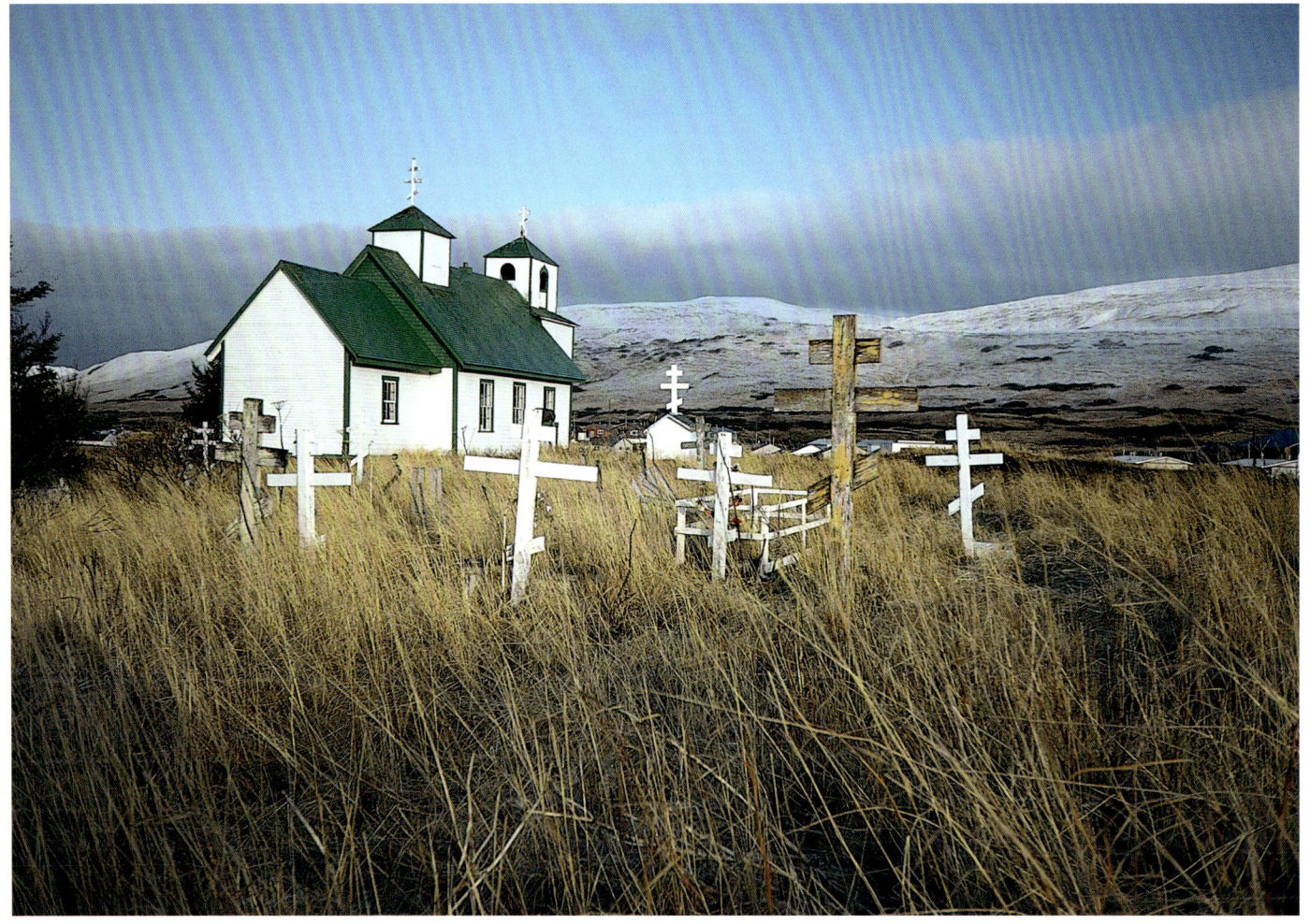

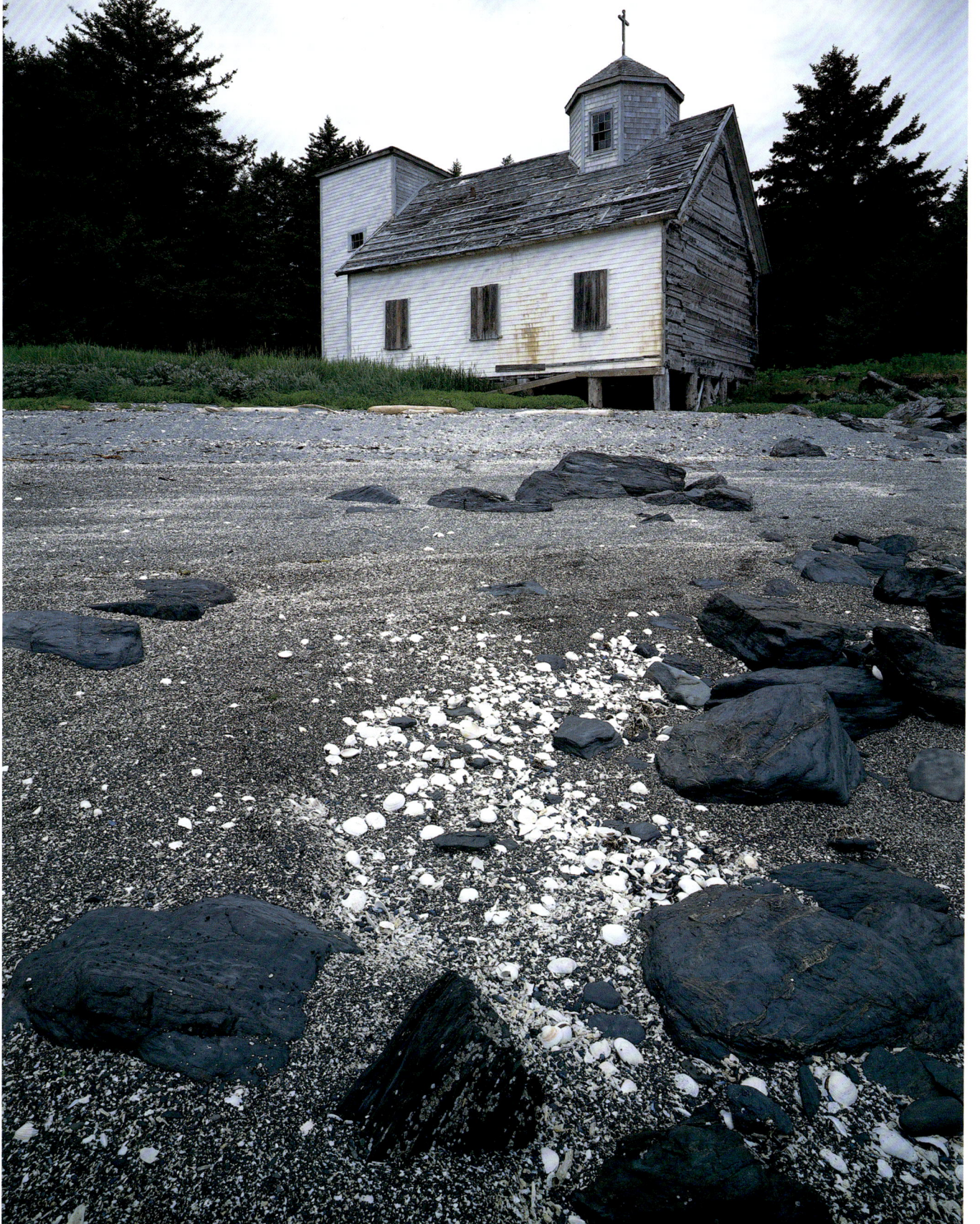

far left Akhiok is Kodiak's southernmost village. It is located on Alitak Bay amid low hills and rolling flatlands at the southern tip of Kodiak Island. Ancient Alitak petroglyphs were recently identified nearby. (Tom Watson)

left The Russian Orthodox Church damaged by the tsunami (tidal wave) from the 1964 earthquake still stands on Afognak Island. (Fred Hirschmann)

below Hand-decorated Ukrainian eggs (pysansky), an Easter tradition. (Marion Owen)

right Holy Resurrection Russian Orthodox Church, built in 1945, in the city of Kodiak. (Randi Hirschmann)

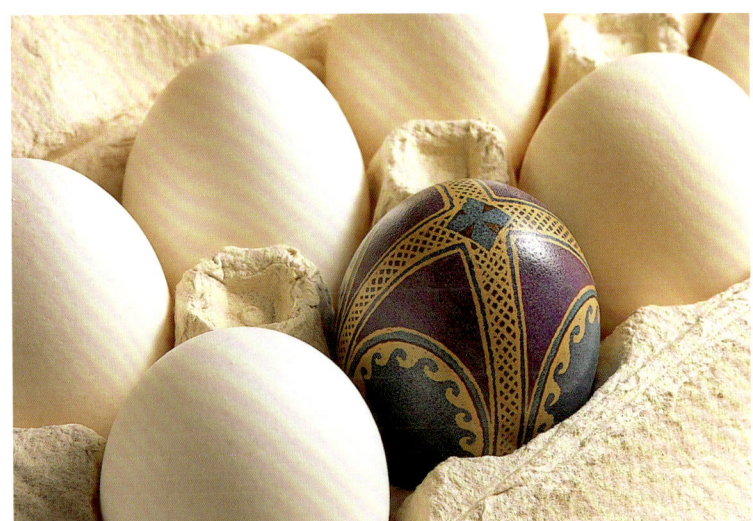

far right Christmas starring ceremony, Holy Resurrection Russian Orthodox Church. (Marion Owen)

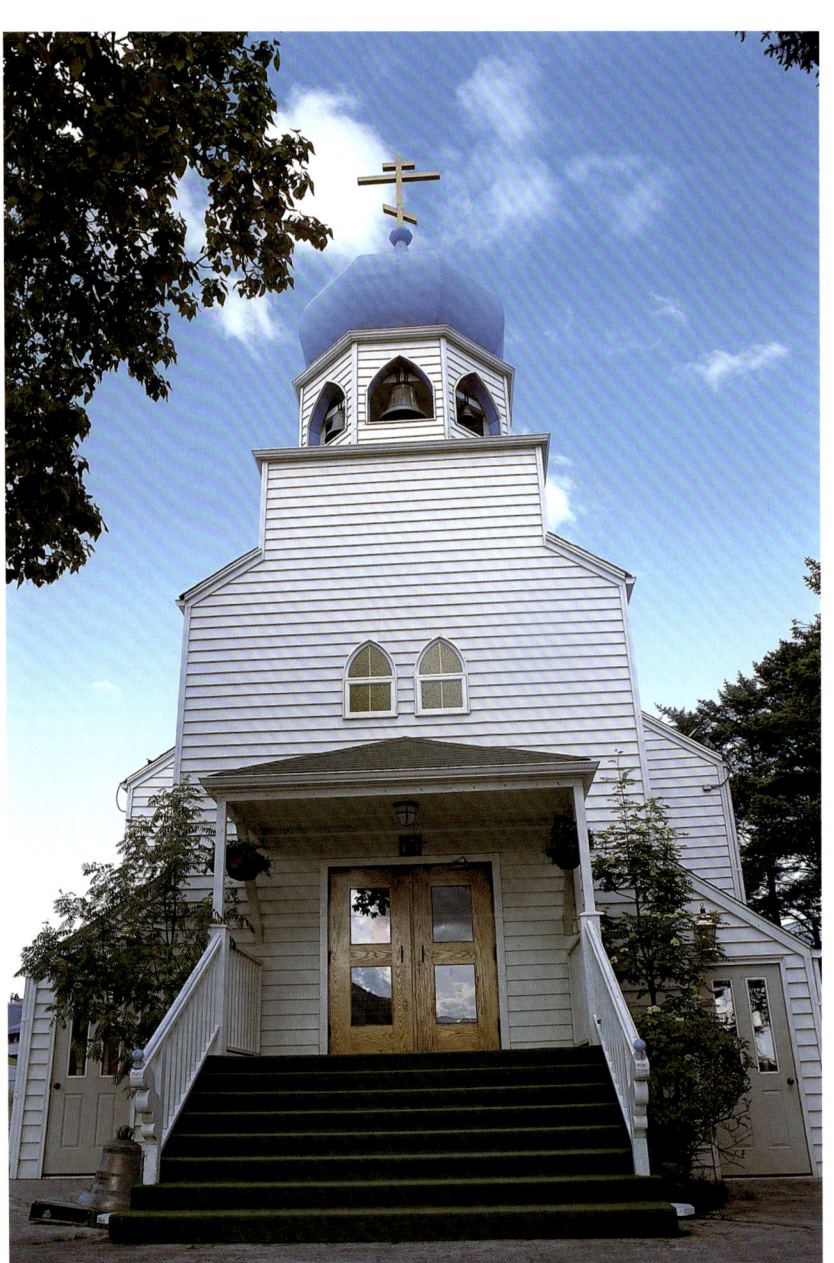

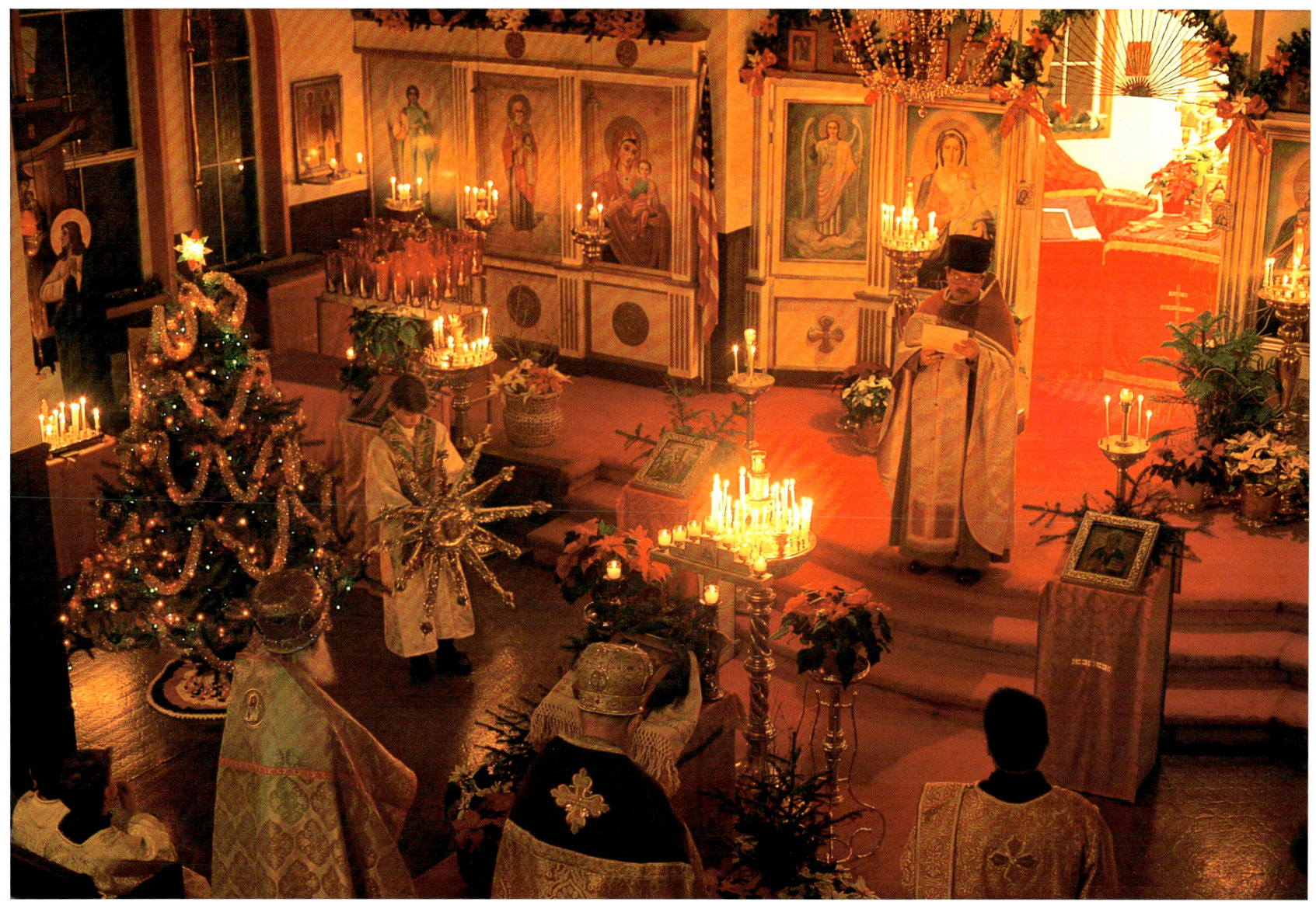

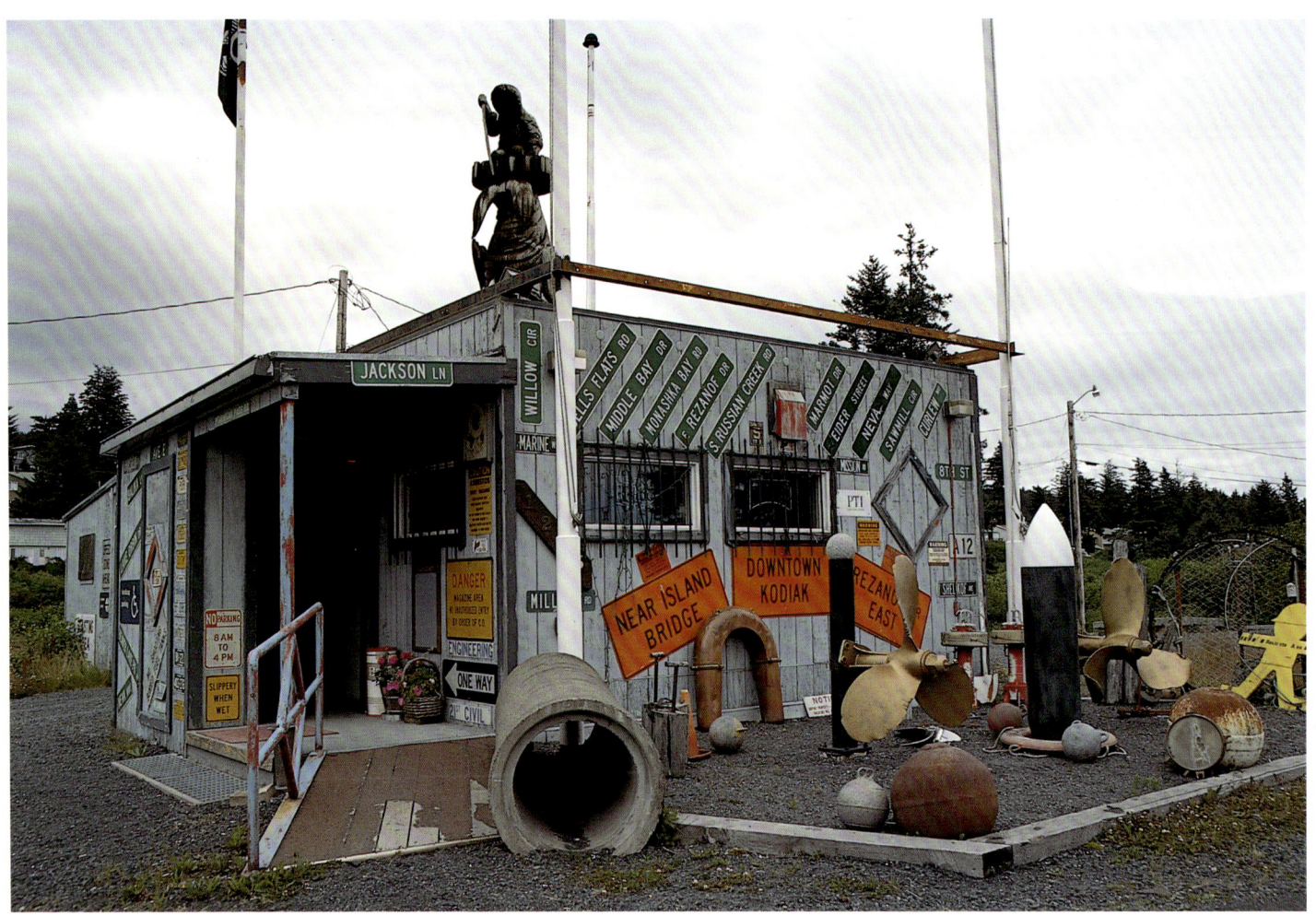

above Diamond Jim's reflects the eccentricities of its owners and patrons. (Elysia Leake)

right Fireplug and flowers. (Heather L. Johnson)

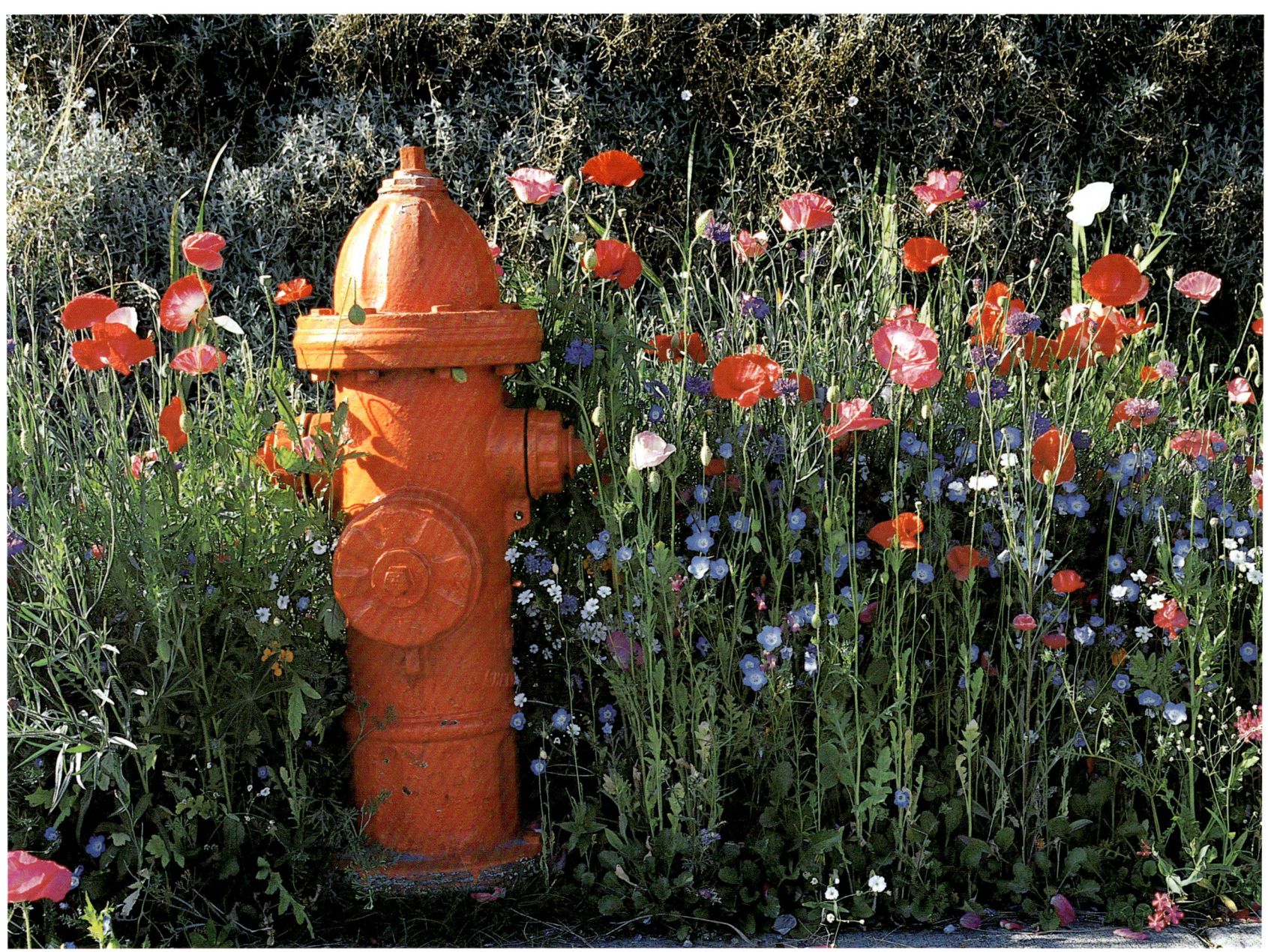

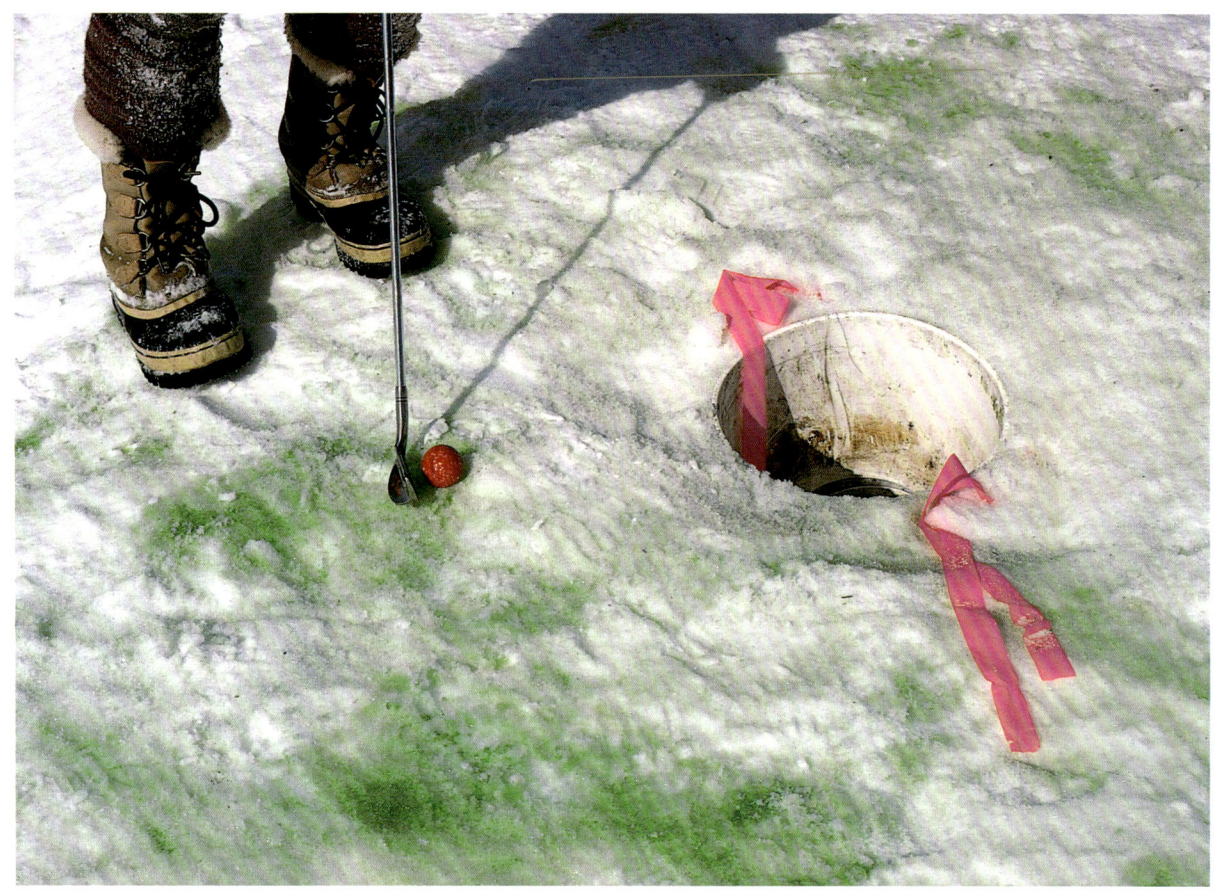

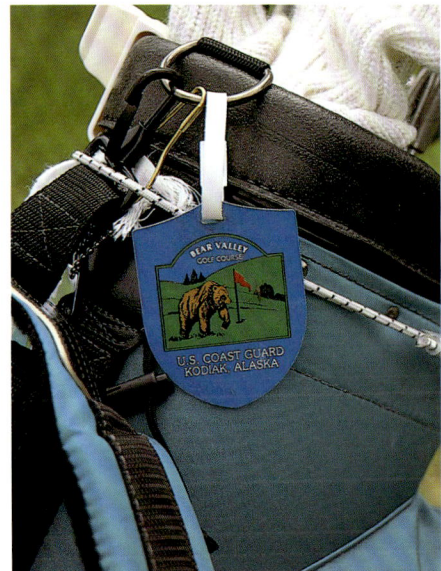

above ID tag for Bear
Valley Golf Course.
(Marion Owen)

above Making the final
putt on the "green" of the
one-hole par-70 Pillar
Mountain Golf Classic.
Held in March, the
irreverent golf tournament
is a struggle up the side
of 1,400-foot Pillar
Mountain.
(Marion Owen)

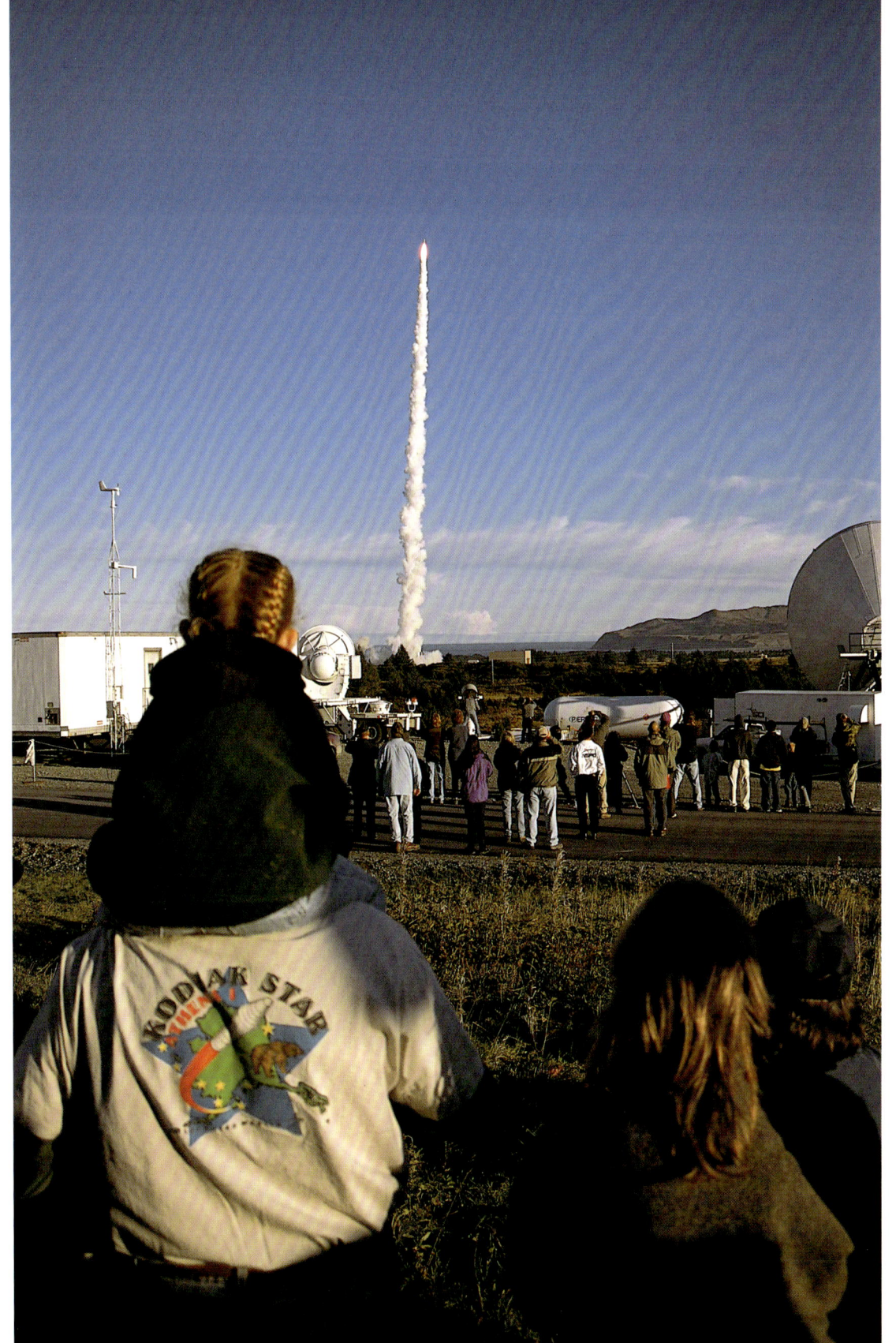

left A NASA rocket spears into space September 29, 2001 at Narrow Cape's Kodiak Launch Complex. The complex launched its first rocket in 1998. Kodiak's northern latitude makes it an ideal place to launch satellites intended for polar orbit.
(Marion Owen)

92

below Fish processing is a major part of Kodiak's economy. (courtesy of Alaska Seafood Marketing Institute)

right Fish processors work the king crab line in a waterfront seafood processing plant. (courtesy of Alaska Seafood Marketing Institute)

far right Coast Guard Cutter Mellon, homeport Seattle, on patrol during the opilio crab season. (U.S. Coast Guard Petty Officer Keith Alholm)

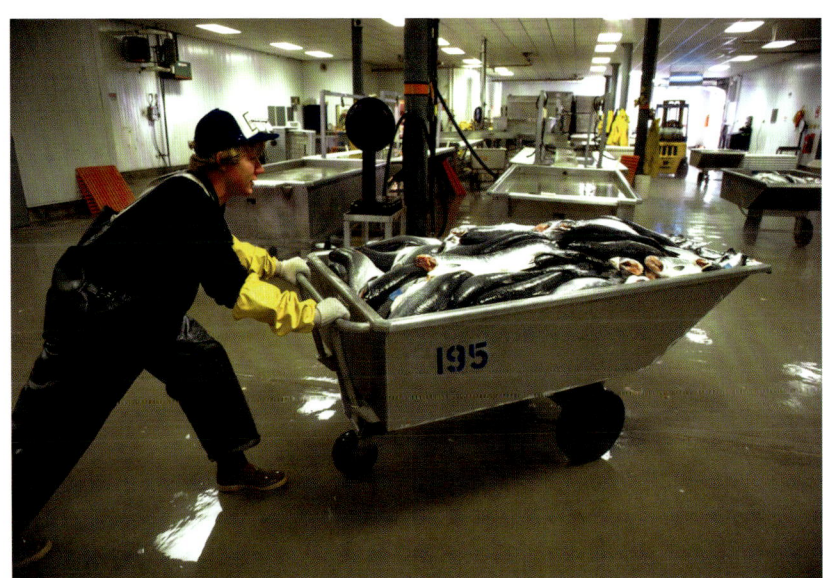

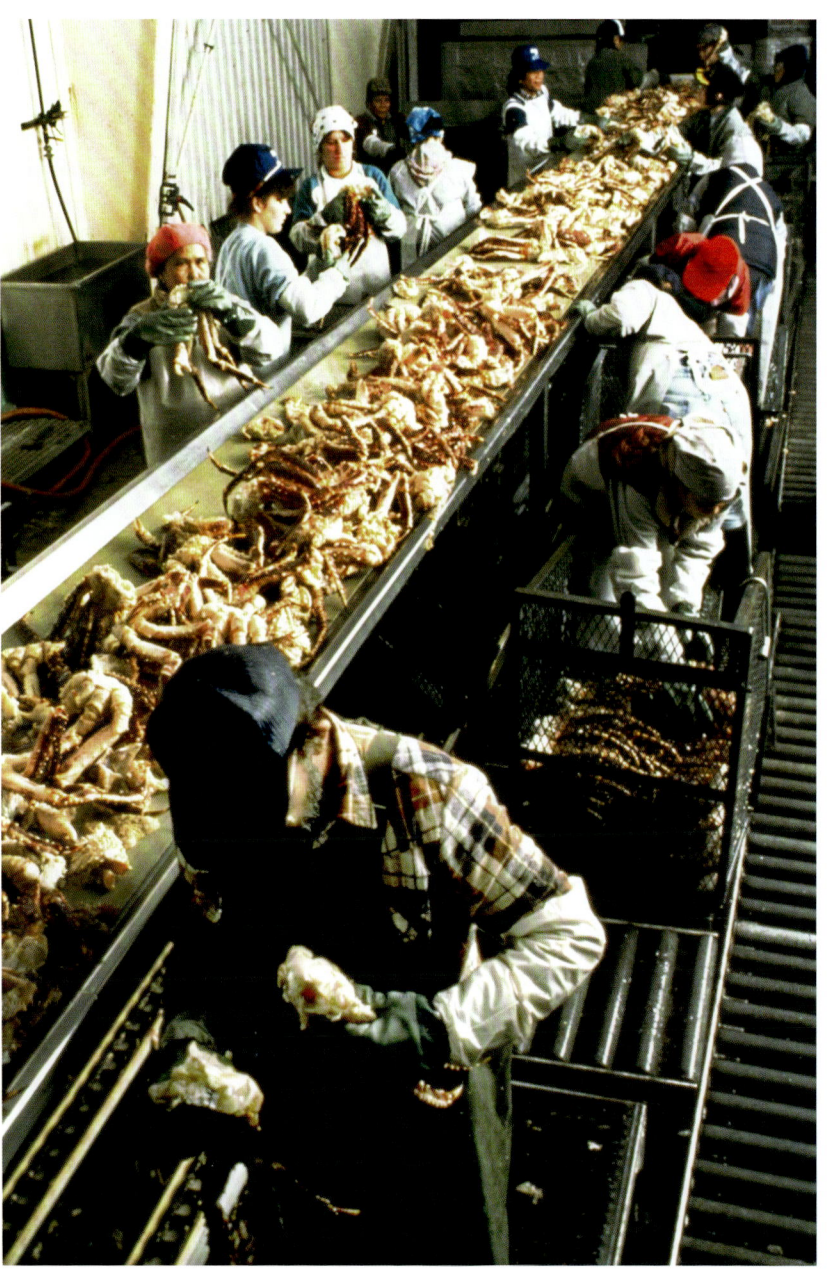

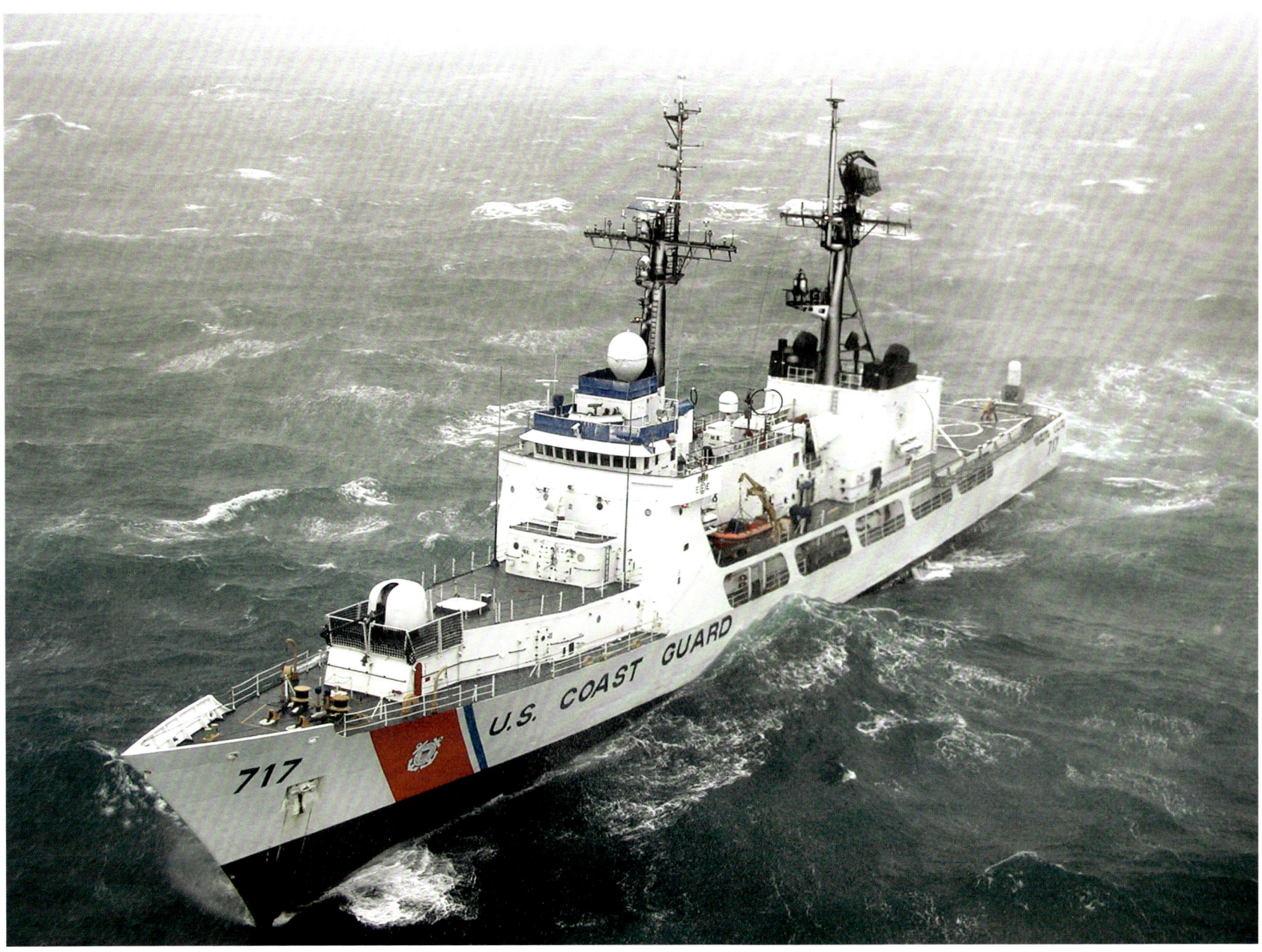

below Christmas spirit in a fishing town.
(Elysia Leake)

right Santa waves from the Coast Guard helicopter in the "Santa to the Villages" program. The country's largest Coast Guard station is located in Women's Bay, just outside the city of Kodiak, with nearly 1,100 active duty personnel.
(Marion Owen)

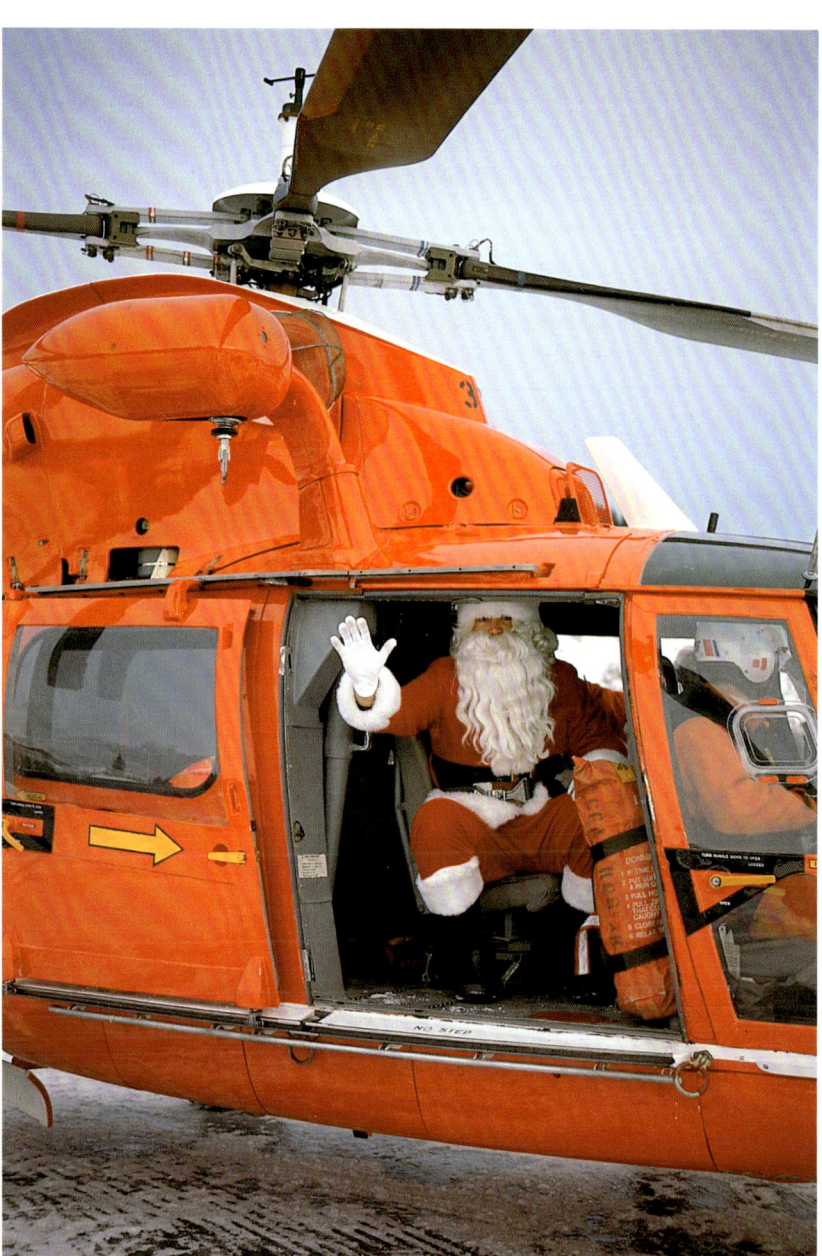

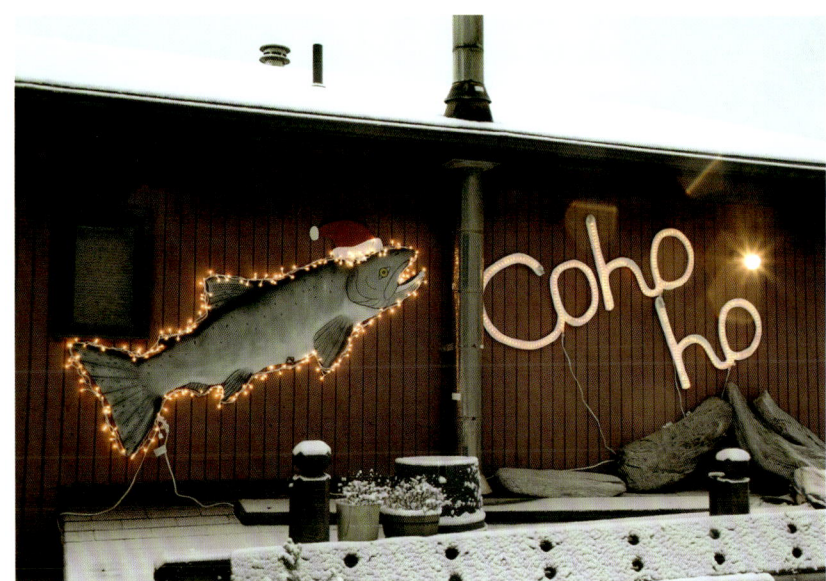

page 96 Holy Resurrection Russian Orthodox Church and fireworks.
(Hank Pennington)

Bibliography

Alaska Department of Fish and Game, *Wildlife Notebook Series*, 1994, Alaska Department of Fish and Game, Juneau, Alaska.

Alaska Geographic, *Alaska's Salmon Fisheries*, Alaska Geographic Society, 1983, Anchorage, Alaska.

Alaska Geographic, *Kodiak*, 1992, Alaska Geographic Society, Anchorage, Alaska.

Alaska Geographic, *Russian America*, 1999, Alaska Geographic Society, Anchorage, Alaska.

Alaska Geographic, *Where Mountains Meet the Sea: Alaska's Gulf Coast*, 1986, Alaska Geographic Society, Anchorage, Alaska.

Alaska magazine editors, *The Alaska-Yukon Wild Flowers Guide*, 1982, Alaska Northwest Publishing Co., Anchorage, Alaska.

Armstrong, Robert H., *A New, Expanded Guide to the Birds of Alaska*, 1984, Alaska Northwest Publishing Co., Anchorage, Alaska.

Bodeau, Jean, *Katmai National Park and Preserve, Alaska*, 1992, Alaska Natural History Association and Greatland Graphics, Anchorage, Alaska.

Chaffin, Yule, Hampton Krieger, Trisha and Rostad, Michael, *Alaska's Konyag Country*, 1983, Chaffin Incorporated, Kodiak, Alaska.

Elliot, Nan, *Best Places: Alaska*, 2000, Sasquatch Books, Seattle, Washington.

Graham, Frances Kelso, and the Ouzinkie Botanical Society, *Plant Lore of an Alaskan Island*, 1985, Alaska Northwest Publishing Co., Anchorage, Alaska.

Kessler, Doyne W., *Alaska's Saltwater Fishes and Other Sea Life*, 1985, Alaska Northwest Publishing Co., Anchorage, Alaska.

Kodiak Chamber of Commerce, *1999-2000 Annual Report*, 2000, Kodiak, Alaska.

Kodiak Chamber of Commerce, *Kodiak Community Profile and Economic Indicators*, 2001, Kodiak, Alaska.

Kodiak Island Convention and Visitors Bureau, *Kodiak: Kodiak Island Archipelago and the Katmai Coast*, 2001, Kodiak, Alaska.

Langdon, Steve J., *The Native People of Alaska*, 2002. Greatland Graphics, Anchorage, Alaska.

The Milepost editors, *The Milepost 1999-2000*, Morris Communications Corp., Anchorage, Alaska.

Old Believers in a Time of Change, Alaska Magazine, October 1988, Vol. 54, No. 10, Anchorage, Alaska.

Pratt, Verna E., *Field Guide to Alaskan Wildflowers*, 1989, Alaskakrafts Publishing, Anchorage, Alaska.

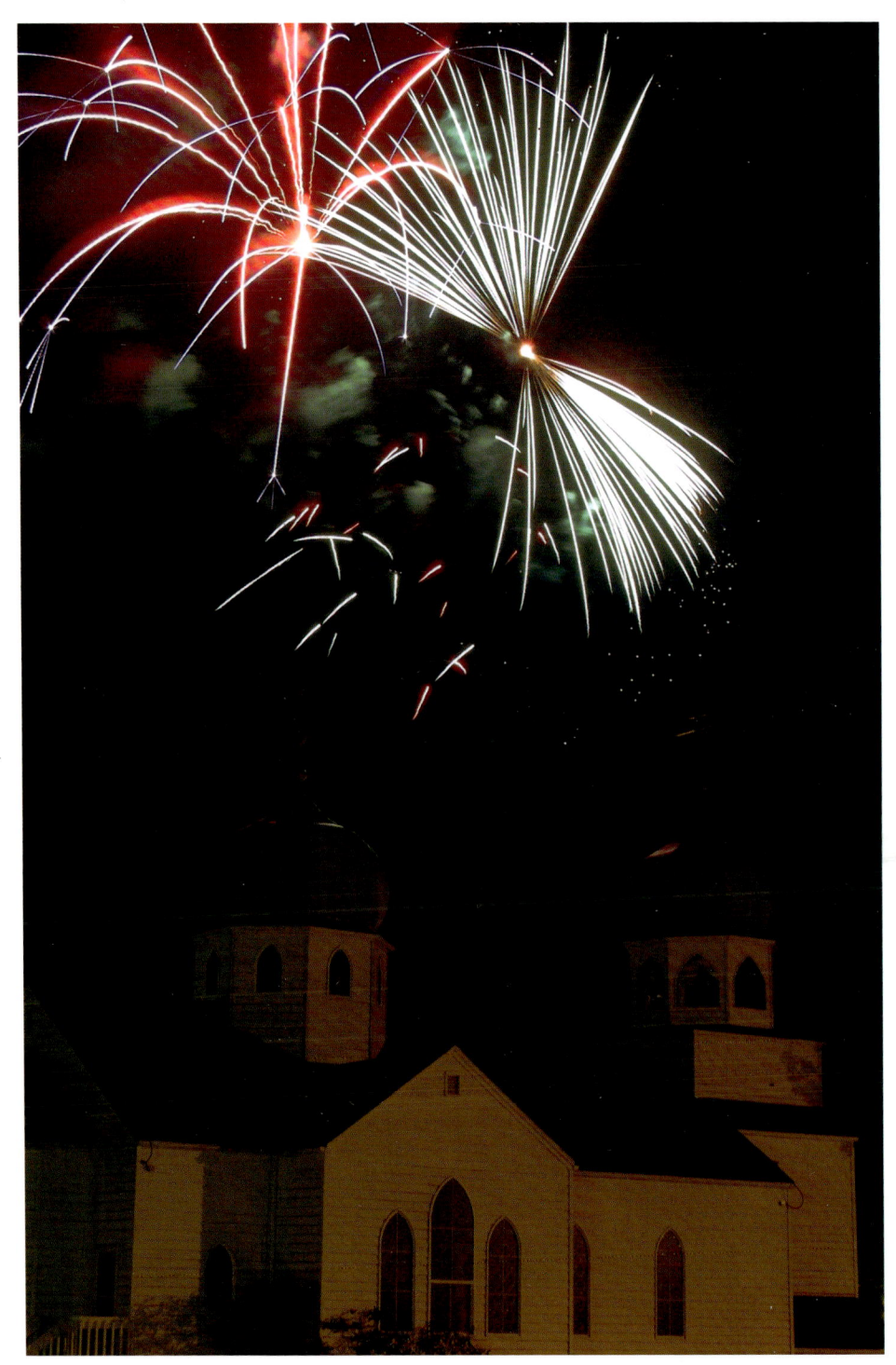